ALSO BY SETH ROGOVOY

*The Essential Klezmer: A Music Lover's Guide
to Jewish Roots and Soul Music*

BOB DYLAN

PROPHET, MYSTIC, POET

SETH ROGOVOY

SCRIBNER
New York London Toronto Sydney

SCRIBNER

A Division of Simon & Schuster, Inc.
1230 Avenue of the Americas
New York, NY 10020

First Scribner hardcover edition November 2009

SCRIBNER and design are registered trademarks of The Gale Group, Inc., used under
license by Simon & Schuster, Inc., the publisher of this work.

For information about special discounts for bulk purchases,
please contact Simon & Schuster Special Sales
at 1-866-506-1949 or business@simonandschuster.com.

The Simon & Schuster Speakers Bureau can bring authors to your live event.
For more information or to book an event contact the Simon & Schuster
Speakers Bureau at 1-866-248-3049 or visit our website at www.simonspeakers.com.

Designed by Carla Jayne Jones

Manufactured in the United States of America

10   9   8   7   6   5   4   3   2   1

Library of Congress Control Number: 2009026310

ISBN 978-1-4165-5916-0
ISBN 978-1-4165-5983-2 (ebook)

Permissions acknowledgments appear on pages 299–306.

For my mother
Stella Peretz Rogovoy
1938–2009
May her memory be for a blessing

"Make music for Hashem, for He has acted with grandeur; make this known throughout the world. Exult and shout for joy, O inhabitant of Zion, for the Holy One of Israel is great in your midst!"

—Isaiah 12:5–6

"My word is like fire, says the Lord, and like a hammer that shatters a rock."

—Jeremiah 23:29

"Those guys are really wise. I tell you, I've heard gurus and yogis and philosophers and politicians and doctors and lawyers, teachers of all kinds . . . and these rabbis really had something going."

—Bob Dylan

"Listen, I don't know how Jewish I am, because I've got blue eyes. My grandparents were from Russia, and going back that far, which one of those women didn't get raped by the Cossacks? So there's plenty of Russian in me, I'm sure. Otherwise, I wouldn't be the way I am."

—Bob Dylan

"A truth that's told with bad intent / Beats all the lies you can invent."

—William Blake, "Auguries of Innocence"

"I'm exiled, you can't convert me."

—Bob Dylan, from "We Better Talk This Over"

CONTENTS

TERMS AND USAGE

Robert Allen Zimmerman began calling himself Bob Dylan among friends and acquaintances when he started performing at coffeehouses in the Dinkytown section of Minneapolis while still enrolled at the University of Minnesota in 1959–60. Zimmerman and Dylan are the same person. Some authors have found it cute or clever to refer to Dylan as Zimmerman and vice versa. More nonsense than sense has been made about the name change—although there is plenty of sense to be made out of it, not the least of which is that Zimmerman was born under the sun sign of Gemini, the twins (a fact that Dylan directly addresses in the song "Where Are You Tonight?" from the 1978 album *Street Legal,* when he sings, "I fought with my twin / That enemy within / 'Til both of us fell by the way"). Herein Zimmerman—who legally changed his name to Dylan in 1962—is called by that name until the period of time during which he began calling himself Dylan and when most of those who knew him knew him as Dylan.

The term "Bible" as used herein is synonymous with the Hebrew "Torah," or, more precisely, Tanakh, which refers to the Five Books of Moses contained in the Torah scroll plus the books of the Hebrew Prophets and the Writings, which include the Psalms and other nonprophetic works (such as Proverbs, the story of Job, the Song of Songs, Lamentations, Ecclesiastes, and, significantly, the concluding book of Chronicles—a title Bob Dylan borrowed for his 2004 memoir).

Some refer to these works as the "Old Testament," but such usage puts the Jewish works in the context of the Christian Bible—composed of most of the Jewish Bible (the "Old Testament") and the writings referred to as the "New Testament"—and thus implies that they have been superseded by the latter, which is insulting to Jews. Thus, it's a term shunned herein.

"Torah," however, can also be used to mean the complete corpus of Jewish law and scripture, which goes far beyond the Tanakh and includes the Midrash, the Mishnah, the Talmud, the mystical writings, and other works by great sages such as Rashi, Maimonides, and Nachmanides. "To study Torah" could mean to study any of these works, or even to study modern commentaries on these works. In this sense, "Torah" can mean the complete body of Jewish learning.

In referring to the Jewish deity, I follow convention in my narrative by writing "G-d," an acknowledgment that His name is ineffable, unknown, and should be treated with respect (and not be defaced or erased). In quotations, however, the spelling out of "God" follows the original publication's practice, for example, in Bob Dylan's song lyrics.

Jesus is referred to by name, but without the additional term "Christ," a word derived from the Greek term *kristos*, loosely translated as "messiah." To append the term "Christ" after the name of Jesus or to refer to Jesus by that term alone implies acceptance of Jesus as the Messiah foretold by the Jewish prophets.

For the comfort and ease of the general reader, historical names and texts are given in their commonly accepted English forms: thus, for example, the Jewish patriarchs, Avraham, Yitzhak, and Yaakov are called Abraham, Isaac, and Jacob, respectively, and the book in which we read about them is referred to as Genesis instead of its Hebrew title, Bereishis. Likewise, the oft-quoted Prophets Yishayahu, Yirmiyahu, and Yehezkiel are referred to here as Isaiah, Jeremiah, and Ezekiel.

PROLOGUE
ROCKIN' THE SHTETL

He decided to raise the level of the . . . entertainer to the dignity of a singer about his people, their life and struggles. . . . With a deep affection and regard for his suffering people, he sang of his times, pointed up the evils, satirized the guilty, stressed the good.

When doing research for a previous book, I stumbled across this passage in the folklorist Ruth Rubin's book *Voices of a People*. Rubin was writing about Eliakum Zunser. Born in Lithuania in 1836, Zunser began his performing career as a traditional *badkhn,* a folk artist who worked primarily as a wedding emcee in Jewish Eastern Europe, and became a pioneer of original Yiddish protest songs in the 1860s and 1870s, which eventually led to his becoming the most popular Jewish folksinger of his time, by building a new kind of protest music atop a foundation of folk tradition.

A *badkhn,* according to Zunser's biographer Sol Liptzin, "was a pious merrymaker, a chanting moralist, a serious bard who sermonized while he entertained." Zunser's innovation was to take the received, highly stylized form of wedding poetry and to elevate the medium to a genre of social commentary. Zunser was immensely successful, and, teaming up with *klezmorim*—the folk musicians of the Old World who played primarily for weddings—he became the closest thing the shtetl had to a rock star.

Liptzin describes the adolescent Zunser as one who "was becoming more and more dissatisfied with the answers offered by his teachers to the questions that concerned him most deeply." Zunser, who was called a poet even though his main outlet was songwriting, would channel his frustration through the medium of song and become, according to Liptzin, a "lyricist of social justice," "the voice of the inarticulate denizen," "the sensitive seismograph that faithfully recorded the reactions of the common man to the counsels of despair and to the messianic panaceas." He was, in a term, the voice of a generation.

Born just over a century later halfway around the world, another Jewish folksinger would build upon tradition by writing a new kind of song that spoke the particular language and accent of its time and place, along the way meriting for himself the moniker "poet," winning acclaim as the voice of a generation, and joining forces with musicians to create a revolutionary new musical genre. Ruth Rubin's description of Zunser could well apply to Bob Dylan, as could Liptzin's. Zunser was, in a sense, a proto-Dylan, or, conversely, Dylan was, in a sense, the Zunser of the second half of the twentieth century, albeit one whose canvas was stretched larger and whose influence was more universal.

The track of Zunser's creative career eventually took him all over Russia, where he performed his songs and extemporized sermons at hundreds of weddings—at first as a soloist and later with his own band, just as Dylan would gain fame first as a solo folk artist in the early 1960s before employing the services of an electric rock band on record and in concert in 1965. Zunser's early, "rationalist" period, during which he adopted the popular beliefs of the Jewish enlightenment, produced songs such as "Salvation" and "Judged and Found Guilty" that gently chided his listeners to throw away their ancient superstitions and view the world—their world, in particular—critically and through "modern" eyes. He was telling them, in short, that the times they were a-changin'.

By 1861—exactly one hundred years before Bob Dylan recorded his eponymous debut album—Zunser had gained enough confidence and local renown to quit his day job as an embroiderer and commit himself full-time to his work as a songwriter and *badkhn*. He soon found himself entangled in a bad managerial deal that consigned him to years of skimpy, fixed wages, while his manager, Moishe Warshaver, pocketed the growing fees and gratuities showered upon Zunser as his talent and fame grew. Zunser and Warshaver spent years trying to settle their business relationship through lawsuits (as would Dylan and his manager, Albert Grossman, one hundred years later). Eventually Zunser gained the favor of the governor-general of Vilna, and he prevailed in court; his contract with Warshaver was nullified and the latter was banned from the city, thereby ceding the lucrative territory to Zunser alone.

Because he was no longer working in poverty and despair, Zunser's songs became lighter. One of the best-known songs from this period was called "The Whiskey Song," which, as Liptzin described it, "commemorated in a jovial mood the fall in the price of liquor and the resulting increased consumption. The satiric references were good-natured, and the crusading spirit completely absent. Drink, he felt, had its value. Why should not the laborer and the poor man also be able to afford once in a while the exhilaration of moderate indulgence?" Or, in other words, "Everybody must get stoned."

Zunser's period of lightness and frivolity was to be short-lived, however. Already having lost one child to the jaws of a wolf, he saw his entire family—his wife and seven remaining children—succumb to an epidemic of cholera in 1871. His songs thereafter became tinged with grief, much as Dylan's were after he separated from his wife in the mid-1970s. This period of sorrow, however, was to prove Zunser's most productive. "Undoubtedly, his ability to transmute pain into verse and melody aided his recovery and hastened the revival of his will to live," wrote Liptzin. In his song "The World Kaleidoscope," Zunser "reached an extreme of gloom in his characterization of the world as a prison in which the unfortunate victims lie fettered in chains. *In vain did each prisoner plead for death.*" (Emphasis mine.) Or, as Dylan sang during his subsequent period of gloom and doom, "Men will beg God to kill them / And they won't be able to die."

In an introduction to a collection of Zunser's songs published in 1928, the famed Yiddish writer and editor Abraham Cahan, exercising his muscles as a proto–rock critic, wrote, "To do justice to his unique genius, to appreciate the charm which his songs had for our people, one must be familiar with the combined effect of the text and music in them, with special attention to the peculiar witchery of the rhythm throbbing in both. . . . Seemingly the height of simplicity and all but made up of accents of ordinary speech, I can never hum an air of his without succumbing to what impresses me as the magic mysticism of something hovering in the background." The early twentieth-century musicologist Abraham Idelsohn wrote of Zunser, "He pleads with his people to awaken from apathetic slumber and to become aware of their misery." (Dylan put it more directly in song in 1979, asking his listeners, "When you gonna wake up?")

In 1889, Eliakum Zunser came to the United States for a concert tour. But unlike his spiritual successor—still playing one hundred concerts a year well into his seventh decade—there would be no Never Ending Tour for Zunser. Rather, he wound up settling into a life of relative obscurity in New York City, where the services of *badkhonim* were rarely called for (and from where Dylan, a Minnesota native, would launch his stellar career approximately seventy years later), and where instead he set up shop as a printer and publisher. Zunser continued to write sporadically, and by the time of his death in 1913 he had written approximately six hundred songs—a figure that Bob Dylan himself was closing in upon at the time of this writing.

INTRODUCTION
FROM CHAOS TO CREATION

The question I was asked more than any other (perhaps with the exception of "Are you going to interview him?" Answer: No) when I told people I was writing a Jewish biography of Bob Dylan was, "Isn't he still a born-again Christian?" To which I always replied, "Who knows?"

Indeed, who knows? And in any case, it's beside the point. This book sets out to make no claims about Bob Dylan's past or present religious beliefs or self-identification. There are enough on-the-record comments from Dylan to support any viewpoint—he's Jewish, he's Christian, he's Rastafarian, he doesn't believe in any religion, or he finds G-d in music, religion in the songs.

All that being said, there are certainly indications, in his songs and in the little we know about his offstage life—which is surprisingly little, considering how much has been written about him, how many websites and discussion groups are devoted to him, and how fanatically curious his ardent followers can be about him—suggesting that Dylan has never fully abandoned the faith of his forebears. Rather, he has apparently taken very seriously his relationship to Judaism, a relationship that, as this book sets out to demonstrate, so fully and completely informs his life and his work—lyrically, thematically, musically, and otherwise—that it cannot be ignored as an essential aspect of both.

A funny thing happened when I began a mostly self-directed study of Jewish scripture—the Bible, the Talmud, the mystical writings comprising the Kabbalah, the traditional prayer liturgy—in my mid-thirties. Every so often, an image, a theme, or a phrase would jump out at me as something familiar. This wasn't an echo of previous learning of Jewish texts—of that I had next to none. For me, the texts that I had memorized as a schoolboy—the words that I could access almost immediately in much the same manner that a yeshiva graduate can quote nearly any chapter and verse from the Torah— were the lyrics of Bob Dylan, which I began studying at age fourteen in 1974 and have continued to study with a regularity bordering on obsession ever since.

The great surprise that awaited me when turning my attention in midlife toward the rich trove of Jewish texts was that there was a significant overlap between the torah of Dylan and the Torah of Moses. For example, in the book of Prophets, Ezekiel recounts a vision of angels: "The soles of their feet . . . their appearance was like fiery coals, burning like torches." And in the Bible, G-d warns Moses, "No human can see my face and live," after the latter asks the Former if He would reveal his physical manifestation. These verses were uncannily familiar when I read them the first time in their original versions, as I knew them from Bob Dylan songs. "The soles of my feet, I swear they're burning," Dylan sings in "The Wicked Messenger," from 1967. And on the chorus of "I and I," from 1983, Dylan proclaims, "One says to the other / No man sees my face and lives."

One of the most rewarding ways of approaching Bob Dylan's lyrics is to read them as the work of a poetic mind apparently immersed in Jewish texts and engaged in the age-old process of midrash: a kind of formal or informal riffing on the texts in order to elucidate or elaborate upon their hidden meanings. Perhaps the most famous of these riffs takes place in one of Dylan's best-known songs, 1965's "Highway 61 Revisited," his whimsical retelling of the Akeidah, the story in which G-d commands Abraham to bind Isaac as if for a sacrificial offering, which Dylan posits as a conversation between two jaded, cynical hipsters. U.S. Route 61, incidentally, is the main highway leading from New Orleans to Dylan's birthplace in Duluth, Minnesota.

While the Abraham and Isaac story is one of the core legends of Western civilization, as far back as 1962, lyrics by the son of Abe Zimmerman reveal a familiarity with Torah far beyond the basics of the average religious school education. The song "Blowin' in the Wind," destined to become a civil rights anthem, borrows imagery from two biblical prophets, Ezekiel and Isaiah, to which Dylan would often return for inspiration. The song "Love Minus Zero/No Limit," one of his most beautiful love songs, gains added heft and resonance when one realizes that much of its symbolism is drawn from early chapters of the book of Daniel. And any attentive Dylan fan stumbling upon these verses in chapter 26 of Leviticus—"Your strength shall be spent in vain . . . I will make your heaven like iron . . . You shall eat and not be satisfied . . ."—will recognize them as the raw material from which he shaped the 1967 song "I Pity the Poor Immigrant."

Although facts about Dylan's Jewish upbringing and practice are hard to come by given his notorious penchant for privacy, purposeful obfuscation, or even outright deception regarding his personal life, evidence from his lyrics, his public statements, and some undisputed biographical items add up to a convincing portrait of a mind profoundly shaped by Jewish influence, study, and belief, and a life lived largely as a committed Jew. Although Dylan grew up near the Canadian border in the cold, hard, iron-mining town of Hibbing, Minnesota—as one might imagine, not exactly a hotbed of Jewish communal life and culture—his nuclear and extended family of grandparents, aunts and uncles, and cousins who lived in Hibbing or in the nearby port city of Duluth—where he was born and to where his family frequently returned—retained enough connection with Jewish tradition to observe the dietary laws, to mark the weekly

Sabbath, and to stage a party the likes of which had never been seen in Hibbing when it came time for Dylan to become bar mitzvah in 1954. The teenage Bobby Zimmerman spent the next three or four summers at a Jewish camp in Wisconsin, and as a freshman at the University of Minnesota in 1959, he lived in a Jewish fraternity house.

Much has been made and written of Bob Dylan as a product of the American folk and blues traditions. Without question, Dylan's specific art has always drawn very heavily on Anglo-American folk, African-American blues, gospel music, Tin Pan Alley pop, country music, and other styles of American music. Dylan's genius has been to take them further, to combine them with other strains of music, and to foster a revolution in American music that saw rock triumph over sugary pop in the mid-1960s as the premier expression of the youthful counterculture.

But there is another context from which Dylan has sprung. While he may never have heard of Eliakum Zunser—and there's no evidence that he has—and while he may be utterly unfamiliar with the folk-protest tradition that was part of the culture of his Russian Jewish ancestors back in the Pale of Settlement, there is still something of Zunser in Dylan, as much as there is of the folk-singer Woody Guthrie and the blues legend Robert Johnson. One of the very first original compositions that Dylan debuted in folk clubs in New York upon arriving there in 1961 was "Talkin' Hava Negeilah Blues," based on Guthrie's patented style of "talking blues." From the earliest days of his career, Dylan—contrary to the received notion that he engaged in a deliberate cover-up of his background—wore his Jewish heart on his sleeve.

The Jewish influence on Dylan's art, or on the practice of his art, goes deeper than a superficial or coincidental resemblance to that of Eliakum Zunser's a century earlier. Like much blues and some folk itself, Dylan's work stems from the ancient tradition of Jewish prophecy—not in the sense of foretelling the future, but rather in the sense that a prophet, or in Hebrew, a *navi*, is a truth-teller to and an admonisher of his people: literally, a "proclaimer." The Prophets, whose sermons and declarations are collected in the biblical books of

Amos, Isaiah, Jeremiah, Ezekiel, and others, were, in a sense, social critics—the original protest singers, if you will. They pointed out the hypocrisies and errors of their subjects' ways, warning of punishments that could befall them and suggesting paths toward collective redemption. Some of them also recount in detail their encounters with G-d, or what we call their "mystical" experiences, and describe a future time when others will enjoy such intimate encounters with the Creator.

The biblical Prophets did not so much engage in the act of prophecy, in the sense of foretelling the future (although they did warn about what would happen to their listeners if they did not heed their words or the laws of G-d), as they engaged in sociocultural criticism. They warned against backsliding and immorality and blatant lawbreaking and foretold the bloody consequences of this behavior. In many ways, Jesus, too, fits into this tradition of Jewish prophecy, although Christians believe that Jesus was not just another Jewish prophet but rather the divine bringer of a new message and a new covenant with G-d.

Consciously or not, Bob Dylan has in large part adopted the modes of Jewish prophetic discourse as one of his primary means of communication, determining the content of his songs, the style of delivery, and his relationship to his audience. As the great twentieth-century American theologian Abraham Joshua Heschel wrote about the biblical Prophets, "The words in which the prophets attempted to relate their experiences were not photographs but illustrations, not descriptions but *songs*." (Emphasis mine.) Throughout his career, Dylan has repeatedly returned to that very same prophetic tradition to infuse his songs with a measure of impact and dignity that so obviously sets his work apart from other singer-songwriters of the rock era.

To put it another way, Dylan's innovation was to invert what was until then the purpose of pop music—to make listeners feel better about themselves, to entertain them, and to glorify the joys of sex and romantic love—and instead to use it to challenge his listeners' preconceptions and orthodoxies by unsettling and provoking them, which he has done from day one until today. Bono, the singer of the

Irish rock band U2 and himself a strong believer in a type of Christianity with ancestral Jewish roots, understands this about Dylan. "[Dylan's] was always a unique critique of modernity," he writes. "Because in fact Dylan comes from an ancient place, almost medieval. . . . The anachronism, really, is the '60s. For the rest of his life he's been howling from some sort of past that we seem to have forgotten but must not . . ."

Thus, in the pages that follow, in addition to recounting the basic biographical arc of his life and career and discussing the musical and creative achievements that have led him to be widely considered as one of the greatest, most influential artists of the last half century, I hope to illuminate Dylan's life and work by revisiting them in a context that has until now been minimized or overlooked by biographers and critics. Bob Dylan didn't just spring from nowhere. Some have done a good job exploring Dylan's immediate roots in Hibbing, but few have spent more than a few lines bothering to dig deeper into the unique sociocultural context in which Dylan was raised. Nor have any chroniclers deemed it fit (or been properly equipped) to place Dylan's unique approach toward his art in the greater context of Jewish culture and history, especially given how so much of his work regards the spiritual aspects of existence and is strewn with quotations, paraphrases, allusions, and themes drawn from normative Judaism, and given how his transformational approach echoes that of artists, poets, seers, and prophets going back hundreds and thousands of years in Jewish history. Nor have any traced this strain in his work as a continuous, unbroken chain throughout his life and career, in order to show how Dylan has, consciously or not, chosen in large part to use the prophetic mode of discourse as his primary mode, or at least one of his primary modes, of communication, determining how he shapes his narratives and addresses his audience, as well as the themes and subject matter of so many of his songs.

None of this is meant to suggest the exclusion of other significant strains of interpretation or context for Dylan's work. Dylan has been essentially influenced by American folk, blues, country, pop, and early rock 'n' roll music, and by individual artists (for example, Woody Guthrie, Hank Williams, Robert Johnson, Chuck Berry) and songs from those genres. Dylan's songs are full of allusions to, quotations of, and themes from old folk and blues songs. Dylan has been significantly influenced by great poetry and literature—one need look no further than Christopher Ricks's magnificent book, *Dylan's Visions of Sin,* which has a lot more to say about Dylan-as-poet than it does about Dylan's so-called visions of sin but nevertheless does so masterfully—and even by popular literature, as was shown when several lines from a song on the 2001 album *"Love and Theft"* were traced to an obscure Japanese yakuza novel. Even Hollywood has provided Dylan with material and inspiration—entire songs have been composed in large part of choice bits of movie dialogue.

And as much as I do believe that a complete understanding of Dylan's work is impossible without a recognition of the debt it owes to Judaism—and the way in which it *engages* Jewish themes and thought in a process akin to midrash, the elaboration upon Jewish scripture as a form of commentary—I recognize fully that his complete oeuvre can also be read in large part as:

1) a reckoning with various loves and losses, most notably his relationship with his wife, Sara, before, during, and after their marriage,
2) a commentary on topical concerns of American society and politics (although this strain in his work has been unduly overemphasized to the detriment of the others), and/or
3) a meditation on identity, with various characters and narrators that come to the forefront and disappear, and an obsession with the theme of the mask, from his early obsession with Woody Guthrie at least through his aptly titled 2003 film, *Masked and Anonymous.*

And, one could argue—and several authors have—that some of Dylan's work suggests a struggle or identification with a personal relationship with Jesus (as I hope to show, one that is at least subsumed by and doesn't discount his primary relationship with his Jewishness).

Certainly, some of Dylan's most overtly theological songs were the gospel songs he recorded between 1979 and 1981. Neverthe-less, in 1982, Dylan's son Samuel became bar mitzvah, and by 1983, when Dylan was reportedly hanging out with Orthodox rabbis in Brooklyn and Israel, overtly Jewish themes colored the songs on the album *Infidels,* the sleeve of which featured a photograph of Dylan overlooking the Old City of Jerusalem, taken on a visit ear-lier that year for his son Jesse's bar mitzvah. The song "Neighbor-hood Bully"—a drippingly sarcastic overview of Jewish history and persecution through the lens of contemporary Zionism—evinced a strongly nationalistic identification with Jewish peoplehood. The songs "Jokerman" and "I and I," too, revealed a mind once again inspired by the Jewish Bible.

Over the ensuing decade, Dylan made several appearances on telethons for Chabad, in one calling the Orthodox Jewish outreach movement his "favorite organization." During this time, he made several more visits to Israel; he opened a shopping complex in Santa Monica replete with an office, a coffeehouse, a gymnasium, and a synagogue; and he saw his daughter, Maria, marry and begin raising a family with the Orthodox Jewish singer-songwriter Peter Himmelman.

In that postgospel period, Dylan's songs continued to reflect a mind steeped in a Jewish worldview: on *Oh Mercy,* "Everything Is Broken" portrays the Kabbalistic concept of a world in a state of disrepair, and "Political World" includes a vivid description of *Kiddush HaShem,* the religiously inspired martyrdom of those who were dying in Auschwitz around the time Dylan was born. And when Dylan garnered a Lifetime Achievement Award at the Grammy Awards in 1991, the focus of his acceptance speech was an inscruta-ble passage that astute listeners recognized as a paraphrase of psalm 27, an essential prayer inextricably tied to the acts of repentance and return that are the themes of the liturgy of Rosh Hashanah and Yom Kippur, the holiest days of the Jewish year.

Dylan has apparently continued to find inspiration in Jewish scripture in recent years. In "Not Dark Yet," on his 1997 Grammy Award–winning album, *Time Out of Mind,* Dylan sings, "I was born here and I'll die here against my will," paraphrasing Pirkei Avot

(Sayings of the Fathers, from the *Mishnah* 4:29): "Against your will you were born, against your will you die." And that album's opening track, "Love Sick," borrows its unusual central complaint from King Solomon's love poetry as expressed in Song of Songs 2:7: "[Bereft of your presence], I am sick with love" or, to put it more succinctly, as does Dylan, "I'm sick of love . . . I'm love sick."

Also in recent years, Dylan has been spotted annually at Yom Kippur services—typically at whatever Chabad (an Orthodox Hasidic sect) synagogue he finds himself nearest to as he constantly tours the country. A few years ago, at Congregation Adath Israel, in St. Paul, Minnesota, he is said to have received the third *aliyah* to the Torah—an honor providing an individual blessing—and to have returned in the evening for the concluding Neilah service, whose central imagery is of a penitent standing at a gate or doorway, entreating G-d's mercy to be written into the Book of Life before the doors are shut and barred, an experience Dylan put into song on *Time Out of Mind*'s "Tryin' to Get to Heaven":

> *Now you can seal up the book and not write anymore*
> *I've been walking that lonesome valley*
> *Trying to get to heaven before they close the door.*

It's imperative that one consider the Jewish nature of so much of Dylan's life and work in order to appreciate it fully and to its truest and greatest extent. In some small but significant way, this book will add to that understanding and appreciation of Dylan's work by telling the story of his life and work with reference to how Judaism influenced and shaped both.

ONE

Robert Allen Zimmerman was born in Duluth, Minnesota, to Abram Zimmerman and Beatrice "Beatty" Zimmerman (née Stone), on May 24, 1941. At birth he was, as is the tradition, given a Hebrew name to go along with his English name—in his case, Shabtai Zisel ben Avraham (*ben Avraham* simply meaning "son of Abraham," Abram being the Anglicized version of the Yiddish equivalent, Avrem).

Twenty years later, in New York City, Robert "Bobby" Zimmerman would assume a new name, a stage name more befitting a performer of any type, especially an ambitious folksinger looking to create a myth or a more colorful backstory for Bobby Zimmerman's early life than that of his relatively conventional, middle-class upbringing as the child of middle-class merchants. Some say Zimmerman changed his name to hide his background, ethnic, religious, or otherwise (although Zimmerman is a German name, and not a particularly Jewish one at that). Yet embedded in four of Bob Dylan's best-known songs are references to several of the simple, biographical facts contained in the preceding paragraph.

"Like a Rolling Stone," Bob Dylan's greatest hit—literally (it went to number 2 on *Billboard* magazine's singles chart), figuratively (it's widely considered the most important individual song of his career and, by many, in all of rock 'n' roll history), and critically (entire books have been written about this one song)—includes his mother's maiden name in the title and in the line that serves as the fulcrum of the song: "How does it feel / To be . . . like a rolling stone?" There's more than a bit of self-reference going on in this song that almost singlehandedly revolutionized rock 'n' roll music. Several years after writing it, Dylan would say as much, realizing in hindsight that the subjects of his early songs referred to often only by pronouns—you, he, it, they—were in fact all versions of himself. "I hadn't really known before, that I was writing about myself in all those songs," he told his biographer Anthony Scaduto.

Around the same time as "Like a Rolling Stone," another popular hit by Dylan, "Rainy Day Women #12 & 35," would also make use of the same name—or word—in its key line, "Everybody must get stoned." Besides the obvious connotation—that everyone must get drunk on alcohol or high on drugs—Dylan slyly suggested that everyone must come under the influence of a guy named Stone. And, perhaps more trenchantly, he was punning on other alternative meanings of the term—that everybody must find themselves on the receiving end of stones, in the literal, biblical sense of being stoned, or in the more figurative sense of being on the receiving end of critical barbs, as was Dylan throughout his career.

Also around the same time, another of Dylan's best-known songs, "Highway 61 Revisited," drew directly from the Bible for its famous opening image. "God said to Abraham / Kill me a son," the song begins, in a sort of hipster retelling of the Akeidah, or the binding of Isaac. Of all the stories, Dylan chose this "greatest hit" of the Bible to riff upon, a story about a father and son in which the central character bears the same name as his own father, thereby aligning himself with the sacrificial son, one who was offered up to G-d in a demonstration of absolute faith. Further personalizing the narrative, Dylan located the "killing" (as well as the other events that follow in the song) on the very road that runs from New Orleans to Canada— by way of his birthplace, Duluth.

And finally, Dylan playfully references his given family name,

Zimmerman, in another of his top hits, "Gotta Serve Somebody"—incidentally, the first recording ever to garner him a Grammy Award, for best male rock vocal, in 1980—when in an otherwise mostly serious song he jokes, "You may call me Terry, you may call me Timmy / You may call me Bobby, you may call me Zimmy . . ." Bobby Zimmerman was undoubtedly called "Zimmy" (among other things) as a youth, but this rare morsel of autobiographical reference in one of his songs—particularly to his original surname, which he had been accused of changing in order to hide his Jewishness—coming at the beginning of his so-called born-again Christian phase, was quite telling and suggestive, if not downright subversive.

So what? So what if his name and his parents' names found their way into his songs, and, coincidentally, into a handful of his most successful songs at that? Writers, poets, and songwriters—artists of all sorts—are always drawing upon the things they know best in their work; they are veritably encouraged to "write about what you know." Why should Dylan's colorful family history be any exception? Why shouldn't Dylan do the same?

Rare are the number of times that Dylan writes something that can be traced back to an autobiographical impulse and then used in the service of his poetry. And that Dylan does so, for the most part, in songs that engage in or rely upon religious themes, suggests that, consciously or not, Dylan sees himself (and his family) very much in a Jewish context, playing out Jewish themes and tropes, placing his own relationship to his Judaism front and center. This is in marked contrast with the received wisdom that Robert Allen Zimmerman attempted to turn his back on his middle-class upbringing, his family, and his Judaism when he changed his name to Bob Dylan and started making up stories about being an orphan and a frequent runaway from a foster home in South Dakota, in the service of portraying himself as a successor to Woody Guthrie (whose own legend and autobiography was in large part constructed out of whole cloth), rather than as the son of a conventional, ordinary appliance salesman and his department-store saleswoman wife.

It's easy to see without looking too far into or beyond his own lyrics that Dylan had no intention of such deception. In one of the very first original songs he wrote and recorded, "Song to Woody," which appeared on his eponymous debut album, recorded in the fall of 1961 and released in March 1962, and which otherwise was filled with renditions of old folk and blues tunes, Dylan explicitly denied any such intention. After several verses expressing hero worship, thanks, and gratitude to Woody Guthrie and his peers, Dylan ended the song by saying:

> I'm a-leaving tomorrow, but I could leave today,
> Somewhere down the road someday.
> The very last thing that I'd want to do
> Is to say I've been hittin' some hard travelin' too

thereby making it clear from the outset of his career that he doesn't put himself in the same class, or the same situation, as hard-travelin' folk music forebears like Woody Guthrie.

But lest we get too far ahead of ourselves . . .

Robert Allen Zimmerman was born in Duluth, Minnesota, to Abram Zimmerman and Beatrice "Beatty" Zimmerman (née Stone), on May 24, 1941. The first of the couple's two children, Bobby was raised for a few years in Duluth, where his father worked for Standard Oil, before contracting polio in 1946. After his recovery, Abe Zimmerman moved his family about seventy-five miles northwest to his wife's hometown of Hibbing, a mining town about one hundred miles from the Canadian border, where he also had family, including his brothers Maurice and Paul, who invited him to join them in running their recently purchased appliance store, Micka Electric, later renamed Zimmerman Furniture and Electric.

Despite the German-sounding name, the Zimmerman clan, including Abe's parents, Zigman and Anna, originally hailed from Odessa, Ukraine, from which they, like many others, fled anti-Jewish pogroms in 1905. Zigman settled in Duluth, where he worked as a peddler, and sent for his wife and children, who would eventually number six, including Abram, who was born in Duluth in 1911.

Beatty Stone's ancestors, including the Edelsteins on her mother's side, came from Lithuania, considered the "Jerusalem" of nineteenth-century Eastern Europe for its high concentration of rabbinical scholars and yeshivas, schools in which Jewish law was studied and parsed on a never-ending basis. Beatty's grandfather, Benjamin "B. H." Edelstein, was a religious man who worked as a blacksmith. B.H., along with his wife, Lybba, and his brother Julius, arrived in Hibbing around the same time the Zimmermans settled in Duluth. In the early 1920s, B. H. Edelstein and his brother began opening movie theaters in town—including one named after Lybba—and these would remain in the family for decades, eventually being run by Beatty's uncles. This family connection to show business would give a teenage Bobby Zimmerman free access to repeated viewings of his favorite movies of the 1950s, including Gregory Peck westerns and the proto-punk rebellion flicks of James Dean and Marlon Brando that had a strong influence on Zimmerman's burgeoning adolescent identity. His early education in film would also stand him in good stead when his career as a music celebrity broadened to include a parallel career in the movies (as was the practice of the time, as per Frank Sinatra, Elvis Presley, and the Beatles) as an actor, screenwriter, director, and songwriter for film—and as a poacher of classic film dialogue for his song lyrics.

The success of the Edelsteins' small chain of four cinemas allowed B.H.—who lived to the ripe old age of ninety-one (his death in 1961 coincided with the year his great-grandson Robert finally fled the Midwest to seek fame and fortune in New York City)—to devote much of his time to daily prayer and Torah study. The sight of his bearded, yarmulke-wearing, immigrant great-grandfather wrapping tefillin—the leather straps and boxes that Orthodox men use in the morning prayer service—and davening (praying Old World–style in a rigorous manner using a singsong chant with stylized bowing and arm gestures), as well as seeing him poring over old volumes of the Talmud for hours at a time in the afternoons, must have made quite an impression on young Bobby Zimmerman, giving this all-

American boy from the Midwest a good taste of what daily life had looked like for his family just a few generations earlier back in Eastern Europe. Interacting with B.H. was like entering another dimension in space and time, transporting his interlocutors back to late-nineteenth-century Lithuania, the intellectual and religious heartland of Judaism at the time.

Beatty Stone was an attractive, vivacious, modern young woman with an outgoing personality and a sense of possibility that couldn't be contained in the relatively provincial confines of Hibbing, a town of eighteen thousand. As soon as she was old enough, she began escaping to Duluth with friends and aunts close in age to attend dances and parties. At one such event she was introduced to Abram Zimmerman, who was undoubtedly attracted by her good looks and extroverted personality, which contrasted with (or complemented) his introverted, serious mien. The two were married in Hibbing in 1934, when Beatty was nineteen and Abe twenty-two, and made their home back in Duluth, where Abe was working his way up the management ladder at Standard Oil's regional office. Beatty got a part-time job at a department store, which kept her occupied in the intervening seven years before she finally became pregnant with a baby who would grow up to be one of the most famous and influential cultural figures of the twentieth century.

Tales abound of Bobby Zimmerman as an attractive toddler and preschooler, one devoted to his mother, and one with a penchant for breaking out in song. As early as age four, he began giving command performances at family gatherings, including a Mother's Day party and at Beatty's sister Irene's wedding, singing popular hits of the day, such as "Accentuate the Positive." Even then, he was working on his stage persona, playing the part of the reluctant performer, eventually giving in to the crowd's pleas for him to perform (or to monetary bribes that he allegedly refunded at the end of the song), but not before insisting that everybody remain silent and give him their full and complete attention before he would sing.

The Zimmermans presented Bobby with the gift of a younger brother, David (a gift he reputedly had little use for until the two grew close as adults), in 1946. Their joy was short-lived, however, as Abe contracted polio around the same time. After six months of recuperation, he lost his job at Standard Oil. For the rest of his life, Abe—who had been a hearty, athletic man—would walk with a noticeable halt and with considerable pain, which Bob Dylan would emphasize in paying tribute to his father in his memoir, *Chronicles*. Fortunately, right around the same time, Abe's brothers Maurice and Paul had bought their employer's appliance store, and extended an offer to Abe to join them in the business. Zimmerman Furniture and Electric was located in Beatty's hometown, however, so the Zimmermans packed up their two young boys and their belongings and made the trek to Hibbing (soon to be followed by Abe's mother, Anna), where they both now enjoyed the proximity of extended families: grandparents, parents, siblings, aunts, uncles, and cousins. As Dylan once told an interviewer, "When I was young, my life was built around the family. We got together all the time. There weren't many Jews around."

By the time Abe and Beatty moved to Hibbing in 1947, the once-thriving mining town where the average temperature in January is below zero was already showing signs of economic hardship and hints of the postwar industrial collapse to come. The town's heyday was the late 1910s and early 1920s, when Hibbing iron fueled the Allied effort in the First World War. Just before the war, the richest deposits of ore were discovered below the town itself. The Oliver Mining Company convinced the townspeople to allow them to move the entire town, buildings and all, a mile down the road to a village called Alice, in a slow process that took longer than four decades and was still being carried out well into the 1950s while Bobby Zimmerman was still a teenager. Among the accommodations the mining company granted the townspeople, who now had the distinction of living next to the world's largest open-pit iron mine, were several opulent civic buildings, the Androy Hotel, and a $4 million high school—an astronomical sum for the time—said to be the most luxurious in the nation. Among the school's unique appointments was an 1,800-seat auditorium with velvet seats and cut-glass chandeliers, loosely modeled on New York's Capitol Theatre, which eventually gave the teenage Bobby an early taste of what it's like to perform in a theater-sized venue. (Later in his career, when he could still fill larger, arena-sized venues, Bob Dylan would often opt for playing in vaudeville-era theaters of this same size and vintage, including Boston's Orpheum and the State Theatre in Portland, Maine, among others. Before going on tours or into the recording studio, he'd often hole up with his band for a week at a time at the restored Bardavon Opera House in Poughkeepsie, New York, to rehearse and work through arrangements.)

While the Great Depression came as a blow, it wasn't lethal to the local economy in Hibbing, especially once orders began coming in from weapons manufacturers to supply the Allied armed forces fighting the Second World War. While it might seem ironic that this provincial city with an economy entirely based on producing the raw material for armaments would produce Bob Dylan—widely if somewhat mistakenly seen as a leading voice of the antiwar and pacifist movements of the 1960s—perhaps it makes perfect sense that Dylan *would* hail from such a place. In fact, Dylan would directly and honestly address the nature of his hometown in song, most notably in "North Country Blues," but also in liner notes and concert programs, notably in "My Life in a Stolen Moment," included in the program for a concert at New York's Town Hall in April 1963. And his proximity to the machinery of war undoubtedly stoked the creative flame that produced songs such as "Masters of War," "A Hard Rain's a-Gonna Fall," and "It's Alright Ma (I'm Only Bleeding)."

When Abe and Beatty first arrived in Hibbing, they stayed with her parents. Within a year, Abe bought the two-story, gray stucco house on Seventh Avenue that would become Bobby's home until he went off to college in 1959. The house had three bedrooms, but Bobby and David shared a room much of the time so that their grandmother Florence, Beatty's mother, could live with them after her husband, Ben Stone, passed away. Growing up with an immigrant grandmother who still spoke Yiddish, as did his father and uncles, must have imprinted upon Bobby a strong sense of his Eastern European immigrant roots, which would variously find expression in his 1967 song "I Pity the Poor Immigrant," in the Yiddish cadences of the music on the 1976 album, *Desire,* and elsewhere in his work, including in a poem he wrote in college that began, "*Sholem Alechem* all you mothers . . ."

Hibbing was composed mostly of working-class Scandinavian, Slavic, and Italian immigrants and their children. Not only did Bobby Zimmerman's religion, ethnicity, and name set him apart in this predominantly Catholic city but his house was also one of the newest in one of the nicer neighborhoods. If not totally spoiled, Bobby seemed to get whatever he wanted, whether it was a radio, a record player, a guitar, a piano, a motorcycle (along with the requisite leather jacket and boots), and, eventually, a car. The majority of his peers had tough fathers who labored in the massive iron pit and came home from work filthy (to this day mining remains the number-one industry in Hibbing), while Bobby's father and uncles came home relatively clean after a day's work selling furniture and appliances—often on credit—to the parents of his schoolmates.

Bobby's mother worked part-time at Feldman's Department Store. Many of the downtown businesses, including Hyman Bloom's Boston Department Store, Jacob Jolowsky's auto wrecking, Nathan Nides's fashion shop, David Shapiro's market, Jack and Israel Sher's insurance agency, and Louis Stein and James Shapiro's pharmacies, were owned by Jews. This set up a situation in Hibbing—all too typical throughout Jewish history in America and in Europe beforehand—in which, owing to unique socioeconomic circumstances that limited Jews to mercantile occupations, banking, and other financial trades, members of the gentile working class became indebted to Jewish merchants, inevitably provoking resentment toward the merchant class and Jews, who were seemingly synonymous. Working-class towns composed mostly of immigrant Catholics tended to be hotbeds of anti-Semitism across America. Growing up middle-class and Jewish in Hibbing made Bobby Zimmerman feel different from the others, separate, an object of suspicion, and alienated from his peers. His schoolteachers generally recall Bobby as a shy, quiet, retiring kid who did everything he could to deflect attention from himself.

Nevertheless, he grew up in the comfort of a large family network of grandparents, uncles, aunts, and cousins. The extended

Zimmerman clan, and that of his mother's family, the Stones and Edelsteins, wasn't entirely alone in Hibbing, where there was an active if small Jewish community of just under three hundred—enough to support a synagogue, the nominally Orthodox Agudath Achim, where Bobby and David attended Hebrew school. The synagogue was also home to a chapter of the women's charitable Zionist group Hadassah, for which Bobby's mother served as president, and a chapter of the Jewish service organization B'nai Brith, for which his father served as president.

With his parents so obviously at the center of what passed for "Jewish life" in Hibbing, it's no surprise that Bobby's bar mitzvah party, held at the Androy Hotel on May 22, 1954, attracted four hundred guests—reportedly a record for the time in Hibbing. Many of the attendees were friends and relatives who came from Duluth and the Twin Cities, since there weren't even four hundred Jews in Hibbing alone. Stories vary as to who trained Bob to chant Torah, the centerpiece of the ritual marking a Jewish boy's coming of age. Legend has it that the Zimmermans imported an Orthodox rabbi from Brooklyn, New York, just for the occasion, but this probably stems from an idle bit of disinformation Bob Dylan once tossed off to an interviewer. More likely, Bobby was trained in religious school by a part-time rabbi who attended to the local congregation's needs from his base in Duluth, or Beatty Zimmerman drove her son to Duluth regularly to train with a rabbi, or some combination of the two. Bobby obediently studied and carried out this ritual, publicly marking a Jewish boy's coming of age, assuming the legal religious obligations and privileges of a Jewish man, as has been the tradition for centuries.

As Zimmerman Furniture and Electric's bookkeeper, it was Abe's role to police the store's debt, and his son Bobby was occasionally drafted to go out with the store's workmen on repossession calls when it was clear that a family was unable to repay its debt. Bobby hated this chore, and it fostered in him sympathy for those who couldn't pay their bills on time, as well as resentment toward a system—in this case, embodied in the person of his father—that seemingly preyed upon the working poor. Perhaps most acutely and painfully, it fostered embarrassment for Bobby to be seen (or to see himself) as a face of the very system against which he recoiled. This only fed into his split sense of self, as a Gemini (the twins) on the one hand and as a middle-class Jewish rebel on the other, and undoubtedly fed into his lifelong assumption of masks and aliases (the most famous, of course, being "Bob Dylan"). Bobby could have easily left high school and gone straight to work in the family business, or completed college (which he never did) and returned to Hibbing to run the business and build it into something larger. Instead, he chose another path.

His early alienation from his peers, as well as his innate, creative bent, prompted Bobby to become a somewhat dreamy boy whose self-contained world left him plenty of time to exercise his creative impulses in the form of writing poems, drawing, and playing piano and, later, guitar. About as sporty as Bobby would become would be as a member of a teenage bowling team called the Gutter Boys. Eventually, his teenage friendships revolved around shared interests in music and the movies. By the time he was fifteen, Bobby had gathered around him a coterie of musician friends who would become the Shadow Blasters and later the Golden Chords, specializing in playing renditions of songs by Little Richard, Bobby's idol, with Bobby on lead vocals and piano. These and subsequent garage bands, including the Satin Tones and Elston Gunn and the Rock Boppers (guess who was Elston Gunn?), would wind up playing for local dances and school talent shows.

One high school performance especially stands out in the memories of teachers, parents, and students who attended. The auditorium curtain opened, and Zimmerman and company began blasting their way through a Little Richard tune (not that anyone could tell), with Bobby shrieking like a banshee, pounding the piano keys with his fists, and kicking the foot pedal so hard it broke. The amplifiers onstage were turned up all the way, and they in turn ran via microphones through the auditorium's loudspeaker system. After one number, greeted by much booing, gnashing of teeth, and complaints about the volume (to say nothing of shock at Bobby's frenzied, crazed performance), a school authority cut the power to the PA system, but the band soldiered on. Accounts of the gig read remarkably like a dress rehearsal for Bob Dylan's infamous, controversial "going electric" performance a decade hence at the Newport Folk Festival in 1965, replete with booing, attempts at cutting the power, and urgent calls to foreshorten his performance. One can only imagine Dylan's feeling of déjà vu at Newport, bringing him back ten years earlier to the near-riot he caused at Hibbing High when he first "went electric."

While the Mister Joneses in the audience—the teachers, school administrators and staffers, and other adults—were puzzled and scandalized by Bobby Zimmerman's loud stage antics, those *were* appreciated by a good percentage of his fellow students, at least the ones who were hip to the burgeoning rock 'n' roll revolution as captured in the 1955 film *Blackboard Jungle*, which spawned the first rock 'n' roll hit song, sending "Rock Around the Clock" by Bill Haley and the Comets to number 1 for eight weeks. As a result, Bobby began enjoying his first taste of minor celebrity. Around this time, young Zimmerman also began modeling himself after James Dean in *Rebel Without a Cause* and *East of Eden* and Marlon Brando in *The Wild One,* and he persuaded his parents to get him a motorcycle. In another foreshadowing of events that would change the course of his life—and music history—a decade later, Bobby proved to be a terrible biker, once hitting a child who ran out from between two parked cars (fortunately the child was only mildly injured) and another time wiping out on the edge of railroad tracks just as a train sped by.

Accompanying his growing interest in music and movies was his budding interest in the opposite sex. Perhaps his self-transformation from middle-class Jewish boy to rebel rock 'n' roll biker and musician fooled Echo Helstrom; perhaps she was clueless about who he really was; or perhaps, to her credit, she simply didn't care. Echo and her family, of Finnish descent, lived in a wooden shack southwest of town. Her father was a mechanic and welder who didn't approve of some guy named Zimmerman coming around bird-dogging his daughter (although Echo's mother supposedly was fond of him). Like Bobby, Echo had dreams of celebrity, fashioning herself a star of the silver screen. From all reports she had the looks; she was often compared to Brigitte Bardot. The two probably made a striking couple, right out of one of those rebel movies they shared together on dates at the Victory, Garden, or Lybba theaters, and the two went out with each other for most of their junior year in high school, until Echo grew tired of Bobby's many long weekends spent in the Twin Cities, where presumably he saw other girlfriends.

All the while that Bobby Zimmerman was dealing with teenage life in Hibbing—by all accounts, doing pretty well even with the social roadblocks lodged against him—he lived something of a double or parallel life out of town. Summers from 1954 to 1958, he attended Herzl Camp, in Webster, Wisconsin. The camp, which shared both a religious and Zionist orientation, drew Jewish teens from all over the greater region. By all accounts, Bobby thrived in this environment, and as anyone who has ever had the experience of going to sleepaway camp can attest, it can be a liberating experience that frees an individual of his homebound identity and lets him experiment with new personas precisely at the age where such personal self-exploration is so important. Bobby made many friends there, including several girlfriends—most notably Judy Rubin, whom he would continue to see on and off for several years in the Twin Cities area—and several young men, including Howard Rutman, Larry Kegan, and Louis Kemp. These connections, which built upon those he already had with the Duluth Jewish community through his extended family, served Bobby well over the next few years. Rutman and Kegan lived in St. Paul, and Bobby would visit them frequently while still in high school (traveling by Greyhound bus—a national business founded in Hibbing to transport residents from the new Hibbing to the iron mines in the original Hibbing—until he was old enough to drive).

With Kegan and Rutman, Bobby formed what was perhaps his very first musical group. Calling themselves the Jokers, they performed mostly a cappella versions of the teen hits of the day.

Woody Guthrie's autobiography, *Bound for Glory,* in what was to prove a fateful gesture.

It was in Dinkytown that Bobby Zimmerman began establishing a public persona as Bob Dylan, figuratively and literally. As Dylan recounts in *Chronicles,* he walked into a coffeehouse called the Ten O'Clock Scholar and asked if he could play. The owner asked him his name. Zimmerman blurted out, "Bob Dylan." And that was that. Bob Dylan became a regular scenester and performer at the Scholar and at other coffeehouses in and around Dinkytown, where the unique voice and approach of this folk and blues singer would begin to emerge and be sharpened and honed, so that by the time he arrived in Greenwich Village just a year or two later, the myth he constructed of himself as a Woody Guthrie–style wandering troubadour seemed fully believable.

Zimmerman began integrating "Bob Dylan" into his regular life, too. In 2005, a sixteen-page sheaf of poems titled "Poems Without Titles" that Bob wrote during his university stint, bearing the signatures "Dylan" and "Dylanism," was sold at auction for $78,000 by Christie's. (It's not clear if these were college assignments or work Zimmerman did on his own.) A spokesperson for Christie's said the poems manifested the incipient Dylan's "witty and sometimes coarse sense of humor," his desire to stop smoking, and his relationships with various women. The poems ranged from adolescent angst ("I search the depths of my soul for an answer. But there is no answer. Because there is no question. And there is no time") to simple autobiography ("Once there was Judy / And she said / Hi to me / When no one else / Could take the / time . . . ," presumably a reference to Judy Rubin). According to Christie's, the poems also reference Dylan's Jewish heritage with Yiddish phrases, such as the aforementioned "*Sholem Alechem.*"

By the spring of his freshman year, Dylan already had one foot out of academia. By the summer, he hit the road, having followed up a lead for a gig in Colorado. Like his first arrival at summer camp, Dylan's summer in Denver and Central City, Colorado, gave him an opportunity to try out a new persona. He supposedly worked for a couple of weeks at a seedy Central City joint named the Gilded

Garter, playing piano in between performers of dubious talents, and bedding down with a stripper while in town. Back in Denver, he occasionally got stage time at a coffeehouse called the Satire, and enjoyed a taste of the big time at Denver's marquee folk club, the Exodus, where he crossed paths with Judy Collins (who would go on to become an influential exponent of Dylan's work, recording and performing dozens of his songs) and the blues singer Jesse Fuller, from whom Dylan learned how to play harmonica and guitar at the same time by attaching the mouth harp to a rack around his neck.

He also got into more trouble over his sticky fingers when he was busted by friends who found a significant portion of the folksinger Walt Conley's record collection in Bob's apartment in Denver. That incident pretty much spelled the end of his short-lived stint in Colorado, and by the time he returned to Dinkytown, everyone marveled at how Dylan seemed utterly transformed, replete with newfound confidence, a new folk and blues repertoire, a mouth harp wrapped around his neck with a coat hanger, and an Oklahoma accent worthy of his newest idol, Woody Guthrie. When Dylan learned that Guthrie was beset by Huntington's Disease, living as a virtual prisoner in a hospital outside New York City, his foremost obsession became to go to New York and meet his idol. And so, after visiting his family in Hibbing in December, he hit the road for New York in the first month of the new decade, one that would become almost synonymous with the man himself.

TWO

EXODUS

By the winter of 1960, Bobby Zimmerman was ready to head east to the ground zero of the folk revival, which somewhat unaccountably meant New York City. Could there have been a more unlikely venue for the revival of primarily Southern blues and Anglo-Appalachian folk music than Washington Square Park, smack-dab in the heart of Greenwich Village in southern Manhattan? Much has been made of the pilgrimage aspect of Zimmerman's trip east: that it was all in the service of his obsessive need to meet Woody Guthrie, whose persona by this point he apparently had adopted to a great extent. While this undoubtedly gave him an excuse for heading to New York, where he would have access to meeting Guthrie, who was living in a hospital facility in Morris Plains, New Jersey, the proto–Bob Dylan must also have had his sights set more generally on being where the action was in folk music: the major folk clubs, many of the most important and influential folk musicians, the headquarters of folk music publications such as *Sing Out!* and *Broadside,* and the offices of the major folk music labels, including Maynard Solomon's Vanguard, Moe Asch's Folkways, and Jac Holzman's Elektra. This is to say nothing of just wanting to escape, once and for all, the predominantly Upper Midwestern axis to which he'd been confined his entire life. Setting out for newer, if not greener pastures was, in this sense, a healthy move, both creatively and psychologically; it's one embedded in the very Creation story of the Jewish people, in the very name of the third chapter of the Bible, Lekh Lekha, and in its first sentence (perhaps ironically, in this case, addressed to a man with the same name as Dylan's father):

G-d said to Avram, "Go away from [Lekh Lekha] your land, from your birthplace, and from your father's house, to the land that I will show you. I will make you into a great nation. I will bless you and make you great."

Thus, the primal birthing moment of the Jewish people was contingent on one man abandoning the prosperous land of his forefathers and heading off to a barren land populated by hostile tribes (taking with him, coincidentally, a wife named Sarah, and settling near a place called Bethel, which in Dylan's day was a village near his adopted hometown of Woodstock, New York, that would host the landmark rock festival bearing his town's name, precisely to link it with Woodstock's most famous resident, the festival's most famous no-show). And while Dylan had yet to meet his Sara when the time came to leave the land of his forefathers (there would, most notably, be a Suze and a Joan before Sara), and while he probably didn't go under the direct command of G-d, he would encounter his fair share of pushback at the hands of "hostile tribes," in his new homeland, on his way to certain renown.

Much has been made of Dylan's arrival in New York during one of the harshest winters in years, but this could barely have made an impression on someone from northern Minnesota, where winters are biblically long, cold, and snowy. Dylan said as much in *Chronicles*: "When I arrived, it was dead-on winter. The cold was brutal and every artery of the city was snowpacked, but I'd started out from the frostbitten North Country, a little corner of the earth where the dark frozen woods and icy roads didn't faze me. I could transcend the limitations." As it turned out, Dylan's landing in the Big Apple wasn't so much an arrival as a takeover by storm. Within a year's time, he worked his way to the top of the bill in the leading folk clubs; he'd garnered the attention of the top chroniclers of the folk scene, most notably Robert Shelton of *The New York Times,* who has written the closest thing to an "authorized" biography of Dylan and is widely credited with propelling him to fame through several rave reviews for the paper of record as well as relentless behind-the-scenes machinations with people who could help Dylan and his career; he'd befriended key musicians, including Dave Van Ronk and Odetta, and already begun a lifetime's worth of alienating other musicians who resented his success owing to slights perceived or real; and he won an unprecedented record deal *not* with one of the folk labels of the time (Vanguard, Folkways, and Elektra all famously turned him down) but with one of the nation's top pop and jazz labels, Columbia, which remains to this day Dylan's record company.

When Dylan first arrived in New York, he made straight for Greenwich Village, and within days if not hours he was performing at pass-the-hat folk coffeehouses and clubs. His timing was truly impeccable, and if ever the accident of birth played into a cultural revolution, it was Dylan's having been born in 1941. This made him the perfect age to be enraptured by Little Richard and Elvis Presley as a teenager in the mid-1950s, and then to assume a more mature, sophisticated air in his college years and early twenties, precisely when the first generation of rock music gave way to white-bread usurpers like Pat Boone and Fabian. This cleared a path for the more intellectual, literary, and politically aware revival of folk music, which actually became a commercial force in the pop music marketplace, primed to address the nascent challenges of what would become known as the Sixties and all that implied. The civil rights movement; the election of the youthful John F. Kennedy, the first pop-star president; the Cold War and its most prominent manifestation in the form of the Vietnam War, provoking the antiwar movement and the counterculture that stemmed from it—all these combined to coalesce a new cultural paradigm in search of a leader, symbolic and otherwise, and for better or worse and much to his dismay, this role was put on the shoulders of Bob Dylan, who just happened to be the right man with the right voice at the right time—or the wrong time, depending on your point of view (and, in Dylan's case, apparently *his* point of view).

Dylan came to New York with hardly an original song in his playbook, but within months began to emerge an array of works displaying a firm grounding in traditional and modern folk—especially the work of Woody Guthrie, and especially the talking blues form—while at the same time a uniquely personal style and approach that was already transforming what *seemed* traditional, or even mimicry, into something new that could have come only from Bobby Zimmerman's unique background and perspective.

One of the first original songs to appear in his live set was "Talkin' Hava Negeilah Blues," a seemingly tossed-off ditty (first officially released on *The Bootleg Series, Vols. 1–3* in a studio version recorded in April 1962, but clearly played live as early as September 1961, when it is mentioned in a *New York Times* review by Robert Shelton) that in retrospect tells volumes about where Bob's head was at right from the beginning. On the surface, the short number is both a parody and a mockery of the "ethnic" trend in folk music at the time, which saw the likes of Pete Seeger and the Weavers adopting songs from a multiplicity of cultures, for example, "Guantanamera" from Cuba, "Wimoweh (The Lion Sleeps Tonight)" from southern Africa, "Tzena, Tzena" and "Alle Brider" from Eastern Europe, and perhaps most famously (and, today, notoriously), the all-purpose ethnic projection "Kumbaya," which forty years later is sure to provoke moans of agony among any but the most persistently sincere and politically correct members of any audience subjected to its insipid melody.

Introduced by Dylan as "a foreign song I learned in Utah," the song "Talkin' Hava Negeilah Blues" consists almost in its entirety of the singer trying to get the words "hava nagila" out of his mouth. "Ha . . . va . . . Ha . . . va . . . neh . . . gee . . . lah," he sings—as if the words were utterly and totally strange and foreign—before putting it all together in a still slow and carefully enunciated "Ha-va Na-gee-lah," immediately followed by a totally anomalous yodel, juxtaposing another of the more absurd, cloying tendencies of sincere folksingers of the time (hence, the mockery). As Shelton so aptly put it in his review, the song "burlesques the folk music craze and the singer himself." And so we have both a parody and mockery, or a mocking parody, of two specific aspects of folk music contemporary to its time, coming from a young, newly arrived upstart from the Midwest.

A young, newly arrived *Jewish* upstart from the Midwest, that is. Several barnloads of hay have been pitched by biographers and critics reading Dylan's early days of self-mythologizing in New York to be a denial of his middle-class Jewish background, starting with his name change and continuing through his tall tales about running away from home, joining the circus, and traveling freight trains like a latter-day Woody Guthrie. They read his silence about his real family and real name, never mentioned by him in early interviews or writings, as some kind of cover-up, out of shame or embarrassment, that somehow being the son of a Jewish furniture merchant in a somewhat prosperous mining town would disqualify him from being an authentic folk voice (as if Woody Guthrie's father, for example, wasn't actually a politically active businessman and landowner, with relatives in showbiz, and as if Pete Seeger, for instance, hadn't descended from upper-class Ivy League WASPs who were academically trained musicians and composers of "serious" music). These chroniclers willfully ignore a long tradition of performers in all fields and of all ethnicities assuming stage names, for reasons ranging from protecting the privacy of their family (one of Dylan's main motivations) to, in the case of those whose names didn't exactly trip off the tongue, assuming a more stage-friendly name (also the case with Zimmerman/Dylan).

The irony is that Dylan's given name was just a coincidence of history—obviously a name arbitrarily chosen by or selected for one of his father's male antecedents at some point along the way, after the Napoleonic Code became the rule of law across Europe and Jews were no longer called by a single name and identified further by their fathers (in Dylan's case, Robert, son of Abram, in English, or, as reflected in his Hebrew name, Shabtai Zisel ben Avraham). This isn't to deny a certain degree of ethnic masking behind Asa Yoelson's transformation to Al Jolson, Sonia Kalish's rebranding as Sophie Tucker, Nathan Birnbaum's reincarnation as George Burns, or the reinvention of that other famous Zimmerman—Ethel—who merely lopped off the first syllable of the family name to become Merman. But was Allen Konigsberg really serious about passing for a non-Jew by renaming himself Woody Allen, only to create a great comic persona built on the figure of a Jewish nebbish? Or when Leonard Alfred Schneider became Lenny Bruce and proceeded to pepper his comic routines with obscene Yiddish words and mockery of his Jewish family? In both cases, they were more likely following tradition for tradition's sake—and rightly choosing more easily memorable, mellifluous stage names. With no evidence to the contrary, it shouldn't be assumed that Robert Allen Zimmerman had any other motivation than choosing a more stage-friendly name when he began calling himself Bob Dylan. From his arrival in New York City and his very first performances of his own songs, he seemed if anything to go out of his way to draw attention *toward* his religious heritage and ethnic background rather than away from it.

Hence, "Talkin' Hava Negeilah Blues." Of all ethnic folk songs he could have chosen, why else did Dylan choose the best-known Hebrew song (a modern Israeli dance tune, really) for his material to mock? Were Dylan to have been seriously intent upon distancing himself from his cultural heritage, wouldn't he have put ten feet between himself and the kitsch of "Hava Nagila"? Didn't singing "Talkin' Hava Negeilah Blues" merely draw attention to his ethnic background? Even if read as a *mockery* of that background, it *still* served to draw attention to his Jewish origins. Far from distancing himself from his family and his Judaism, Dylan was planting hints right from the outset about who he really was, from where he was coming, and perhaps even where he was headed.

In fact, right out of the box, in stark contrast to the conventional notion that Dylan consciously tried covering up his background as a middle-class Jew, he made his relationship with Jewishness and Jewish history quite clear, not only in "Talkin' Hava Negeilah Blues," but in other early songs, including "Talkin' John Birch Paranoid Blues" and "With God on Our Side." His obsession with the Holocaust, particularly with the murder of six million Jews—one that resurfaces in *Chronicles*—is manifested in several early songs. In "Talkin' John Birch Paranoid Blues," a 1962 song that satirizes the mentality of a member of the extreme right-wing, red-baiting John

Birch Society, Dylan sings, "Now we all agree with Hitler's views / Although he killed six million Jews / It don't matter too much that he was a Fascist / At least you can't say he was a Communist!" The song also hints at several things to come, such as Dylan's fascination with movies (which will inform his song lyrics throughout his career, especially in the 1980s and beyond), and with the 1960 Zionist epic *Exodus,* about the founding of the state of Israel. In the penultimate verse, he sings:

> *To my knowledge there's just one man*
> *That's really a true American: George Lincoln Rockwell.*
> *I know for a fact he hates Commies cus he picketed the movie* Exodus.

It's not exactly clear why, as he has it in the song, picketing *Exodus* would indicate anti-Communist tendencies—perhaps Dylan's poking fun at the equation between Jews and Communists, or Hollywood and Communists, or Jews and Hollywood and Communists. Or perhaps it was Dylan's very knowing and sophisticated reference to the movie's screenwriter, Dalton Trumbo, who as one of the infamous "Hollywood 10" had been blacklisted and imprisoned for being a member of the Communist Party. Although Trumbo had regained his footing in Hollywood under an assumed name in the late-1950s, the director Otto Preminger listed Trumbo's name in the credits of *Exodus* as an act of defiance against the blacklist, thus helping to bring this sordid chapter of American history to its conclusion. (Dylan's love affair with *Exodus* didn't end here. In the mid- to late-1990s, the lead guitarists in his road band would introduce "All Along the Watchtower" with a snippet of Ernest Gold's Oscar-winning "Theme of Exodus," thereby associating the Dylan song, drawn from the book of Isaiah, with contemporary Jewish nationalism.)

Dylan didn't let go of the trope of the six million Jewish victims of Hitler after dropping it into "John Birch," either. He refers to it again within the year in one of his most cutting songs, "With God on Our Side," a song pointing out the convenient appeal to righteousness to cover up a multitude of sins.

In another contemporaneous protest song, Dylan refers to a signal event in Exodus—this time, the biblical book after which the movie, based on the novel of the same name by Leon Uris, was named. In "When the Ship Comes In," Dylan paints a picture reminiscent of the end of days, when a nameless foe will be conquered with the aid of earthly miracles of biblical proportions, including seas that split (as they did for Moses and the Hebrew slaves fleeing Egypt in the original book of Exodus). The song ends with a vision of deliverance symbolized in two iconic episodes of Jewish liberation—another reference to the split seas, this time crashing in upon the Egyptian pursuers, and with a reference to the story of David and Goliath, a story that has become the quintessential symbol of the underdog triumphing miraculously over a larger, greater foe:

> *And like Pharaoh's tribe,*
> *They'll be drownded in the tide,*
> *And like Goliath, they'll be conquered.*

Dylan's vision here isn't a charitable version of the triumph of good over evil, but rather, one that's often incorrectly, but nevertheless for our purposes aptly, characterized as "Old Testament"–like in its harsh judgment and violence: an early hint of Dylan's idiosyncratic politics. Dylan never marched in lockstep with the New Left of the 1960s, never spoke out against the Vietnam War, and in subsequent years when confronted with lyrics such as those of "Masters of War," even denied that it was an antiwar or pacifist manifesto, insisting that it was simply an indictment of the military-industrial complex. In other words, Dylan was about as antiwar as President Eisenhower.

But most important, and back to our original point: in his very first years, when Dylan was going from being a guitar-strumming folkie on the club circuit to an international star songwriter and festival and theater headliner, he was already drawing heavily on the scriptural, symbolic, and contemporary political heritage of his family and forebears. This was hardly the work of someone attempting to leave any traces of Judaism behind; rather, we see it as the work of someone with a profound appreciation for that heritage, and an appreciation for how it can be engaged in the service of his own art to add timeless import, literary heft, and a powerful maturity belying the immature scratchings of a twenty-one-year-old Woody Guthrie wannabe.

Even when the young Bob Dylan wasn't being so overt in his references to Jewish symbols and sources, he still found inspiration in scripture that fueled some of his greatest original works. The song that made him an international star, a wealthy man, and the so-called spokesman of his generation, a song adopted as one of the key anthems of the civil rights and antiwar movements of the 1960s, is something of a midrash on themes drawn directly from passages from the books of Ezekiel and Isaiah.

It was the genius of Dylan's manager at the time, Albert Grossman, to introduce the world to "Blowin' in the Wind" in a recording by his greatest invention, the folk trio Peter, Paul and Mary. Grossman put these three together with uncanny foresight: as much as Dylan became the "spokesman of a generation" for the cognoscenti, it was Peter, Paul and Mary who would symbolize and encapsulate "the Sixties" for the masses, in terms of style and sensibility: they wore the faint whiff of "hippiedom" in their hair and their clothes; some of their songs could be read as drug allegories ("Puff, the Magic Dragon"); and they bridged the folk revival, as represented in their versions of traditional material such as "Five Hundred Miles," Pete Seeger numbers including "If I Had a Hammer" and "Where Have All the Flowers Gone," and the new-folk movement, with their renditions of songs by Dylan and other contemporary song-writers, including John Denver. Their two-men-and-one-woman lineup hinted at unrepressed sexuality (as compared with the buttoned-up, all-male Kingston Trio after which they were patterned), even though there were no intra-trio love affairs; and the Christian resonance of their names, with the associations of peace and love attached to those lovers and disciples of Jesus (in order for which Noel Stookey, already a well-established folksinger and comic in his own right, had to be rechristened "Paul"). It was their version of "Blowin' in the Wind" that made the song famous, and within weeks after Dylan's own version had been released on his second album, their smoothed-over, harmony-laden rendition peaked at number 2 on *Billboard*'s pop singles chart, with sales exceeding a million copies, making them rich, Albert Grossman happy, and Bob Dylan a household name.

Today, "Blowin' in the Wind" is one of those rare songs that seem to have been around forever—like "Kumbaya," for better or worse. It's been recorded in hundreds of versions Stevie Wonder brought it back to *Billboard*'s Top 10 in 1966, and everyone from Sam Cooke to Marlene Dietrich has taken a stab at it—and it remains a staple of Dylan's concerts. The musical and thematic roots of the song are both deep and profound, undoubtedly adding resonance to this otherwise seemingly vague, abstract ballad that is open to countless interpretations beyond the original and most obvious, that of a cry for racial equality. There's good reason to read the song that way due to the music: the melody is built on an old spiritual called "No More Auction Block," which Dylan sang on occasion in his folk-club period. Dylan acknowledged that debt by releasing a live version of that tune on *The Bootleg Series, Volumes 1–3*. While not an exact rewrite of the melody, Dylan's is built upon the basic musical theme of the original and goes beyond it—but how brilliant of him to take a song about resistance to slavery and to update it for the modern civil rights movement.

Equally important, however, is how the key verse of Dylan's song, written at age twenty-one, is inspired by two biblical verses: one from Ezekiel and one from Isaiah, two of the greater Prophets often referred to by Dylan throughout his career.

Dylan sings:

> *How many times must a man look up*
> *Before he can see the sky?*
> *Yes, 'n' how many ears must one man have*
> *Before he can hear people cry?*

In Ezekiel 12:1–2, G-d says to Ezekiel, "Son of Man, you dwell in the midst of the rebellious house, who have *eyes to see but do not see,* who have *ears to hear but do not hear*, for they are a rebellious house." And in Isaiah 11:3, it is written, "He will be imbued with a spirit of fear for G-d; and will not need *to judge by what his eyes see* nor *decide by what his ears hear*." (Emphasis mine. See also Isaiah 43:8 and Jeremiah 5:21.)

Oliver Trager, author of *Keys to the Rain: The Definitive Bob Dylan Encyclopedia*, apparently had no idea what he was stepping in when he wrote, "this song for the ages could have been spoken by the ancient sages—it seems to have been around at least that long." Indeed, it has.

The song's biblical inspiration isn't restricted to those two verses. The image of the dove in "How many seas must a white dove sail, before she sleeps in the sand" is taken from the story of Noah and the Flood; when the floodwaters visibly diminish and the peaks of mountains can be seen, Noah sends out a dove to see just how far the waters have subsided. "The dove could not find any place to rest its feet, and it returned to him, to the ark. There was still water over all the earth's surface" (Genesis 8:9).

As noted earlier, around this same time Dylan added his "Song to Woody" to his performing repertoire, and it was one of only two original numbers to be included on his first album. A tribute to Guthrie and his ilk, sung and delivered very much in Guthrie's style, with a melody adapted from Guthrie's own "1913 Massacre," the song—which Dylan would continue to revisit in concert throughout his career, most notably at the star-studded Thirtieth Anniversary tribute concert at Madison Square Garden in 1992, when it was the very first song he performed in his evening-closing set—functions as something of a mission statement for Dylan. Many have taken it over the years to be a sycophantic work of hero worship, but a close reading shows, again, that it's as much a statement of what Dylan's mission is *not* as it is a statement of what it *is*. After taking a listener through several verses in which he honors Guthrie and his other folk forebears for all they've accomplished and all he's learned from them, Dylan turns around and says precisely the *opposite* of what so many have assumed was Dylan's point in writing the song, and his overall plan for the beginning of his career: to be something of a successor to Guthrie (in the vein of and thereby usurping artists and friends like Ramblin' Jack Elliott, who has never gone beyond that initial step, and perhaps thereby stealing the "birthright" of Guthrie's son, Arlo, who on the other hand *has* gone on to establish his own unique voice and persona, while continuing to honor the work of his father). Exhibit A is once again that final verse in which Dylan spells it out plain as the light of day:

> *I'm a-leaving tomorrow, but I could leave today,*
> *Somewhere down the road someday.*
> *The very last thing that I'd want to do*
> *Is to say I've been hittin' some hard travelin' too.*

Dylan had other plans than merely to say he was a guitar-playing hobo or a vagabond troubadour. And while at the time of the writing of "Song to Woody" he may not have had clearly in mind what those plans were, he certainly knew it was to make a mark of his own. But what's equally or even more fascinating is why so many observers of Dylan have so willfully misrepresented him at this crucial point in his career, viewing him as a user who insinuated himself into the crowd surrounding Guthrie, "stealing" his style (and "stealing" it, we are to understand, from more rightful "heirs"—an odd note of patriarchal feudalism emanating from an ostensibly leftist milieu), and pawning it off as his own on his way toward establishing himself as a folk presence with which to be reckoned. Hostile tribes, indeed.

THREE

NUMBERS

The buzzing Greenwich Village folk scene was small and welcoming enough so that by the fall of 1961, Dylan had already played harmonica on recording sessions for Harry Belafonte, Victoria Spivey, and Big Joe Williams, and shared live residencies with the blues singer-guitarist John Lee Hooker, the bluegrass outfit the Greenbriar Boys, and the blues-folk singer Dave Van Ronk. Having befriended the writer Richard Fariña and his folksinger wife, Carolyn Hester, he was invited to a run-through at their apartment for Hester's upcoming recording session at Columbia Records, which would be produced by John Hammond. The producer was impressed enough with what he saw and heard of Dylan at the informal session to invite him to record a few demos of his own. After the *New York Times* critic Robert Shelton wrote a rave review of Dylan's set opening for the Greenbriar Boys at Gerde's Folk City, Hammond lobbied Columbia to sign Dylan as part of the label's expanding effort to infiltrate the youth market via jumping on the folk-revival bandwagon. The deal Hammond inked with Dylan—a deal of questionable legal value, as Dylan was still a minor—was for one year with four yearly options to be exercised (or not) by the record label.

Bob Dylan's first album was recorded in two sessions over three days in November 1961, with Hammond acting as producer. There wasn't much to "produce"—Hammond basically set up a few microphones to capture Dylan's voice, guitar, and harmonica. This was solo Dylan playing traditional folk and blues songs in the same manner he performed in folk clubs, and he wouldn't record this sort of material this way again until about thirty years later, when he returned to the well of traditional folk music and released two albums of mostly obscure tunes on *Good as I Been to You* and *World Gone Wrong* in the early 1990s.

On his eponymous debut, the song selection was nearly as remarkable as the performance. If there was a theme tying the songs together, it was mortality and death. The titles alone tell half the story: "In My Time of Dyin'," "Fixin' to Die," "Man of Constant Sorrow," "See That My Grave Is Kept Clean." But it's really the performance that trumps all. Recorded when he was only twenty years old, released before his twenty-first birthday (on the day this author turned two years old), Dylan's voice packs in the wisdom and personality of the ages, far beyond any simple mimicry. Sure, there are echoes of Woody Guthrie, Lead Belly, and Robert Johnson haunting these tracks. But the sum is greater than the parts, and what is most striking about the sound of *Bob Dylan,* apart from any message he chose to impart on this collection of songs drawn from all over the traditional Americana map, from bluegrass, country, blues, American, and Anglo-Irish folk, is the sound of *urgency*. If there was ever such a thing as punk-folk, this was it, at least a decade before anyone even used the term *punk* to refer to a style of music. The command and authority that powered "Fixin' to Die" by Bukka White, or "See That My Grave Is Kept Clean" by Blind Lemon Jefferson, is almost supernatural. Dylan wasn't just channeling the authors of these tunes, or the original interpreters. He was drawing from some deeper well, along the way making a statement about this music—music that he would leave behind for the most part for the vast duration of his long career—that it was a wellspring of aesthetics and emotion upon which he intended to build a new, original music, the logical next step beyond the mere revivalism that dominated the Village and the Newport folk set. Dylan did not perform these songs as museum pieces, but as vital and vibrant numbers that would form the foundation of what was to come.

By the time the album was released, nearly a half year after its recording, Dylan had moved far beyond these songs, writing, performing, and recording original songs that, while certainly sharing some DNA with traditional folk, blues, and Anglo-Irish ballads, added a whole new voice and approach to what "folk music" could be—much to the consternation of some folk purists who could not have imagined at this point how much more Dylan would infuriate them in the coming months and years, as he paved the way to a revolutionary, new style of music that, in order to be appreciated fully, had to be seen not as a next step in the folk process but as a giant leap forward, a wholesale, discontinuous break with a treasured past.

For all the fuss about how he styled himself a latter-day Woody Guthrie by way of Ramblin' Jack Elliott, Dylan steered clear of any of Guthrie's songs or any numbers from Elliott's songbook. The only overt Guthrie connection was "Song to Woody," although the other original number, "Talkin' New York," a satire of the Village folk scene, borrowed Guthrie's talking-blues format, and acknowledged Guthrie in its final lines when Dylan refers to East Orange, the New Jersey town where he would visit Guthrie on Sundays at the home of Bob and Sidsel Gleason.

Otherwise, the album was composed of a mixture of old folk, country, blues, and spirituals. Other than "Song to Woody," only "Baby Let Me Follow You Down," which Dylan acknowledges learning from Eric "Rick" Von Schmidt in a spoken intro before the song, would live on in his concert repertoire, enjoying a place of honor in a totally revamped electric-rock version with the Hawks on their world tour of 1965–66 (and reprised with Dylan one last time at the Band's farewell concert, the Last Waltz, in 1976). The album also included a rendition of the folk chestnut "House of the Rising Sun," which *had* been recorded by Guthrie, along with many others, including Lead Belly and, perhaps originally, Clarence "Tom"

Ashley, but for which Dylan caught flak for supposedly "stealing" his mentor Dave Van Ronk's arrangement of the number, which Van Ronk had yet to record. When anyone else did this sort of thing, it was credited to the "folk process"—in the small, insular world of folk music, envy of Dylan's remarkable (but not overnight) success got in the way of such generosity of spirit that others enjoyed.

In spite of the extraordinary performances it contained, with initial sales of only about five thousand, Dylan's debut album was considered a commercial flop and did little if anything to propel his career, such as it was at the time. The lack of impact the album had outside a very small coterie of the folk world (and much of which was negative) led wags at Columbia Records to refer to Dylan as "Hammond's Folly." Nevertheless, Hammond and Dylan persevered. A month after the release of his debut, Dylan returned to the recording studio for the first of eight sessions that would take place over the course of the next year, eventually resulting in the sophomore effort that would introduce to the world its greatest new songwriter.

In the interim between the recording of *Bob Dylan* in November 1961 and its release in March 1962, Dylan began churning out original songs, most of them topical protest numbers, at a dizzying rate. At times it seemed that all he needed for inspiration was to pick up a newspaper, find a story that illustrated a social ill (racism, greed, violence, labor strife, poverty, or some combination of them), and he had the ingredients for a song. He wrote songs such as "The Death of Emmett Till," about the brutal lynching of a black teenager who made the mistake of interacting with a white woman in Mississippi; "The Ballad of Donald White," about a black man on death row; "Let Me Die in My Footsteps," reflecting the prevalent fears over nuclear annihilation; and "John Brown," a searing indictment of patriotism run amok, in the form of a mother's complicity in sending her son off to war. None of these wound up on *The Freewheelin' Bob Dylan*; they existed as songs for performance— sometimes written to order for a specific occasion, as in the case of "Emmett Till," which Dylan debuted at a benefit concert for the Congress of Racial Equality (CORE) in February 1962 (a practice

Dylan would quickly abandon). Although most were recorded over the next year, many surfaced officially only in the 1990s or later as part of Columbia Records' ongoing *Bootleg Series* of previously unreleased recordings.

While Dylan first "went electric" in the recording sessions for *Freewheelin'* on "Corrina, Corrina," an overlooked, gentle gem based on an old blues tune featuring tasteful, jazzy electric guitar accompaniment by Bruce Langhorne, along with bass and drums—the first song on a Dylan album to feature instrumental accompanists—Dylan's true colors got their first demonstration with "Mixed-Up Confusion," recorded at the same sessions as "Corrina, Corrina" and then rushed out as a pop single in December 1962. One part Presley, one part Chuck Berry, and the rest uniquely Dylan, the single died an instant death when it failed even to chart. But as an historical artifact, which finally surfaced on the 1985 compilation *Biograph*, the song was a harbinger of things to come—the first genuine folk-rock record, the first confessional singer-songwriter number, Dylan's first expression of personal, freewheeling abandon in an incisive, highly personal song wrongly dismissed as a throwaway:

> *I got mixed up confusion*
> *Man, it's a-killin' me*
> *Well, there's too many people*
> *And they're all too hard to please . . .*
> *Well, my head's full of questions*
> *My temp'rature's risin' fast*
> *Well, I'm lookin' for some answers*
> *But I don't know who to ask . . .*
> *Seein' my reflection*
> *I'm hung over, hung down, hung up!*

Hardly out of the starting gate and yet to release his first album of original songs or have one of his songs recorded by another artist, Dylan already on "Mixed-Up Confusion" is confronting the demons he'll confront—and face down—over the next few years and for the rest of his life. Before he's even worked through his early stint as a protest singer, he's feeling used and used up. Before he's sold more than a few thousand records, he's feeling the heat of popular stardom. He's anticipating his role as the asker of questions and the demands that he answer them. And he's already feeling the burdens of being a prophet without honor.

In the meantime, his time mostly his own, Dylan enjoyed one of his most prolific creative periods, writing not only the songs that would populate *The Freewheelin' Bob Dylan* but also dozens of others. Some were recorded as demos for his publishing company; others for *Broadside* magazine, a new folk newsletter founded by Pete Seeger and friends that was devoted entirely to new, mostly politically and topically oriented songs; "Blowin' in the Wind" was first published in *Broadside*. Dylan also spent plenty of time making the rounds of folk clubs in New York City, enjoying his nascent relationship with his first serious girlfriend, Suze Rotolo—who would prove highly influential in introducing Dylan to the ideology of the New Left, the civil rights movement, and Brechtian theater (and, along the way, inspiring several of Dylan's classic love—and put-down—songs)—and traveling to England, where he spent about a month at the end of the year, ostensibly working on a BBC teleplay but mostly hanging around the London folk scene and meeting British folksingers.

Indifference toward Dylan's debut album in the marketplace and the media gave way to near-hysteria, however, with the release of Peter, Paul and Mary's pop single version of Dylan's "Blowin' in the Wind," shortly following on the heels of the release of *The Freewheelin' Bob Dylan* in May 1963. The song and album announced the arrival of a major new force in folk—in no small way pointing folk toward a new direction, away from something to be revived in favor of approaching the folk idiom as a living, breathing genre open to new, original contributions: songs that, like old folk songs, could address the concerns of the heart and the pocketbook with a contemporary, topical flair, one thematically and stylistically attuned to its immediate audience.

Looking back on *The Freewheelin' Bob Dylan*, it's truly astounding that it was the work of a twenty-one-year-old who had only just begun writing songs in earnest in the months before its release. It introduced Dylan as a songwriter of commanding vision and artistry. Alongside "Blowin' in the Wind," it also included several other songs that would go on to become classics of his oeuvre frequently played in concert, such as "A Hard Rain's a-Gonna Fall," "Don't Think Twice, It's All Right," and "Girl of the North Country." And it did all this at the same time that an English group called the Beatles was about to dominate American radio and record sales with hit singles about puppy love, such as "I Want to Hold Your Hand" and "She Loves You." (Indeed, Beatles lore has it that after George Harrison got a copy of *Freewheelin'* and played it for his bandmates, they all—especially John Lennon—saw the blueprint of an entirely new path for their songwriting.)

The Freewheelin' Bob Dylan opens with "Blowin' in the Wind," in a solo arrangement with Dylan accompanying himself on guitar and harmonica. His vocal intonation is gentle, almost wistful, heavy on the Midwestern phrasing and beyond his years, and his guitar playing is fleet and confident. His fingerpicking on "Girl of the North Country," his first original love song, presumably written for one of the girlfriends he left behind in Minnesota (or for all of them)—and perhaps inspired by his longing for Suze Rotolo, from whom he was separated by an ocean at the time of this writing—is remarkably sophisticated, striking unexpected notes and chords in what otherwise is simple music based on the old English folk tune "Scarborough Fair" (not to be confused with the Simon and Garfunkel tune by the same name, also based on the same folk song), which he learned from the British folksinger Martin Carthy while in England in late 1962 and early 1963. Dylan's vocal attack on this highly personal song disguised as a folk ballad is more animated than "Blowin' in the Wind," and he ends the song with a piercing, long, single note held for several measures before punctuating it with an ellipse and an exclamation point.

From that love song, Dylan changes the mood 180 degrees with one of his earliest prophetic songs, "Masters of War," in which he targets all those who benefit from the waging of war and profit off the lives of young men who die for a cynical cause. The song was written in 1963, years before the daily body count in Vietnam would be announced on the nightly news. Rather than directly responding to current events, Dylan was drawing upon a generalized impression of history fed by the implied threat of the Cold War (which was "cold" precisely because it refrained from pitting the might of the United States directly against that of the Soviet Union). Nevertheless, having grown up in the wake of the Second World War and having come of age during the Korean War—neither of which was especially controversial on its merits—Dylan specifically indicts war profiteers (the emphasis here being on the monied class versus the poor grunts doing their dirty work, upon which their fortunes are made). A Marxist complaint? Perhaps. But even if so—and Suze Rotolo, who appears on the cover of *Freewheelin'* with Dylan, and many of his coterie, were proponents of the New Left—Dylan's approach and language draws upon that of the biblical Prophets, and his indictment of the "Masters of War" is as much a spiritual as a political one, as we hear in the line, "All the money you made / Will never buy back your soul."

Some of the central imagery of "Masters of War" seems inspired by or based upon the book of Isaiah—specifically chapters 25 and 26, to which Dylan will return for inspiration throughout his career, for songs including "Knockin' on Heaven's Door" and "Shelter from the Storm." The idea, for example, that oppressors hide behind masks is found in Isaiah 25:7: "On this mountain He will eliminate the veiled faces . . . of all the nations, and the masks that mask all the nations." Or, as Dylan sings, "I just want you to know / I can see through your masks."

Alone, a connection between the two lines would be specious at best, but the accumulation of related imagery between the lyrics to "Masters of War" and the two chapters from Isaiah (which together run to about a page and a half) gains impact when looked on in their entirety. For example, the image of puppet masters hiding themselves inside their homes while blood is spilled on the ground is found in Isaiah 26:20–21:

> Go, my people, enter your rooms and close your door behind you; hide for a brief moment until the wrath has passed. For behold, G-d is going from His place, to bring punishment for the sin of the inhabitant of the world upon him; and the land will reveal its blood, and no longer cover over its slain.

The gruesome, vengeful conclusion to "Masters of War,"

> *I'll watch while you're lowered*
> *Down to your deathbed*
> *And I'll stand o'er your grave*
> *'Til I'm sure that you're dead,*

echoes Isaiah 25:12: "And the stronghold of your powerful walls He will topple, He will lower; it will reach the ground, until the dust." Hardly the stuff of pacifism.

While the latent content of the song may be found in Isaiah, in the lyrics Dylan turns to the Western Christian tradition, in the characters of Judas and Jesus, to charge further those guilty of lies and deceit ("like Judas of old") such that they are beyond redemption ("Even Jesus would never / Forgive what you do"). Dylan sets his indictment of war profiteers to a modal blues arrangement, meaning that he sings the melody over a single, droning chord, which changes quickly only at the end of each verse. This style and his incessant strumming give the original recording of the song an ominous, old-time feeling. Dylan revived the song for his appearance at the Grammy Awards ceremony upon receiving a lifetime achievement award in 1991, when, at the height of the Persian Gulf War, he played a searing, electric, almost unrecognizable version of the tune.

While the basic metrical structure and lyrical format of "A Hard Rain's a-Gonna Fall" is borrowed from the old English child ballad "Lord Randall," which Dylan learned from Martin Carthy, Dylan's "Hard Rain" utterly transforms and transcends the original, while at the same time, in its sensual psychedelia, offers the first hint of a new sensibility—an openness to new poetic possibilities—in folk, pop, and rock lyrics. Often ascribed to the Cold War fear of nuclear annihilation surrounding the Cuban Missile Crisis, the song portrays a landscape of devastation, tortured by biblical images of blood, flood, fire, violence, and death. It's a nightmarish vision of apocalypse juxtaposing Edenic symbols of innocence ("a newborn baby," "a white ladder," "a young child," "the song of a poet") with their hellish antitheses ("wild wolves," "blood that kept drippin'," "a dead pony," "died in the gutter").

Its language and imagery were clearly influenced by the French symbolist poets Dylan was reading at the time, including François Villon and Arthur Rimbaud, as much as they were by the Bible. And Dylan personalizes the vision by ending the first line of each stanza—all of which are in the form of questions, such as "Oh, where have you been . . . ?"—with "my blue-eyed son," a reference to his own blue-eyed self, not the last he'd make in song (as would others, including Joan Baez, down the road). After four verses paint a vision of living hell—"I met a young woman whose body was burning," "Heard one hundred drummers whose hands were a-blazin'"—Dylan's narrator sums up his mission in light of the horrors he's envisioned:

> *I'm a goin' back out 'fore the rain starts a-fallin',*
> *. . . And I'll tell it and think it and speak it and breathe it,*
> *And reflect it from the mountain so all souls can see it,*
> *Then I'll stand on the ocean until I start sinkin'*
> *But I'll know my song well before I start singin'*

In other words, Dylan declares his role as that of prophet: using his gift of song to prophesy about the world around him—not necessarily a future world of destruction, but the present world where he sees "guns and sharp swords in the hands of young children" and where he "heard one person starve" while he "heard many people laughin'," a world of indifference at best and willful violence at worst—and the consequences mankind faces by ignoring what he sees and hears (going back to Isaiah and Ezekiel's categories used for "Blowin' in the Wind"), consequences of biblical proportions, the "hard rain" of the refrain. And presumably, unleashed with those rains, a flood upon the earth—metaphorically or otherwise—that hasn't been witnessed since the days of Noah.

Dylan commented on his impending role as prophet, wittingly or otherwise, on another song from this era, "Long Time Gone," which was recorded in March 1963 along with numerous other songs from this period as a demo for his publishing company, Witmark. While "Long Time Gone" never was officially released, the lyrics to this and other such songs were included in an authorized publication, *Writings and Drawings,* in 1973. In the early song, recounting a hobo-like life of rambling the countryside, Dylan sings, "I know I ain't no prophet / And I ain't no prophet's son," quoting from Amos 7:14: "'I am not a prophet nor am I the son of a prophet,'" as revealing a gesture of self-awareness as one would find in Dylan's early work. In other words, by stating the negative—that he's not a prophet, before anyone has even suggested he may be one—he's already implying the opposite: that he *is* a prophet, or at least, that the question of his being a prophet of some sort is relevant.

Contrast the heights of symbolist poetry from "Hard Rain" with the album's closer, "I Shall Be Free," a five-minute rambling joke in the form of a talking blues that mocks folk music, celebrity culture, the Cold War, politicians, and Bob Dylan himself. In poking fun at politicians who claim to represent all the people all of the time, made manifest in their choice of diet, the first food mentioned on a menu that includes pizza and chitlins is a traditional, Eastern European Jewish baked good that is sometimes used as an epithet for Jews: "bagels."

Dylan's first album of original songs also includes one of his earliest and best-known kiss-off numbers, "Don't Think Twice, It's All Right," presumably written about Suze Rotolo during one of their many spats. As delivered on *Freewheelin',* the song is a jaunty, fingerpickin' folk song, albeit with an acid edge. Later renditions would forefront the acid, especially Dylan's solo acoustic version from his 1974 tour as captured on the live album, *Before the Flood,* where the subtlety of the original version is replaced by the onslaught of Dylan's relentless guitar strumming and sneering, shouted vocals.

The album is fleshed out with "Oxford Town," a topical protest song inspired by the integration of the University of Mississippi by James Meredith. The first black man enrolled at Ole Miss, Meredith arrived on campus accompanied by literally hundreds of federal troops and state National Guard officers, all of whom could not prevent a night of violence and rioting on the part of racists among the student body, resulting in hundreds of injuries, arrests, and two killings. Dylan lightens the mood with "Talkin' World War III Blues," a humorous vignette that coheres as a surrealistic dream told to a psychiatrist, a spoof on Cold War paranoia that works as a sort of comic antidote to "A Hard Rain's a-Gonna Fall."

A month before *Freewheelin'* was released, Dylan played a concert at New York's Town Hall, for which he wrote program notes. "My Life in a Stolen Moment" mixed authentic autobiography with outright fabrications intended to make his upbringing fit a certain image. After a very accurate description of life in Hibbing (again, in contrast to claims that Dylan purposely obfuscated his origins) followed by a version of university life rendered with a fair degree of poetic license, Dylan recounts a fictional tale of having bounced around from Texas to Washington to New Mexico to New Orleans, with a layover in jail, before returning to reality by reporting the car trip from Madison, Wisconsin, that brought him to New York City and Gerde's Folk City. Dylan continues with a mostly truthful accounting of his quick rise to fame, crediting Robert Shelton's review in *The New York Times* leading to his record deal with Columbia, and ends with a philosophical meditation on the role of influences: "Open up yer eyes an' ears an' yer influenced / an' there's nothing you can do about it."

FOUR

JEREMIADS

With the triumph that was *The Freewheelin' Bob Dylan*, the album that announced the arrival of a new, vital talent to the record-buying public, Dylan embarked on a busy schedule for the rest of the year. Having gained fame largely as the writer of Peter, Paul and Mary's million-selling hit version of "Blowin' in the Wind," Dylan was almost immediately pegged as the new, young spokesman of a generation—the poster boy for the folk-protest movement. In July, Dylan flew to Greenwood, Mississippi, at the behest of fellow folksingers Theodore Bikel and Pete Seeger, to perform at a voter registration drive organized by the Student Non-Violent Coordinating Committee (SNCC). He was filmed on the occasion singing a new song, "Only a Pawn in Their Game"—about the slain civil rights activist Medgar Evers and his killer—from the back of a truck to black fieldworkers; the footage would appear in the 1967 concert documentary *Dont Look Back*. A few weeks later, Dylan was the toast of the Newport Folk Festival in Rhode Island, appearing at various workshops, sitting in with other performers, as well as performing his own set.

From Newport, Dylan went on to perform as a "special guest" on Joan Baez's summer tour, where the headliner introduced him as her discovery and the two would duet on several of his songs, before Baez handed the stage over to Dylan to perform his own short set of music. They grew close, personally, with Dylan spending several weeks in the relative isolation of Baez's home in Carmel, California, where he wrote songs, drank wine, and the two of them presumably grew even more intimate.

This didn't go over too well with Suze Rotolo, and just a few months after her return to New York from Italy to reconnect with Dylan, she moved out of their West Fourth Street apartment and moved in with her sister Carla, spelling the beginning of the real end to their relationship. Not wanting to stay alone in his apartment when he was back in New York, Dylan took refuge variously with Peter Yarrow and Albert Grossman at their rural outposts in Woodstock, about two hours north of the city. Dylan was one of a number of folksingers, including Baez, to perform at the historic March on Washington on August 28, 1963, when Dr. Martin Luther King, Jr., gave his "I Have a Dream" speech. Dylan participated in a group sing-along on the steps of the Lincoln Memorial as well as performing "Only a Pawn in Their Game," which, if anyone listened closely, was not a "finger-pointing song." It didn't offer a typical, black-and-white viewpoint of the struggle for racial equality in the South, but rather, contextualized the murder of Medgar Evers within a cultural and institutional framework in which the assassin with his finger on the trigger was, as the title says, merely a pawn in a much larger, class-based industrial conspiracy.

After his busy summer touring with Baez and garnering more fame and media attention with Peter, Paul and Mary also paying tribute to him in song and in word at every concert they performed, Dylan returned to New York City for a triumphant solo concert at Carnegie Hall on October 12, for which he flew his parents in from Hibbing, and which ended in a preview of Beatlemania-like hysteria, with Dylan having to be ushered out of the theater with the use of decoys. Dylan was confident enough at this concert to open with the title track to his next album, *The Times They Are a-Changin'*, which wouldn't be released until the following January. When he came back onstage for an encore, Dylan introduced his final number, "When the Ship Comes In," with a sermon about latter-day Goliaths:

> Recognizing that there are Goliaths nowadays, people don't realize just who the Goliaths are. But in olden days Goliath was slain, and everybody nowadays looks back and sees how cruel Goliath was. Nowadays there are crueler Goliaths who do crueler and crueler things, but one day they're going to be slain too, and people are going to look back in two thousand years and say, "Remember when Goliath the Second was slain?"

As we shall see, the story of David and Goliath is one to which Dylan would return throughout his career.

With songs just pouring out of him, Dylan returned to the recording studio in August and October; in five sessions total, he recorded *The Times They Are a-Changin'*, which consisted almost entirely of protest songs and was released in mid-January 1964. The sound of Dylan's performance has a dark, lonely tone to it, as grim as the grim-faced, downward-casting look Dylan sports in the photographer Barry Feinstein's classic black-and-white portrait on the LP's cover. Gone were any of the humorous, freewheeling talking blues or antic dream songs that leavened the aptly titled *Freewheelin' Bob Dylan*. The grave sound of *The Times They Are a-Changin'* instead matched the tone of the lyrics and the mood of the nation just a few months after the assassination of President Kennedy (even though the album was recorded before his murder).

The album kicks off with the title track, one of Dylan's best-known, most successful anthems—perhaps his most nakedly self-conscious anthem, one of the few songs he wrote that openly aspires to be an anthem, and in this case, self-consciously spoken in, with, or by "the voice of a generation." Cast as a prophetic warning, the song is about a generational challenge—"Come mothers and fathers / Throughout the land . . . Your sons and your daughters / Are beyond your command" and a battle cry, ". . . he that gets hurt / Will be he who has stalled / There's a battle outside / And it's ragin' . . ."—which in hindsight was remarkably prescient; the song was written in 1963, several years before political protests would turn violent or even fierce.

Of the five stanzas, the middle three are addressed directly to specific groups: writers and critics, senators and congressmen, and the aforementioned mothers and fathers. The first and last stanzas are more universal; the former to "people wherever you roam" and the latter to no one in particular, as it strays from the formula and summarizes the message for the listener: "The line it is drawn / The curse it is cast . . ." Dylan launches his polite tirade—polite as it is couched in somewhat archaic language to match its folk song format ("Come gather 'round people . . .")—with an image of a biblical, or *the* biblical, deluge:

> *Come gather 'round people*
> *Wherever you roam*
> *And admit that the waters*
> *Around you have grown*
> *And accept it that soon*
> *You'll be drenched to the bone.*
> *If your time to you*
> *Is worth savin'*
> *Then you better start swimmin'*
> *Or you'll sink like a stone*
> *For the times they are a-changin'.*

Noah didn't have to swim—he built an ark—but Noah was the only righteous man on earth. By "swimmin'," the narrator here presumably means to warn the listener to get with the current, or get with what's current, at the risk of being overcome by a tidal wave of change.

In the second stanza, Dylan takes on "writers and critics," by implication grouping them with clueless, if not malevolent, parents and politicians who stand in the way of progress. Dylan himself, however, was in no small sense a writer and a critic—a social critic, at least, through his songwriting. He also dismissively refers to those "who prophesize with [their] pen," a neat bit of alliteration, but also an apt putdown, the insult here not being that they prophesize, but the means by which they prophesize. If the pen was once mightier

than the sword, it no longer seems to have that effect, Dylan says—
at least not in the hands of the everyday writers and critics who lack
the vision and foresight to comprehend the changes in the world
around them. A voice and a guitar now seem to have supplanted pen
and paper as the weapons of choice in the battle for righteousness.

In the final verse, the narrator portrays a universe turned upside
down, with everything in reverse:

> *The slow one now*
> *Will later be fast*
> *As the present now*
> *Will later be past*
> *The order is*
> *Rapidly fadin'*
> *And the first one now*
> *Will later be last . . .*

A dozen years later, in "Idiot Wind," Dylan will revisit some of this
imagery in a more personal fashion and find it wanting, even down
to the wheel, with a much more pessimistic conclusion:

> *Now everything's a little upside down, as a matter of fact the wheels*
> *have stopped,*
> *What's good is bad, what's bad is good, you'll find out when you reach the*
> *top*
> *You're on the bottom.*

And nearly forty years later, Dylan would reconsider his relationship to change, in "Things Have Changed," the Academy Award–
winning song written for the 2000 film *Wonder Boys,* in which he
sings, "I used to care, but things have changed."

The political protest songs on *The Times They Are a–Changin'* are
most significant for the approach they take, or, more properly, for
the approach they *don't* take. As previously alluded to, while "Only
a Pawn in Their Game" takes as its jumping-off point the murder of
Medgar Evers the previous spring, the song is really more about the

man who pulled the trigger than about his victim. Evers is not lion-ized in the song; rather, the song empathizes with his anonymous (as far as the song is concerned, "he ain't got no name") assassin: a poor white man born and bred to a culture that teaches race hatred and white supremacy.

Dylan offers a similarly perverse reading of contemporary society in "Ballad of Hollis Brown," a grim narrative about a poor South Dakota farmer who has hit hard times and, out of desperation and at his wit's end, turns his rifle against his wife, their five children, and himself. Again, while Dylan doesn't *approve* of Brown's actions, neither does he condemn them outright, knowing full well that it's not for him to approve or condemn, but to unravel the deeper truth behind such acts of desperation—what drives a man to kill another in the case of "Only a Pawn in Their Game," what drives a man to massacre his own family in "Hollis Brown." Moral condemnation or persuasion, such as it is, can come only as an outgrowth of such understanding, especially when the masters of war hide behind men, or when the button man is just a pawn in a much larger game. A protest singer is merely a journalist or essayist in song; the role of a poet-prophet is to shine the light in dark corners. "What saved the prophets from despair was their messianic vision and the idea of man's capacity for repentance," wrote Abraham Joshua Heschel in *The Prophets*. "The prophet is a person who, living in dismay, has the power to transcend his dismay." Dylan begins early on to trans-form songs and performances that are full of the meaning and sound of dismay into the means of transcending that dismay, through the promise of a better day and through a glimpse of that day through the ecstatic experience he offers to his listeners and, presumably, which he enacts regularly through the act of performance. Such an approach in popular song was, if not unprecedented, certainly unpar-alleled at the time, and probably has never been equaled or surpassed.

By this time, Dylan had already tired of the unimaginative, by-the-numbers, preaching-to-the-choir style of protest song that sim-ply parroted the news of the day, turning victims into martyrs and making icons of real men and women. Instead, Dylan dug behind the headlines and beyond the obvious, offering a penetrating and iconoclastic reading of a current event, one with a surprising twist and one that through the error of commission refused to pander to any notion of received politics coming from the right *or* the left. To the organized left, it was the beginning of Dylan's political betrayal; to his followers, it was more evidence of Dylan's singular genius.

Despite its title, "With God on Our Side" is less about religion than it is about the strain in American political thinking that justifies our nation's history and actions as products of hidden divine intervention—a strain, as Dylan sings, that goes back at least as far as the destruction of the continent's native inhabitants, who were seen as savage, godless subhumans, and that we know has continued through recent times at least as far as President Ronald Reagan's labeling of the Soviet Union as the "Evil Empire" and President George W. Bush's extension of that to an "axis of evil," including North Korea, Iran, and Iraq, as part of the justification for the ill-fated invasion of Iraq.

Dylan's well-constructed song evinces a sophisticated mastery of history and political thought for the unschooled songwriter of twenty-two. It also betrays his personal biases and allegiances. After he pokes holes in the heroic version of American history as an unquestionable progression of righteous battles, from the Civil through the Spanish-American and First World wars, as opposed to their legacy of death and destruction, he questions the end result of the Second World War:

> *When the Second World War*
> *Came to an end*
> *We forgave the Germans*
> *And we were friends*
> *Though they murdered six million*
> *In the ovens they fried*
> *The Germans now too*
> *Have God on their side.*

This is neither the first nor will it be the last time Dylan will refer to the Holocaust in song, and to do so in graphic, drippingly sarcastic terms. He could have chosen any variety of details to point out the hypocrisy of America's postwar embrace of its brutal enemy; that he singles out Germans as murderers of six million Jews presumably shows where his sympathies lie, especially for someone who alleg-edly was trying to hide or escape from his Jewish identity at the time. Nothing, in fact, could have been further from the truth, at least in song, which goes on to display a sophisticated level of political analy-sis, contrasting our postwar treatment of our German enemies with postwar attitudes toward our actual wartime allies, the Russians.

Dylan's interest in postwar Germany's relationship with its Nazi past extends to "11 Outlined Epitaphs," his liner notes included with *The Times They Are a-Changin'*. In deadpan manner, he hardly hides his disgust with the attitude many in Germany carried with them after the war:

> *I talked with one*
> *of the sons of Germany*
> *while walkin' once on foreign ground*
> *an' I learned that*
> *he regards*
> *Adolf Hitler*
> *as we here in the states*
> *regard*
> *Robert E. Lee*

The cynicism dripping from every line of "With God on Our Side" contrasts sharply with the poetic optimism of "When the Ship Comes In." The latter song portrays the messianic fulfillment of the title track; if these songs all are meant to converse, it is as if, given the understanding of history embedded in "With God on Our Side" combined with the notion of the contemporary challenges facing society in several of the album's topical protest songs (the civil rights struggles in "Only a Pawn in Their Game" and "The Lonesome Death of Hattie Carroll," the economic injustices underlining "Bal-lad of Hollis Brown" and "North Country Blues"), and the mission of redress outlined in "The Times They Are a-Changin'," they will culminate in the scenario portrayed in "When the Ship Comes In."

As Dylan does throughout his career, he symbolizes the moment of transitional change through biblical, nearly psychedelic images of weather and nature behaving in strange and unpredictable ways:

Oh the time will come up
When the winds will stop
And the breeze will cease to be breathin'...
Oh the seas will split
And the ship will hit
And the sands on the shoreline will be shaking.
Then the tide will sound
And the wind will pound
And the morning will be breaking.

The narrative, such as it is, continues in this fashion, with most of the song being played out in nature, with fish laughing, seagulls smiling, rocks standing in the sand, before people even enter the picture, at which point the "whole wide world" watches a transformative scene right out of Exodus and Samuel, two of the biblical books Dylan often references:

And like Pharaoh's tribe,
They'll be drownded in the tide,
And like Goliath, they'll be conquered.

It's the more vindictive side of "The Times They Are a-Changin'"—in that song, people were at least given a chance for redemption, but at this point, it's too late. The "foes," as the song calls them, are greeted with drowning even after they give in, "Sayin' we'll meet all your demands." They're likened to Pharaoh's army and Goliath's Philistines, and transcendence comes as liberation did to the Israelites in Egypt and to David's Israelites later on. The comparison to David is apt, too, as in this song of messianic hope—really more than mere hope, messianic foretelling—Dylan invokes David, from whose lineage it is promised that the Messiah will stem.

The Times They Are a-Changin' boasts powerful songs like these and others: "One Too Many Mornings" and "Boots of Spanish Leather," inspired by Dylan's topsy-turvy relationship with Suze Rotolo, are two of his most plaintive and enduring love songs, and "The Lonesome Death of Hattie Carroll" is one of his greatest protest songs *and* one of his greatest poetic achievements, as Christopher Ricks so convincingly argues in *Dylan's Visions of Sin*.

Given all that Dylan had achieved on *Times* and the previous album, *Freewheelin'*, as well as how successful things looked in terms of his songwriting and performing, it's just a little unnerving to rediscover "Restless Farewell," which concludes *Times*. It's a valedictory address of sorts, as hinted in its title, a saying goodbye to the past and to certain people and practices. It can most easily be read as a farewell to Suze Rotolo and the political protest music that she inspired him to write, and as a farewell to his role as a spokesman for causes, as a writer of protest-songs-to-order, and as one who speaks for anyone but himself. It anticipates another valedictory placed at the end of an album, "Dark Eyes" on *Empire Burlesque*, by more than twenty years, the two songs joined together over time and space by the image of the arrow—here not Cupid's arrow, but the barbs of writers and critics who monger gossip and rumors. As much as the song seems to indicate a parting of the ways, a genuine farewell, it's equally, as the title indicates, a *restless* one, a farewell imbued with ambivalence, a qualified farewell. In the end, Dylan isn't saying goodbye; he's saying, "So long, it's been good to know you." Which is why when he returns on an album in just a little over six months, it will be with *Another Side of Bob Dylan*.

As his fame grew along with his role as the "voice of a generation," so did Dylan's uneasiness with both, feeding his paranoia and discomfort over the spokesman role and his annoyance at being pigeonholed as a political protest singer. The label overlooked the moral, ethical, and spiritual import of his work, the prophetic aspect that, while in part political, was also much more than just *merely* political. None of this was helped by the hatchet job *Newsweek* magazine did on him in November 1963, accusing him of hiding his upbringing, his name, and his parents, and even of buying the song "Blowin' in the Wind" from a New Jersey high school student. Dylan was distraught over this treatment (his disgust would resurface in the opening line of "Idiot Wind" in 1975: "Someone's got it in for me / They're planting stories in the press"), and took time off to read several books by the great Jewish theologian Martin Buber that Albert Grossman gave him in penance for his role in allowing the *Newsweek* interview to take place.

Dylan couldn't have been any clearer regarding his feelings about his role as a spokesperson than he was by titling his next album *Another Side of Bob Dylan* (regardless of whether or not it was the producer Tom Wilson's idea originally, as has been reported) and opening the album sequence with "All I Really Want to Do." Almost all one really needs to know about the song is that within a year of its release it became a Top 20 hit for Cher—her solo debut (with her husband, Sonny Bono, producing), from an album of the same name. (The Byrds would also record a harmony-laden folk-rock version.) Whereas the songs on his previous album were serious, dark, and grim, "All I Really Want to Do" was light, fluffy, and bouncy, and in Dylan's hands, it verged on self-mockery, replete with faux-yodeling, a melody line that challenged his upper range, and, on the recording, at least one botched guitar chord, an audible snort, and a few moments of unrehearsed laughter interrupting the song. The album truly did present to listeners another side of Bob Dylan. (The title also embeds a clever, subtle pun—"side" being a synonym for "album," back when recordings were all on vinyl.)

This isn't to say that "All I Really Want to Do" was a tossed-off, meaningless ditty. Its exuberance is profound, introducing a Dylan marveling in his own seemingly improvisational wordplay, luxuriating in the most ridiculous—and the most virtuosic—rhymes, and unabashedly taking delight in what he does. Where *Freewheelin'* kicks off with an anthem and *The Times They Are a-Changin'* with a clarion call, 1964's *Another Side* opens with the joyful spontaneity of a more lighthearted, personal mission statement. On its surface, it can be read as a retreat or a renunciation of Dylan's role as a political provocateur—"I ain't lookin' to fight with you / Frighten you or uptighten you"—and there are no conventional, topical protest songs on the album. "All I Really Want to Do," however, is still a protest song—a *personal* kind of protest Dylan is waging, one that emerges as the main theme of the album: Dylan protesting against protest, Dylan protesting against the protest label, Dylan protesting against his image and the false expectations placed upon him by the media and unwitting fans. While "All I Really Want to Do" is couched in language of personal reconciliation, the singer could just as well be addressing himself:

> *I ain't lookin' to compete with you*
> *Beat or cheat or mistreat you,*
> *Simplify you, classify you,*
> *Deny, defy or crucify you.*

This certainly won't be the last time Dylan portrays a character beset by forces intent on doing him harm, or identifies himself with a martyr figure, or with *the* most famous martyr figure in all history—one who was crucified. But to his credit, he does so here with a lightness of touch and more than a modicum of self-awareness, which becomes all the more significant as his tone changes over the course of the album, which includes love songs, hate songs, surrealistic comic narratives, and, in "Chimes of Freedom," psychedelic poetry.

"Black Crow Blues" is a burst of honky-tonk, featuring Dylan on piano betraying the inner rhythms and sounds he was hearing in his head. The form is the blues, the words are personal and comic, but the spirit is rock 'n' roll throughout. It's a minor, forgotten bit of Dylan, but like "Mixed-Up Confusion" and "Corrina, Corrina," it's a harbinger of things to come.

Dylan needed to break with topical protest songwriting in order to exercise his greater talents as a poet and commentator on the human condition. The cloak of protest singer never quite fit him, anyway; hence his refusal to stick with the bare facts or the party line, as most evident in "Only a Pawn in Their Game." But more than that, Dylan needed the freedom to go wherever his muse led him, in order to create lasting works of beauty like "Chimes of Freedom," which, although arguably a political song, from a strictly leftist or Marxist point of view would be considered the self-indulgent act of a bourgeois artist more interested in form than content—which is precisely what makes it such a beautiful, astonishing piece of work, probably his supreme poetic achievement up until this point, one that still ranks among his greatest masterpieces.

The song's scene, such as it is, is simple: a couple takes refuge in the doorway of a church during a thunderstorm. Period. But never has a storm been so dynamically, so *electrically,* described. In six eight-line stanzas, Dylan paints a hallucinatory vision, a sensual display of lightning piercing the darkness, revealing an unjust world and a vision of redemption. Wrapped up in this song is all that has come before: the civil rights symbolism of "Blowin' in the Wind," the apocalyptic surrealism of "A Hard Rain's a-Gonna Fall," the tolling of a new day in "The Times They Are a-Changin'." But in "Chimes of Freedom," it's all refracted in shimmering poetry, in a heightened state of synesthesia, where sensory perception is jumbled so that those with ears see, and those with eyes hear:

> *As majestic bells of bolts struck shadows in the sounds*
> *Seeming to be the chimes of freedom flashing.*

What Dylan goes on to describe is a mystical experience—if not a direct vision of G-d, then at least an insight into another dimension, where G-d, acting through nature (much as He does throughout the Bible), speaks and acts in the carrying out of His mission on earth. In this case, it's a prophetic vision, in which the lightning and the thunder speak directly of and to the powerless:

> *Flashing for the warriors whose strength is not to fight*
> *Flashing for the refugees on the unarmed road of flight . . .*
> *Tolling for the luckless, the abandoned an' forsaked*
> *Tolling for the outcast, burnin' constantly at stake . . .*
> *Tolling for the deaf an' blind, tolling for the mute*
> *Tolling for the mistreated, mateless mother, the mistitled prostitute . . .*

In the end, the church bells that are tolling "through the wild cathedral evening" are "tolling for . . . the countless confused, accused, misused, strung-out ones an' worse / An' for every hung-up person in the whole wide universe." It's a tall order, but Dylan is up to the task, as he and his partner "gazed upon the chimes of freedom flashing," leaving the listener to answer the question that is implied: How does one gaze upon a sound? And how does a sound flash? The answer was blowin' in the wind on the night in question; the answer is in poetry; the answer, my friend, is in a transcendent vision of universal freedom and justice for all.

Dylan leavens the tone of the album by following "Chimes" with "I Shall Be Free No. 10," a comic talking blues of the sort he seemingly had left behind after *Freewheelin'*. This one is different, however, in that it's not just a mere toss-off; filled with very knowing references to pop culture, it sets out to skewer Dylan's own image, just as he says it will in the opening stanza:

I'm just average, common too
I'm just like him, the same as you
I'm everybody's brother and son
I ain't different from anyone
It ain't no use a-talking to me
It's just the same as talking to you.

Dylan continues in a vein that is disarmingly cheeky but actually very revealing. A verse is devoted to boxing and Cassius Clay (the heavyweight champion who would later change his name to Muhammad Ali after converting to Islam, and who was himself a spouter of free-verse rhyme who could "float like a butterfly and sting like a bee"), advancing Dylan's lifelong obsession with boxing in song and in life; he returns to mocking the Cold War mentality in verses about Russia, Barry Goldwater, and Cuba (which he will expound upon at greater length two songs later in "Motorpsycho Nightmare," in which he finds himself in a Cold War battle of wits courtesy of Alfred Hitchcock and a randy farmer's daughter); he alludes to the rockabilly pioneer Jerry Lee Lewis ("I sat with my high-heeled sneakers on") in a pointed stanza about a restricted tennis club; he alludes to Roy Orbison ("I got a woman, she's so mean") in a pointed stanza about moneygrubbing women before wryly bemoaning his fate at the hands of "a million friends" of the sort who stab his picture and dream of strangling him with a scarf (anticipating similar complaints lodged in "New Pony" by about fourteen years); pokes fun at his own image ("I'm a poet, and I know it / Hope I don't blow it"), before bringing the curtain down with a musical joke. It's a whirlwind performance, and as revealing of his true state of mind at the time as anything he ever wrote or recorded, serious or otherwise.

Whereas "All I Really Want to Do" was a playful farewell to folk protest (as opposed to "Restless Farewell," the concluding song on *Times,* which was a restless farewell to folk protest), "My Back Pages" was Dylan's most pointed, poetic renunciation of folk protest. Dylan looks back on the "movement," such as it was, for which he was "drafted," and sees it as nothing less than a mirror image of the "establishment" it hoped to destroy. If he finds any consolation at all, it is that, as he expresses in the song's refrain, "I was so much older then / I'm younger than that now." Dylan delivers the song in the same manner he delivered the protest songs—with hard-strumming guitar accompaniment and a rough-edged voice with a hint of a sneer. The song would later be filled out as an anthemic folk-rocker in a hit version by the Byrds in 1967, and by Dylan himself in live versions over the years, but none may have had the spine-tingling resonance of the one performed by a "This Is Your Life" array of musician friends at the Thirtieth Anniversary tribute concert at Madison Square Garden in New York City in October 1992, when Dylan traded verses with Tom Petty, Neil Young, Eric Clapton, the Byrds' Roger McGuinn, and the former Beatle George Harrison— a veritable history of rock 'n' roll all tied up in a single song. Fortunately, Dylan had the foresight to extend the song over six verses when he originally wrote it!

Whereas in "My Back Pages," Dylan points his finger at himself, in the album's closer, "It Ain't Me, Babe," he directs his venom outward, in a hint of things to come. For as much as Dylan came to be known as a writer and singer of protest songs, love songs, and breakup songs, he basically invented and broke the mold of "hate songs." *Hate* is probably too strong a word, but it's the opposite of love, and it's the overriding emotion of many of his most (ironically) beloved songs from the mid-sixties, including "Like a Rolling Stone," "Ballad of a Thin Man," and "Positively Fourth Street."

There's a touch of wistfulness in the original version of "It Ain't Me, Babe" that tempers the song's message, encapsulated in the title. Just exactly what it is that he "ain't" is left ambiguous. The song could be addressed to a former lover; it could be the parting shot of a relationship gone sour. But coming as it does after two other vitriolic numbers—"I Don't Believe You (She Acts Like We Never Have Met)" and "Ballad in Plain D"—the context seems to suggest that Dylan's intentions are strictly personal, not business.

Another Side of Bob Dylan was recorded in one overnight session beginning on June 9, 1964. Several songs, including "Chimes of Freedom," were written in the course of a cross-country road trip Dylan took in February—a few weeks after the release of *The Times They Are a-Changin'* and ostensibly to promote that album in a series of concerts—accompanied by his folksinger friend Paul Clayton, his new road manager and longtime aide-de-camp Victor Maimudes, and, for part of the time, the journalist Pete Karman. The trip took them through the South, where they visited striking miners and knocked on the poet Carl Sandburg's door, before performing at Emory College in Atlanta on their way to New Orleans for Mardi Gras, to Dallas to visit Dealey Plaza, the site of the Kennedy assassination, to gigs in Denver and Berkeley, California, where Karman's place in the entourage was taken by the artist-musician Bob Neuwirth, who would become Dylan's veritable doppelganger over the next few years.

Before returning to New York, Dylan and friends paid a visit to Joan Baez in Carmel, and upon his return, Suze Rotolo finally called it quits (undoubtedly inspiring several of the songs soon to be written for *Another Side of Bob Dylan*, including the cruel portrayal of a final fight among Dylan, Suze, and her "parasite sister," Carla, in "Ballad in Plain D"). The bulk of the songs on *Another*

Side were composed by Dylan while on holiday in the Greek village of Vernilya, after a triumphant concert at London's Royal Festival Hall, with the Beatles, the Rolling Stones, and others in attendance.

Upon its release in August, *Another Side of Bob Dylan* prompted some degree of controversy among former Dylan supporters, especially those who clung to the notion of him as some sort of political spokesperson. He was criticized by the likes of Irwin Silber, editor of *Sing Out!* magazine, for forsaking protest in favor of personal songs, which, given Dylan's head-'em-off-at-the-pass strategy in songs including "All I Really Want to Do" and "My Back Pages," was kind of like accusing blue of being blue. It wouldn't be the first time Dylan would be called to account for betraying some sort of imputed cause or loyalty, nor certainly would it be the last. It would, however, be one of the dumbest.

FIVE

THE CHARIOT

In a fever of creativity after recording *Another Side of Bob Dylan,* Dylan continued to write and record other songs as publishing demos, including an early version of "Mr. Tambourine Man" and two terrific recordings that would surface officially only many years later: "Mama, You Been on My Mind" and "I'll Keep It with Mine," accompanying himself on piano instead of guitar on the latter. (Joan Baez would release a version of "Mama," recast as "Daddy You Been on My Mind," in 1965; after performing concert versions with the Velvet Underground in 1966, the European chanteuse Nico— with whom Dylan was rumored to have had a romantic liaison— released a version of "I'll Keep It with Mine" in 1967.) Dylan also wrote numerous prose poems during this time, some of which were included on the LP sleeve of *Another Side,* and others that surfaced only with the 1973 publication of *Writings and Drawings.*

Also during this time, Dylan collaborated with the photographer Barry Feinstein—who was married to Mary Travers of Peter, Paul and Mary—providing the text to go along with a collection of Feinstein's mostly behind-the-scenes, black-and-white photographs of Hollywood. Given Dylan's love of the movies, and recalling his family's involvement with the film industry as exhibitors of the art form in its glorious heyday, Dylan was an apt choice to provide literary accompaniment to Feinstein's pictures. Feinstein's work captured the movie industry in transition, portraying the last gasps of the studio system in the form of production stills, portraits, candids, and still lifes of sets and back lots. There is a poignant loneliness to Feinstein's images that Dylan's "captions," such as they are, riff upon, reading as they do like verbal improvisations based on the images. In a brief interview in the book, which was finally published in 2008 as *Hollywood Foto-Rhetoric: The Lost Manuscript*, Dylan says he wrote the text "spontaneously." He also claims not to remember writing any of it.

The book does, however, offer the Dylan fan a field day for picking up on allusions to songs and other thematic obsessions. Dylan writes a lot about the actor's "mask" as a defense in the service of his celebrity. And six lines in a row such as

> *touch me mama*
> *it's all right*
> *it doesn't matter*
>
> *it's been too well proven*
> *that even i, myself*
> *am not really here*

are a flurry of almost-song-titles yet to be written ("It's Alright Ma," "Tell Me, Momma," "I'm Not There"). About Judy Garland, he asks as part of a dialogue, "'did she really create the world in six days?'" About an actress on a casting call he names "miss rainbow," he has a casting director say, "what i think i had in mind / was a little younger type / an also a little more Ann Frankish." And of Marlene Dietrich, he writes, "as curiosity's doom inks beauty's claim / that sad-eyed he shall turn t salt [*sic*]," a sneak preview of the 1966 song title "Sad-Eyed Lady of the Lowlands" and a clever allusion to Lot's wife.

It takes nothing away from Chuck Berry to say that those who claim that "Subterranean Homesick Blues"—the gleeful, swing-

ing rock 'n' roll song that kicks off *Bringing It All Back Home*—
is Dylan's version of a Chuck Berry tune are out of their minds,
wrong, ridiculous, pedantic, or worse. (Those numbers include Bob
Dylan himself, who invokes Berry's "Too Much Monkey Business"
as an inspiration for the song in the liner notes to the 1985 retrospective collection, *Biograph*.) And it takes nothing away from the
Beatles, who via their inspiration and domination of the pop charts
in 1964 kick-started Dylan's return to the cherished rock 'n' roll of
his youth, to see the song as a challenge to their teeny-bopper orientation; "Subterranean Homesick Blues," while nearly impossible
to have been made without them, makes the Beatles of the time
sound childlike.

"Subterranean Homesick Blues" is pure Dylan—as pure and
authentic Dylan as ever there was and ever there is and ever there
can or will be. After listening to his first four albums, the song veritably explodes out of the speakers with a brash, dynamic new sound
and personality that introduces an entirely new Bob Dylan, along
the way transforming the shape and sound of rock music forever.
It's arguably the single most subversive and transformative event in
rock history, forever laying down a challenge to all who would pick
up a guitar—acoustic or electric, as the song features both—and
attempt to write and sing a song that matters in any way to anyone
beyond the songwriter himself. It challenges every garage band to
equal the clash of guitars against each other. It challenges every
singer to swing against the beat and to phrase impossibly complex lines with inevitable fluency and fluidity in an utterly natural,
organic voice that elides a melody line but never goes off pitch. It
challenges every band to sound urgent; it challenges every rapper
to keep up the pace; it challenges every writer to express in words
the sheer love of language, the sound of rhymes, words crashing
into each other like those guitar licks, yet somehow retaining their
dignity and meaning in the collision. Dylan would go on to write
better songs—songs with more inventive melodies and chordal
structures, more profound lyrical import, more colorful songs—but
if only due to its placement as the first track of *Bringing It All Back
Home,* and thus his first full-band electric recording, no song he

ever wrote could have the sudden, stunning impact of "Subterranean Homesick Blues."

The song has become so commonplace, so etched in our minds and
our ears and in the culture, that it's easy to overlook or forget how truly
stunning and revolutionary it was and, heard with new ears, still is. In
four fast verses of swift, rapid patter, full of exuberant rhymes, comic
quips, and double entendres, Dylan captures—or creates—an entire
zeitgeist that pretty much encapsulates "the Sixties" or "the counterculture." He portrays a frenzied world of drugs and paranoia, a world
where Johnny and Maggie may be holding illicit substances—"mixing
up the medicine"—or not, but it doesn't matter; an overzealous dis-
trict attorney needs his own kind of score and won't stop at anything,
including illegal wiretapping and planting evidence, to get it:

> *Maggie comes fleet floot*
> *Face full of black soot*
> *Talkin' that the heat put*
> *Plants in the bed but*
> *The phone's tapped anyway*
> *Maggie says that many say*
> *They must bust in early May*
> *Orders from the D.A.*
> *Look out kid*
> *Don't matter what you did . . .*

You could listen to this song for years, even decades, and just luxu-
riate in the delight Dylan takes in the phrasing, spitting out these
percussive lines almost like onomatopoeia or bursts of Tourette's,
without realizing that he's actually constructed something of a narrative here. Along the way, he's also invented a new grammar or
language of hip—partly based on, for sure, French symbolist and
Beat poetry, bebop jazz, and surrealism, but giving them an entirely
new context and attitude. It's not for nothing that two of his most
famous couplets come from this song, phrases that have so wholly
transcended their modest roots in this skittery bit of rock 'n' roll to
become part of the common vocabulary:

You don't need a weather man
To know which way the wind blows.

This couplet, which ends the second stanza, seemingly so simple, contains the seeds of an entire revolution—indeed, the underground terrorist group Weatherman (aka the Weathermen and the Weather Underground Organization) took its name from it. But notice, too, how subtly and beautifully the line is a subversive twist on Dylan's previous song about blowing wind—whereas before what was blowin' in the wind was an enigma, a mystery that seemed to contain the secret of how someday mankind could live in peace, here it's rearranged as a metaphor for an entire generation's total and utter cynicism toward the establishment. Not only do we hip people know which way the wind blows—know how things are really going down—we also know enough to know that the weatherman himself is a tool and a fool, and he probably can't be trusted to boot! Dylan echoes and extends this mistrust of authority in the final couplet of the third stanza with an absurdist, dadaesque image:

Don't follow leaders
Watch the parkin' meters.

As the song title indicates, "Subterranean Homesick Blues" is a blues. But no blues ever sounded like this before, and it's a blues, musically speaking, only in the most formal sense. Lyrically, it has more claim to the blues, being a kind of lament, but one that is universes beyond the typical content of a "my baby left me and I feel so bad" kind of blues. The song gave Dylan his first taste of pop success, the single just cracking *Billboard*'s Top 40, peaking at number 39.

The same can be said, after all, for the next song on this groundbreaking album. In formal, musical terms, the love song "She Belongs to Me" uses a blues structure and pattern. Along with swapping the solo acoustic guitar approach for performing with an electric backup band on *Bringing It All Back Home,* Dylan finds more inspiration and more utility in the blues than he has, up until this point, in the traditional folk ballads that inspired so many of his melodies, lyrics, and song forms. Dylan's genius, though, akin to paradigm-shifting artists like Pablo Picasso and Miles Davis—artists who would themselves come under considerable criticism for some of the shifts and turns their careers would take (Davis, like Dylan, would be condemned for "going electric")—would be to take that wholly American form of the blues and to transform it completely, beyond recognition, into a new style, albeit, as with Picasso and Davis, wholly sui generis. Dylan would make Bob Dylan music and record Bob Dylan records; the rest of the world would follow in step and adopt or adapt the sound into a genre often called "folk rock" for lack of a better term. Dylan never played folk rock, nor did he ever really play folk, rock, or blues. What stands out more is Dylan's *conversion* or *reinvention* of the traditional material and forms through wholesale absorption or reabsorption into an utterly new, unique, and idiosyncratic sound. It is precisely Dylan's idiosyncratic approach that so lends itself to outright mimicry and so resists outright tribute. That is to say— as hundreds if not thousands of Dylan wannabes have eventually learned over the years—it is easier to mimic Dylan than it is to try to follow in his footsteps with any degree of success.

It's difficult to isolate or deconstruct just what are the characteristics of Dylan's approach that make it so unique. To do so also, undoubtedly, takes away some of the fun and the mystery; much better just to surrender to the totality of the experience of hearing him sneer his way through "Maggie's Farm," with those brilliantly long, rounded "I"s that begin each verse. But it's in "Maggie's Farm," in the byplay or interplay between Dylan and the band, where one begins to hear a pattern set, consciously or not, instinctively or accidentally, whereby Dylan creates tension by resisting the stranglehold of the very rhythms he is now adding to his performance. When he's playing solo, accompanying himself on guitar, he can stretch out a beat or a measure, or even add a whole measure, anytime he wants, and as his guitar and voice are connected, one hardly notices. But on a number like "Maggie's Farm," with his mostly rock- and blues-trained musicians laying down a rhythmic pattern in lockstep, Dylan is bound to soar over and collide with the musicians, and he does both. This is partly due to his preferred method of recording, which with few exceptions throughout his career has been to capture a spontaneous moment of a song being played in the studio, *so* spontaneous, much of the time, that the musicians hardly know the song. Perhaps he's played it through for them once on guitar. Perhaps he hasn't. Often they don't know ahead of time what key the song is in, or he changes the key without telling them. Many times he just starts playing without even cueing them to start. (The cluelessness of his musicians is on display for all to hear on *Bringing It All Back Home*'s "Bob Dylan's 115th Dream"—Dylan launches into the song on guitar, and by the second line he bursts into laughter and stops, as the laughter spreads to the producer, Tom Wilson, who can barely utter the words "Start again" through his paroxysms of hysteria, the joke being that the band forgot to play. Or maybe no one ever told them they were supposed to.) Sometimes, if you listen closely, you can hear them following him to see where the next chord change comes. Mostly you can hear them listening to him, listening for when one of his long, drawn-out lines ends with a pause that goes beyond the rigors of the song's ostensible meter. And mostly you can hear him playfully, purposefully singing off and over the beat, floating over the rhythms as if he has no sense of rhythm at all (which absolutely is *not* the case—only someone with an inerrant sense of rhythm could pull off what Dylan does) or isn't paying any attention to his band, the act itself being one of struggle, liberation, and freedom. In other words, Dylan's very phrasing in "Maggie's Farm"—a song whose manifest content is about not playing by the rules or doing what he's told or answering to anyone—says what the song wants to say.

It's often been suggested that "Maggie's Farm" is yet another in a series of thinly veiled diatribes against the folk-protest Stalinists, those who insisted that Dylan had an obligation to use his tools as a songwriter in the service of a cause—in this case, the agenda of the New Left—and that anything else would spell the act of a selfish would-be pop star, one who *used* the political protest movement to gain himself an initial hearing on his way toward greater fortune and fame in the pop music arena. This absurd scenario credits Dylan with far more foresight than any mortal could possibly muster. Was he ambitious? Perhaps. Is personal ambition a sin? Under the rule of a Hitler or a Stalin, probably. Dylan certainly tips his hat toward this reading of the song in the final verse, when he sings:

> *Well, I try my best*
> *To be just like I am,*
> *But everybody wants you*
> *To be just like them.*
> *They say sing while you slave and I just get bored.*
> *I ain't gonna work on Maggie's farm no more.*

"Love Minus Zero/No Limit" is one of Dylan's most enigmatic love songs. We might not even know it's a love song, so dense and obscure is the imagery, if not for the fact that Dylan tells us in the first line—"My love she speaks like silence"—and then refers back to his "love" at least once every stanza. But apart from that, Dylan paints a picture with dazzling wordplay, riffing on received phrases and shocking the listener with abrupt juxtapositions: "The cloak and dagger dangles," "In ceremonies of the horsemen / Even the pawn must hold a grudge," and, in another couplet that would pass into general usage, "there's no success like failure / And . . . failure's no success at all."

Much of the imagery and many of the "situations" in this song are derived from the biblical story of Daniel, to which Dylan would return throughout his career as a gold mine of vivid symbolism, stark confrontations, and more than a little self-identification with the Prophet himself. In exile in Babylon, Daniel's skills as an interpreter of dreams and a fortune-teller come in handy when they are brought to the attention of a succession of kings who otherwise would just as soon do away with him. He foretells how Nebuchadnezzar would build a *statue* of gold, silver, and copper, only to see it *crumble* "like chaff," or, as Dylan puts it, "Statues made of match sticks / Crumble into one another." Daniel reminds Nebuchadnezzar's grandson, Belshazzar, that people used to *tremble* before his grandfather, before translating some mysterious writing on the wall, repeating quotations, drawing conclusions, speaking of the future, and he is eventually rewarded with gifts from wise men. Nevertheless, he later falls victim to a plot by jealous satraps whose attempt to frame him fails when they "could find neither fault nor corruption, inasmuch as he was *faithful* . . ." (Daniel 6:5; emphasis mine). And in his final vision of Judgment Day, he sees "the One of Ancient Days" sitting dressed in a garment "white as snow" on a throne "of fiery flames," or as Dylan puts it, "true, like ice, like fire." (Dylan would return to the story of Daniel when he recorded a version of Johnny Cash's "Belshazzar" with the Hawks during the informal home-recording sessions that eventually produced *The Basement Tapes*.)

As for the meaning of the enigmatic title of the song, which is written like a math equation, love minus zero, of course, equals love. Divided by "no limit," however, anything can happen. Especially when one appreciates that "no limit" is the English translation of one of the Kabbalistic ways of referring to G-d—*ain sof,* or "without end." Hence, "no limit."

The first side of *Bringing It All Back Home* shocked fans with its blistering, blues-based electric rock arrangements, which featured a mostly anonymous group of musicians, including the bassist William E. Lee (whose son Spike is the famous filmmaker), the guitarists Kenny Rankin, John Hammond, Jr., and Bruce Langhorne (who played on "Corrina, Corrina" on 1963's *The Freewheelin' Bob Dylan*), and the drummer Bobby Gregg. The second side, however, was devoted to four mostly solo performances featuring Dylan accompanying himself on acoustic guitar and harmonica (Bruce Langhorne lent subtle counterpoint on electric guitar to "Mr. Tambourine Man"). The full-band arrangements set the tone for the four songs that make up side two of the original LP—a veritable mini–greatest hits album unto itself. And what a segue of songs it is! "Mr. Tambourine Man," "Gates of Eden," "It's Alright, Ma (I'm Only Bleeding)," and "It's All Over Now, Baby Blue." That's more great songs than most songwriters are lucky to pen in the course of an entire career, and here they're just the acoustic side of an album remembered for "Maggie's Farm" and "Subterranean Homesick Blues."

"Mr. Tambourine Man," like the earlier, as-then-unreleased "Lay Down Your Weary Tune," is one of several songs devoted to Dylan's musical muse. Often thought to describe the heightened (or dead-ened) sensory experience brought on by psychedelic drugs, the song was more likely inspired by Dylan's trip to Mardi Gras or by Bruce Langhorne, who was known on occasion to wield an enormous Turkish tambourine. (In the *Biograph* liner notes, Dylan says it's not a drug song and that he wrote the song months *before* his first acid trip.) The narrative, such as it is, portrays an early morning scene after being awake an entire, long night, still seeking stimulation. The verbal twists, again, are astonishing:

> *Yes, to dance beneath the diamond sky with one hand waving free*
> *Silhouetted by the sea, circled by the circus sands*
> *With all memory and fate driven deep beneath the waves . . .*

What fluency and facility, what imagination; once again, the form and content, the medium and the message, are one and the same. And to drive that point home, the refrain always ends with these two lines:

> *Hey! Mr. Tambourine Man, play a song for me,*
> *In the jingle jangle morning I'll come followin' you*

—"jangles" being the little metal cymbals that make a tambourine, well, jangle.

"Gates of Eden," as the title hints, reads like a Kabbalistic exposi-tion on the fall of man, the post-Edenic world, and our innate wish to find our way back to the garden. The song begins and ends with notions of truth. It opens with a cynical take—"Of war and peace the truth just twists / Its curfew gull just glides . . ."—and ends with what at the time must have seemed like a surprisingly direct state-ment of religious belief: ". . . there are no truths outside the Gates of Eden." In between, the song is strewn with biblical and mystical imagery. Ezekiel and Isaiah have visions of G-d riding in a chariot borne by four beings, or Chayos. As it is written in Ezekiel 1:4–13: "I saw, and did behold a storm come sweeping from the north, a huge cloud with flashing fire and brilliance surrounding it . . . and in its midst there was a likeness of four creatures. . . . Their appearance was like fiery coals, burning like torches." Later in the book of Ezekiel—from which Dylan would quote and paraphrase extensively in coming years—the Prophet talks about the trees in Eden: "I made it so beautiful with its abundant tendrils that it was envied by all the trees of Eden that were in G-d's garden" (Ezekiel 31:9).

And thus, Dylan opens "Gates of Eden" with his own poetic rendering of the Prophets' mystical vision of G-d, rendered here as "the cowboy angel":

> *Upon four-legged forest clouds*
> *The cowboy angel rides*
> *With his candle lit into the sun*
> *Though its glow is waxed in black*
> *All except when 'neath the trees of Eden*

It's a dark, dreary world outside the gates of Eden, where false prophets such as Aladdin and "Utopian hermit monks" offer up empty promises of admission into the gates. Someone should have noticed that they were sitting "side saddle on the Golden Calf"—a sure tipoff that theirs was an empty promise, one that could only elicit laughter inside Eden's gates. So, too, does Dylan contrast the emptiness of earthly, material experience with the transcendence of life in Paradise:

> *The kingdoms of Experience*
> *In the precious wind they rot*
> *While paupers change possessions*
> *Each one wishing for what the other has got*
> *And the princess and the prince*
> *Discuss what's real and what is not*
> *It doesn't matter inside the Gates of Eden*

The song turns personal as Dylan, the protest singer, sings out a warning like a "lonesome sparrow" about false prophets and earthly rulers, while "there are no kings inside the Gates of Eden." Finally, he's left alone with someone suspiciously resembling Joan Baez—she "the motorcycle black Madonna two-wheeled gypsy queen," he "her silver-studded phantom." The two of them together unsettle the conventional types, causing "the gray flannel dwarf to scream." It's unclear whose are the "bread crumb sins" being picked on by "wicked birds of prey"—do they belong to the phantom, that is, Dylan, or the dwarf in the gray flannel suit? In either case, the reference is to the Jewish ritual of *tashlich*—after Ecclesiastes 11:1: "Cast your bread forth upon the waters, for after many days you will find it"—in which Jews symbolically shed themselves of their sins alongside a body of water into which they empty their pockets of the accumulated crumbs of the year (remembering to bring along some crumbled-up bread, in case they've been laundering regularly), on the afternoon of the second day of Rosh Hashanah, the Jewish New Year, the holy day that begins the intense period of self-examination and atonement that culminates on the night of Yom Kippur.

Dylan turns dark on "It's Alright, Ma (I'm Only Bleeding)." The music is haunted, haunting, driven by a modal drone—a repeated, percussive, rhythmic tonic note atop which Dylan plucks counterpoint to his spoke-sung lyrics that are the mirror image, thematically, of "Subterranean Homesick Blues." While that song revels in its dizzying, jaunty paranoia, "It's Alright, Ma" paints a world spiraling into oblivion; hence, the circular guitar riff that punctuates the end of each stanza. Dylan's target here is nothing less than modern society in all its godless, faithless materialism. In a vocal delivery that matches the drone of his guitar, he unleashes a torrent of futility in the first verse:

To understand you know too soon
There is no sense in trying . . .

Dylan goes on at length in a nightmarish vision of a world where children are sold "toy guns that spark" and "flesh-colored Christs that glow in the dark," where, in a litany of phrases that collectively could make up its own chapter of Proverbs, he sings about "advertising signs that con you into thinking you're the one / That can do what's never been done," where "money doesn't talk, it swears," where, finally, "all is phony." Dylan bemoans his own role in dealing with all of this, where if his "thought-dreams could be seen / They'd probably put [his] head in a guillotine."

The overall message and tone is familiar from the book of Ecclesiastes, that ode to futility that begins, "Futility of futilities! All is futile!" In Ecclesiastes, Solomon explains what he set out to accomplish: "I applied my mind to study and probe by wisdom all that happens beneath the sky . . . I observed all the deeds beneath the sun, and behold all is futile" (Ecclesiastes 1:17).

Dylan renders this same sentiment in his own poetry:

> *Darkness at the break of noon*
> *Shadows even the silver spoon*
> *The handmade blade, the child's balloon*
> *Eclipses both the sun and moon*
> *To understand you know too soon*
> *There is no sense in trying.*

"All words are wearying," complains Solomon, and Dylan echoes him, singing of "wasted words" and "disillusioned words." Dylan speaks of "them that must obey authority / That they do not respect in any degree / Who despise their jobs, their destinies," echoing Solomon, who writes, "What profit does man have for all his labor which he toils beneath the sun?" In a fit of cynical optimism, Solomon reminds us that "the living know that they will die, but the dead know nothing at all," which Dylan renders as "For them that think death's honesty / Won't fall upon them naturally / Life sometimes / Must get lonely." Even in his liner notes, Dylan offers a couple of specific examples of Solomon's generalized lament that "there is nothing new under the sun" when he writes, "the Great books've been written, the Great sayings have all been said."

And what of "the masters [who] make the rules / For the wise men and the fools"? So Solomon said to himself:

The fate of the fool will befall me also; to what advantage, then, have I become wise? But I came to the conclusion that this, too, was futility, because the wise man and the fool are both forgotten. The wise man dies, just like the fool (Ecclesiastes 2:15–16).

Or, as Dylan put it, "I got nothing, Ma, to live up to."

Bringing It All Back Home concludes with "It's All Over Now, Baby Blue," part attack, part wistful farewell. Much ink has been spilled over who or what the song is aimed at: an erstwhile lover, that is, Suze Rotolo or Joan Baez; a folk musician friend, perhaps blue-eyed Paul Clayton or David Blue (né Cohen); the folk-protest genre, the folk-protest crowd, or acoustic folk music more generally. The song works with any or all readings, but it is most convincingly read as a song Dylan is singing to himself—"baby blue" being the color of his eyes, "bluer than robin's eggs," as Joan Baez would call them in her 1975 song "Diamonds and Rust"—about saying goodbye to all of the above. From the opening line to the final verse, Dylan seems to be addressing a valediction to everything that has come before, on his way toward a new mission, a new "calling," as he implies. He's more than a little brutal, leaving behind "stepping stones" that have presumably given him a leg up, and characterizing those who will not come along, or "follow," as "dead." But as he will put it years later in the song "Jokerman," where he finds himself "Shedding off one more layer of skin / Staying one step ahead of the persecutor within," he needs to turn his back on his prior self, or those who represent his former self in the person of the vagabond wearing his old outfits, in order to light the way toward a new beginning.

Bringing It All Back Home, Dylan's fifth album, was recorded in three days in mid-January 1965, and released almost exactly three years to the day after Dylan's eponymous debut. Dylan had yet to turn twenty-four. Some of these songs Dylan had already been performing since the previous fall, as documented on *Live 1964: Concert at Philharmonic Hall (The Bootleg Series Vol. 6)*, the famous "Halloween concert" in New York City (at what is now called Avery Fisher Hall), which included three quarters of side two—"Mr. Tambourine Man," "Gates of Eden," and "It's Alright Ma (I'm Only Bleeding)"—and two songs recorded at the January 1965 sessions but not included on the finished album, "Mama, You Been on My Mind" and "If You Gotta Go, Go Now." Already by this time the tables had been turned in the folk music world, and Bob Dylan was now introducing Joan Baez as a special "surprise" guest at *his* concerts.

Bringing It All Back Home made Dylan a full-fledged rock star: the album cracked the Top 10 and sold a million copies; "Subterranean Homesick Blues" cracked the Top 40—his highest-charting single thus far. By the time Dylan reached Britain in May, he had his second Top 10 hit there ("The Times They Are a-Changin'" preceding "Subterranean Homesick Blues" by only a couple of months), and his presence induced Beatles-like hysteria among fans, as documented in D. A. Pennebaker's film *Dont Look Back*. *Bringing It All Back Home* marked the first in a trilogy of albums recorded and released at a dizzying, frenzied pace in just a little over a year's time, a period that also saw a whirlwind solo acoustic tour of England while three of his albums—*Freewheelin'*, *Times*, and *Bringing It All Back Home*—sat comfortably in the Top 10; extensive work on his full-length book of prose poems that eventually saw publication as *Tarantula* in 1971; the end of his romantic and, for the next ten years, his professional relationship with Joan Baez; the writing and recording of "Like a Rolling Stone," "Desolation Row," and "Rainy Day Women #12 & 35," among other classics; and his appearance at the summer 1965 Newport Folk Festival, where a scandalized audience of ostriches seemingly had ignored the fact that Dylan had "gone electric" a half-year earlier with the release of *Bringing It All Back Home*.

It was also during this period of time that, unknown to almost any but his closest friends and intimates, Bob Dylan began a relationship with Sara Lownds, a former model and Playboy bunny and friend of his manager's wife, Sally Grossman (who appears with Dylan on the cover of *Bringing It All Back Home*). Lownds, who worked at a film production company, became Mrs. Bob Dylan in a secret ceremony on Long Island, New York, on November 22, 1965 (two years to the day after President Kennedy was assassinated). Born Shirley Noznisky to Jewish parents in Wilmington, Delaware, Sara was a mystical, dark-haired beauty, briefly married to Hans Lownds, a magazine photographer twenty-five years her elder, with whom she had a daughter,

Maria, in 1961. Little is known about Bob and Sara's courtship, other than that Sara lived with her daughter at the famed Chelsea Hotel, where Dylan also took an apartment, presumably to be close to her.

Sara Lownds apparently coveted her privacy as much as she shunned the spotlight, and Dylan is said to have been attracted to her Zen-like equanimity. After the two wed, Dylan adopted Maria, who then became Maria Dylan. The couple would go on to have four children together, all given biblical names: Jesse (born just six weeks after his parents' nuptials), Anna (the Anglicized version of the Hebrew name Chana, after Dylan's paternal grandmother), Samuel, and Jakob. As an adult, Maria would marry Peter Himmelman— like her father, a folk-rock singer-songwriter from Minnesota—and the two would set up an Orthodox Jewish household. Maria's oldest brother, Jesse Dylan, would grow up to be a film and music video director, working with the likes of Tom Waits, Elvis Costello, Tom Petty, and Lenny Kravitz, and creating an Emmy Award–winning video for Barack Obama's presidential campaign. He also created a website called Lybba, named after his great-grandmother, intended to make medical resources available in language understandable to laypeople. Maria's youngest brother, Jakob, would gain fame in the mid-1990s as leader of his own rock group, the Wallflowers, selling millions more albums than his father did and appearing on the cover of *Rolling Stone,* looking like a much more handsome, even bluer-eyed version of his father, with prettier features obviously inherited from his attractive mother.

In the liner notes to *Highway 61 Revisited,* Dylan uses the phrases "slow train" and "solid rock" several times, anticipating the titles of two of the best-known songs from his gospel albums recorded a decade and a half later. "On the slow train time does not interfere," writes Dylan, introducing the album, then in the same sentence referring to "the hundred Inevitables made of solid rock & stone," a play of words on "rock 'n' roll" as well as a coy allusion to the album's opening number, "Like a Rolling Stone," as well as to his maternal family's name. Near the end of his notes, Dylan writes of the album, "the subject matter—tho meaningless as it is—has something to do with . . . the holy slow train" (ellipses mine). In 1979, Dylan will release an album called *Slow Train Coming*, and the next year, his album *Saved* includes a song called "Solid Rock." Dylan is always the master recycler of his own work as well as that of others.

But that is not why *Highway 61 Revisited* is widely considered one of Bob Dylan's all-time greatest albums. Dylan's first album of electric rock from beginning to end, it includes nine songs—beginning with "Like a Rolling Stone" and concluding with "Desolation Row"—every one a classic. More has probably been written about "Like a Rolling Stone" than any single song in rock history. It remains Dylan's greatest hit single (only the Beatles' song "Help!" kept it from going to number 1), has remained a concert highlight (often the closing number), is often credited with having transformed American popular music more than any other single song, is a perennial choice in critics' and readers' polls as the greatest song of the rock era, and has even been the subject of at least one entire book. That Dylan struck gold, figuratively and literally, with this song—which began life as a piano-based waltz modeled on the chord changes of Ritchie Valens's "La Bamba" and "Twist and Shout" by the Isley Brothers and the Beatles, and whose signature organ riff was stumbled upon by the guitarist Al Kooper, who snuck over to the keyboard and began playing without invitation or permission—just makes the lore surrounding it all the more fascinating, as a kind of coming together of spontaneous creative forces, most of all Dylan's writing and vocals, to make for an accidental masterpiece.

Rolling stones gather no moss, and presumably that's what Dylan is referring to when he asks in the refrain, "How does it feel, to be . . . like a rolling stone?" The English rock group the Rolling Stones was already in existence at the time, taking its name from the Muddy Waters blues song "Rollin' Stone." Dylan's song bears no relationship to Waters's; Dylan's is a six-minute torrent of blistering invective in four verses, seemingly addressed to a woman who was once on top of the world, socially and financially, and who has fallen on hard times. Countless scribes have tried to mine the lyrics and Dylan's biography for hints of who inspired him to such misanthropic heights—or depths, as the case may be—and such schadenfreude. Joan Baez and the socialite Edie Sedgwick are prominent, recurring nominees for the honor of "woman to whom 'Like a Rolling Stone' is addressed," but Joan Baez gets way too much credit for inspiring dozens of Dylan's songs during this period, including "It's All Over Now, Baby Blue," "She Belongs to Me," and "Visions of Johanna," and it's not even clear that Dylan had met Sedgwick before he wrote the song. Others suggest it's yet another kiss-off song to the folk community at large—

> *Ain't it hard when you discover that*
> *He really wasn't where it's at*
> *After he took from you everything he could steal*

—he, in this case, being Dylan himself, flaunting what he was accused of having done, using the folk-protest genre just to get ahead.

A few years later, Dylan would talk about the moment when he realized that much of what he had written seemingly about others was actually about himself. As noted earlier, consciously or not, Dylan puts himself in the song via the central image of the rolling *stone,* his mother's maiden name ("like a rolling Zimmerman" just doesn't have the same ring to it). While he certainly wasn't a former socialite fallen on hard times, he could well have identified as one, especially in how that relates to the song's refrain:

> *How does it feel*
> *To be on your own*
> *With no direction home*
> *Like a complete unknown*
> *Like a rolling stone?*

Certainly it's the song's chorus that in large part explains its immediate appeal in 1965, as well as its enduring appeal as a classic. Like the other number with which Dylan is most identified, "Blowin' in the Wind," the song's central narrative device is a question—a narrative strategy that is used throughout Jewish scripture and commentary, and, as Michael Wex points out in *Born to Kvetch,* becomes inherent in the very grammar and vocabulary of the Yiddish language, shaping Jewish rhetoric, so that Jews of Yiddish-speaking, Eastern European ancestry often answer questions with questions. The situation it describes, of alienation from one's past, one's peers, and oneself, perfectly encapsulated the mood of dislocation and transformation that characterized the cultural revolution of the Sixties.

In no small way, the Sixties really began with the song "Like a Rolling Stone," which kicks off musically with a rim shot on the snare drum that sounds like gunfire, a musical shot heard 'round the world, launching the anthem of the counterculture. The "How does it feel?" refrain became one of the few sing-along moments at Dylan concerts, and the "No direction home" line became the title of an award-winning public TV documentary on Dylan's early years, directed by Martin Scorsese with the full and complete cooperation of Dylan's own production company.

"Tombstone Blues" is typical of Dylan's narratives of this time, seemingly stream-of-consciousness yet upon closer inspection carefully put together. It includes a dizzying array of political, cultural, and literary references—in a few lines, he invokes Paul Revere, Belle Starr, Jack the Ripper, the chamber of commerce, John the Baptist, the commander-in-chief, Galileo, Cecil B. DeMille, Ma Rainey, and Beethoven, and puts them into play with fictional characters, all in a display of antiestablishment wit, as reflected in the song's refrain.

Dylan engages in biblical midrash in this song, displaying deep familiarity with the book of Judges. While Samson is never named, Dylan refers to the story of how Samson killed a thousand Philistines with the jawbone of an ass when he sings, "The king of the Philistines his soldiers to save / Put jawbones on their tombstones and flatters their graves." The song derives its title, "Tombstone Blues," from this couplet, which is a freewheeling riff on Judges 15:14–17:

[Samson] came to Lehi and the Philistines shouted at him. . . . He found a fresh jawbone of a donkey, and he picked it up and with it he killed a thousand men. . . . He threw the jawbone away, and the place was hence called Jawbone Hill.

91

To nail the connection between the song's lyrical couplet and the story of the unnamed Samson slaying the Philistines, Dylan invokes Samson's treacherous lover, Delilah, a few verses later:

> *The geometry of innocence flesh on the bone*
> *Causes Galileo's math book to get thrown*
> *At Delilah who sits worthlessly alone*
> *But the tears on her cheeks are from laughter*

Note how Dylan subtly reintroduces the jawbone in this verse in the first line, as well as punning on the word *thrown*, which can also be heard as "throne," upon which presumably the king of the Philistines and/or Delilah may sit, "worthlessly alone."

In the next verse, Dylan refers to the 1949 Hollywood film version of this Bible story, *Samson and Delilah*, starring Victor Mature and Hedy Lamarr in the title roles, when he sings, "I would . . . send out for some pillars and Cecil B. DeMille." The film, which like the original story climaxes when Samson breaks his chains and brings down the hilltop temple by collapsing the structural pillars, was directed by DeMille. (Incidentally, the film itself was based on a 1930 novel, *Judge and Fool*, also known as *Samson the Nazarite*, written by the Zionist leader Vladimir Jabotinsky, the founder of the Irgun, an underground group fighting for an Israeli state, and the spiritual forefather of Israel's right-wing party Herut, led for many years by Menachem Begin. Jabotinsky also cowrote the treatment that was eventually turned into the film script.)

Hidden inside the scorching blues-rocker "From a Buick 6" is a love song to Dylan's soon-to-be wife, Sara. The song describes a quiet, soulful woman who is mother to the singer's children, protective of his privacy, and even, like Sara, the scion of a scrap dealer (rendered here as "junkyard angel"). He emphasizes her qualities of equanimity—"She don't make me nervous, she don't talk too much"—and the oasis or refuge she provides from the burgeoning noise and insanity of his career.

"From a Buick 6" also contains several images of remarkable foresight. Nearly a year to the day after Dylan recorded the song with the lines, "Well, when . . . I'm all cracked up on the highway and near the water's edge / She comes down the thruway ready to sew me up with thread," Sara would scoop Dylan up from the pavement of a Woodstock road after he took a spill off his motorcycle, and drive him to a hospital. Also, in addition to being able to sew, the "junk-yard angel" feeds her man—"she always gives me bread"—an image of the goddess woman that would recur in Dylan's postdivorce song, "Is Your Love in Vain?" from 1977, in which he would sing, "Can you cook and sew, make flowers grow?"

After professing his love for and happiness with Sara in "From a Buick 6," Dylan followed with two songs of hatred and loathing, one addressed to a man, the other to a woman. "Ballad of a Thin Man," with its oft-quoted refrain—"Something is happening here / But you don't know what it is / Do you, Mister Jones?"—echoes "Like a Rolling Stone" in its scorn for someone with bourgeois values:

> *You've been with the professors*
> *And they've all liked your looks*
> *With great lawyers you have*
> *Discussed lepers and crooks*
> *You've been through all of*
> *F. Scott Fitzgerald's books*
> *You're very well read*
> *It's well known.*

The choice of Fitzgerald is an apt one. The novelist's greatest creation, Jay Gatsby, who has convinced everyone he is to the manor born, is revealed to be an impostor, whose wealth was derived illicitly and who is in fact James Gatz, a former soldier and a child of working-class North Dakota. Dylan may posit being "very well read" as a demerit against Mr. Jones, but it's one of his own most admirable characteristics. The song is generally regarded as being about a clueless journalist, or journalists in general—

> *You walk into the room*
> *With your pencil in your hand*

> *You see somebody naked*
> *And you say, "Who is that man?"*
> *You try so hard*
> *But you don't understand*
> *Just what you'll say*
> *When you get home*

—attempting to write about Dylan or the Sixties counterculture, and not knowing which end is up.

"Queen Jane Approximately" is almost as vicious toward a woman as "Ballad of a Thin Man" is toward Mr. Jones. In the form of a sarcastic invitation—"Won't you come see me, Queen Jane?"—the song mocks an earnest queen, or mother, or earth mother, who has come to the end of the line. Even her own family sees she has reached a creative dead end; her ladies in waiting demand recompense for their service; her children resent her. It's hard to read the song as about anyone other than Joan Baez, with Dylan portraying a time when even the folk madonna will grow "sick of all this repetition," having lost her audience and sense of purpose. Then, and only then, he says, should she think about calling him up, presumably for a real talking to—or not, as the case may be.

As noted earlier, the album's title track is Dylan's most obvious attempt at midrash. The first verse of "Highway 61 Revisited" reimagines the story of Abraham and Isaac as a contemporary conversation between two jaded, cynical hipsters:

> *God said to Abraham, "Kill me a son"*
> *Abe says, "Man, you must be puttin' me on"*
> *God says, "No." Abe say, "What?"*
> *God say, "You can do what you want Abe, but*
> *The next time you see me comin' you better run"*
> *Well Abe says, "Where you want this killin' done?"*
> *God says, "Out on Highway 61."*

Dylan relocates the story from the biblical land of Israel to the American Midwest—a region that includes his own place of birth to a father named Abe, as Highway 61 runs from the Canadian border through Duluth, down the Mississippi to New Orleans. In its original version, the song is a rollicking, colorful blues given a carnivalesque treatment with honky-tonk keyboards and circus whistle, suited to the irreverent tone of the lyrics, which go on to catalog a dubious cast of characters including hoboes, salesmen, gamblers, and a promoter who'll do anything for a buck—even if it means staging the "next world war" as a grand spectacle on Highway 61.

Dylan closes the album with "Desolation Row," an eleven-minute phantasmagoria, a snapshot of a world gone wrong, the world as Dylan sees it at the moment, with everyone at cross-purposes and confused about their roles—a world not unlike the one Dylan will eventually portray in his 2003 film, *Masked and Anonymous,* with the ominous threat of violence never far away. Romeo waltzes in on Cinderella's scene and is immediately told he's in the wrong place and he should leave. Ophelia is beneath the window instead of Romeo, and instead of gazing at her would-be lover she's transfixed by "Noah's great rainbow." Cain, Abel, and the hunchback of Notre Dame—an unlikely trio, to say the least—are the only ones not making love or expecting rain. (The hunchback, Victor Hugo's Quasimodo, is also referenced in Dylan's liner notes, as is Ophelia's sin, her "lifelessness.") Albert Einstein is noted for his violin playing and not for his theory of relativity. Casanova, the former ladies' man, lacks assurance; Ezra Pound and T. S. Eliot are duking it out; calypso singers laugh instead of sing and fishermen hold flowers instead of fish. It's a wonder that they still know how to breathe.

"Like a Rolling Stone" was recorded on its own in mid-June and released as a single before Dylan even began recording (and, presumably, writing) the other songs on *Highway 61 Revisited,* the rest of which was recorded over four days in the last week of July and the first week of August (the fourth session was merely to rerecord an all-acoustic version of "Desolation Row," which previously featured electric guitar accompaniment; otherwise the bulk of this classic album would have been recorded in a phenomenally quick three sessions, plus the ones for "Like a Rolling Stone"). In between, Dylan's notorious performance at the Newport Folk Festival, where he was "booed" for "going electric," took place on July 25. Both of those terms are in quotes because the issue of whether or not Dylan was booed has never been settled—many insist that the crowd was merely complaining about being unable to hear Dylan over the din of the band's poorly mixed instruments (the sound engineers at the folk festival presumably having had scant experience mixing levels for an electric band). As for suddenly "going electric," no one could honestly claim to have been surprised, what with *Bringing It All Back Home* having been released the previous March and "Like a Rolling Stone" already making its way up the pop charts. Furthermore, Dylan's was not the only group playing electric instruments at Newport; he was able to throw together his electric rock band on the spur of the moment precisely because the musicians, including members of the Paul Butterfield Blues Band, had already performed earlier in the weekend.

Whatever the case, Dylan *did* draw the wrath of the folk music elite, including the archivist Alan Lomax, Pete Seeger, and *Sing Out!* magazine's Irwin Silber. Even Robert Shelton, previously Dylan's greatest champion in the press, gave Dylan's performance a bad review. Dylan responded to the bad press and the accusations of betrayal just a few days later in the recording studio when he laid down "Positively Fourth Street," a thinly veiled putdown of his erstwhile Greenwich Village friends. They had a lot of nerve to call themselves that!

The debacle at Newport didn't discourage Dylan from what he deemed his appointed path. Rather, it only energized and encouraged him to work up a real act with a real, rehearsed rock band, with which he could deliver the songs from his last two albums in the form they were intended to be heard. Dylan formally debuted this new act on August 28—two days before the release of *Highway 61 Revisited*—at Forest Hills Stadium in Queens, New York, fronting a group that included the bassist Harvey Brooks and Al Kooper from the *Highway 61 Revisited* sessions, along with two members of a Canadian group that formerly backed the rockabilly legend Ronnie Hawkins: the guitarist Robbie Robertson and the drummer Levon Helm of the Hawks. The concert would establish a format that Dylan would stick with through the end of his first world tour in 1965–66—the first half a solo acoustic set featuring Dylan accompanying himself on guitar and harmonica, with Dylan joined after intermission by his backup band. Forest Hills would also establish the pattern of audience reaction for the vast majority of shows from then until the tour's end in May 1966—a pattern of worshipful attention and adoration during the first, acoustic half, followed by an increasingly agitated response during the second, electric half, culminating in heckling, hollering, and outright booing.

After two concerts—the Forest Hills show and one at the Hollywood Bowl in Los Angeles a few days later—Kooper and Brooks, who were primarily studio musicians forging other creative irons, decided to opt out of the touring group, leaving Dylan free to engage the services of the rest of the Hawks. By the third concert, in Austin, Texas, on September 24, the bassist Rick Danko, the pianist Richard Manuel, and the organist Garth Hudson joined Helm and Robertson, and the Hawks would officially become Dylan's backup band, on and offstage, for the next two years, launching a fertile creative collaboration the fruits of which would be enjoyed in concert and on record well into the mid-1970s.

The sessions for *Highway 61 Revisited* also produced two of Dylan's best single tracks, "Positively Fourth Street" and "Can You Please Crawl Out Your Window?" The former, perhaps Dylan's most devastating "putdown" song, written in the wake of the controversy surrounding the Newport fiasco, was presumably addressed to someone from the folk music community or the folk world in toto. The song was released as the follow-up single to "Like a Rolling Stone" and went to number 7 on the pop charts in September. It was first compiled on an LP when it appeared on *Bob Dylan's Greatest Hits* in 1967, and was later included on *Biograph* and *The Essential Bob Dylan*.

In "Can You Please Crawl Out Your Window?" Dylan returned to David, the warrior king—whose story is packed with more blackmail, treachery, and deceit than anything by Shakespeare—spinning a midrash on the tale to suit his own purposes. Used by King Saul as a murder weapon in the hopes that he would be killed, David slew thousands of Philistines, a veritable "genocide" that left him, in Dylan's words, "preoccupied with his vengeance / Cursing the dead that can't answer him back." King Saul harbored a jealous obsession over David's success on the battlefield and with women. Throughout the land Saul was taunted whenever "The rejoicing women sang as they danced and chanted, 'Saul has slain his thousands, and David his tens of thousands'" (I Samuel 18:7–9), and henceforth he resolved to do away with David.

Thus began a series of complex maneuvers against David's life. On one such occasion, David's wife, Michal—who happened to be Saul's daughter—caught wind of a plot and helped David escape. With Saul's agents waiting overnight outside his door to ambush him in the morning, he slipped out the back: "Michal lowered David through the window, and he left; he fled and escaped" (I Samuel 19:12). Or, as Dylan put it in the song's refrain, "Can you please crawl out your window? / Use your arms and legs it won't ruin you."

David was thenceforth on the run, moving with his family and soldiers from place to place. They dwelled in caves, in the wilderness, and in mountains. In Gath, fearful of King Achish, David acted crazy so as not to seem like a threat. "He concealed his demeanor in their eyes and feigned madness for their benefit; he scribbled on the doors of the gate and drooled into his beard" (I Samuel 21:14). Later on, after ducking into a cave to relieve himself, Saul found himself face-to-face with David, who made clear he had no intention of killing Saul. David asked him, "Why do you listen to those who say, 'David seeks to harm you?'" (I Samuel 24:10). Or, as Dylan put it, "How can you say he will haunt you?" Saul replied, "You are more righteous than I, for you have repaid me with goodness while I have treated you badly" (I Samuel 24:18). Or, as Dylan has it, "Why does he look so righteous while your face is so changed."

Nevertheless, Saul had yet to abandon his plan against David, who took his troops and arrived back in Gath, this time pledging loyalty to Achish, king of the Philistines. It was all a ruse, however, and David used the cover to do daily battle against other enemies of Israel. When the Philistines decided to do battle against Israel itself, Achish's generals dismissed David from their service, fearing he'd prove to be a fifth columnist. On their return from the front, David and his men came upon the city of Ziklag and found that it had been burned and pillaged by the dreaded Amalekites. Rather than greet him as a liberator, the residents of Ziklag were angry at David for not having protected them. So angry, in fact, that they wanted to punish him in that timeworn biblical way: "David was in great danger, for the people were ready to stone him, for the soul of all the people was embittered" (I Samuel 30:6). In David's case, they'd stone him even when he was trying to be so good.

Later, David triumphed over the Philistines, retrieved the Holy Ark, and brought it back to Jerusalem. In a frenzy of jubilation, David led the parade following the Ark, "leaping and dancing before G-d" (II Samuel 6:16). His wife, Michal, looked out her window and saw David making a spectacle of himself. Apparently, she didn't approve of his rock-star-like behavior—neither his skimpy outfit nor the thrill it gave his groupies—"and she despised him in her heart" (II Samuel 6:16). She asked him rhetorically, "How honored was the king of Israel today, exposing himself in the presence of his servants' maidservants, as one of the riffraff would be exposed!" (II Samuel 6:20). Or, as Dylan wittily rephrased it, "He looks so truthful, is this how he feels / Trying to peel the moon and expose it."

As we see, David's is one of the sexiest stories in the Torah, and sexual license versus sexual restraint is a motif running through the books of Samuel in which David's story is told. When David and his attendants flee to Nob, where the high priest offers the communal sacrifice, Ahimelech, the priest, allows the hungry refugees to partake of the sacred show-bread on the condition that they "have kept themselves from women" (I Samuel 21:5). One of the best-known stories of David's colorful life is his courtship of Bathsheba—he takes one look at her while she is bathing and has to have her. Exercising his kingly privileges, he does. Then, to cover his tracks and fend off any jealous reprisals, he engineers the battlefield death of her husband, Uriah, one of his generals. The Lord isn't happy about this, however, and the Prophet Nathan quotes the Former to the king, saying, "I shall raise evil against you from within your own house; I shall take your wives away in front of your eyes and give them to another man, who will lie with them under this very sun" (II Samuel 12:11).

David eventually reaps what he sows. His son Amnon rapes his half-sister, Tamar. His son Absalom vies with David for popularity with the ladies—"There was no one in all of Israel so admired for his beauty as Absalom" (II Samuel 14:25)—and eventually, after killing Amnon in retribution for raping his sister, foments rebellion against his father. David flees his household, taking all with him but "ten concubine wives to mind the house" (II Samuel 15:16). When Absalom conquers Jerusalem, his first act is to sleep with the women "in front of all Israel," as prophesied by Nathan (II Samuel 16:21–22). When David finally returns to Jerusalem triumphant, he locks up the ten women, who now are forbidden to have relations with anyone (II Samuel 20:3). These wives, whom David can't live with and can't live without, appear in "Can You Please Crawl Out Your Window?" as the "religion of the little ten women."

"Can You Please Crawl Out Your Window" went through several recorded iterations, including one with the Hawks that was released as a single in December. The song was clearly modeled after "Like a Rolling Stone," and Dylan must have had hopes of repeating the success of the latter with this follow-up. Alas, while it cracked the British Top 20, it made it only to number 58 on *Billboard*'s Hot 100 chart. Dylan also cut an early version of "One of Us Must Know (Sooner or Later)" with the Hawks at the same early October recording session (as well as "I Wanna Be Your Lover," a nod to the Beatles that would eventually surface on *Biograph*), but the version of that song that was released as a single in February 1966 and included on *Blonde on Blonde* was a different version recorded in January. That single failed even to make it into the Hot 100.

A few months later, however, Dylan would rebound with his next single, "Rainy Day Women #12 & 35," the lead track from his next album, *Blonde on Blonde,* which would equal the chart success of

"Like a Rolling Stone," peaking at number 2—a milestone Dylan would never again reach (he'd crack the Top 10 only one more time, with "Lay Lady Lay" in 1969). As already noted, the jolly novelty track "Rainy Day Women #12 & 35," given a New Orleans–ish barrelhouse brass band treatment, replete with hoots and hollers and call-and-response chatter from the musicians, embeds a few resonant phrases inside its otherwise silly representation of drunken debauchery. Coming on the heels of the previous year's megahit, "Like a Rolling Stone," the frequent use of "stone" and "stoned" in the song is already a commentary—a midrash, perhaps—on Dylan's own work. Where "Like a Rolling Stone" was deadly serious and spiteful, "Rainy Day Women" is all levity, insinuating something of a retreat from the bitter invective powering the earlier anthem. Its placement as the opening cut gives it greater heft, as if Dylan is saying this time around things are going to be a lot looser and more fun than last time.

They certainly are on "Rainy Day Women #12 & 35," which is full of laughter, silly rhymes, and seemingly improvisational music and lyrics. It's the sound of a party in the studio; the song was recorded at the final session for the album, the last of six dates at Columbia Records' recording studio in Nashville, Tennessee. But underneath all the laughter, the hollering, and the boozy brass is a revealing commentary on the vicissitudes of fame. No matter what you do, Dylan says, you'll be on the receiving end of critical barbs and attacks; "everybody must get stoned."

The song rides on the pun embodied in this phrase. Each verse consists of four phrases describing occasions when "they" will "stone ya," where the meaning of the phrase "stone ya" is literal, in the biblical sense of punishment via stones, or figurative, in the sense of punishment by words. Each verse ends with the refrain "But I would not feel so all alone / Everybody must get stoned," concluding that no matter what you do—walking, sitting, eating breakfast, driving—you're going to get attacked in some form. But it's also a joke, playing on the double meaning of the phrase "get stoned," meaning to get drunk or high on drugs—which, in context, may be the only reasonable response to an impossible situation.

Now that I've taken all of the fun out of that novelty tune, we can dig deeper into *Blonde on Blonde* proper. When the album was released, it was one of the very first "double albums," featuring two LPs packaged in a gatefold sleeve. Nowadays, the seventy-two minutes of music on *Blonde on Blonde* could be squeezed onto one CD, but back then, any more than about twenty minutes of music per side reduced the sonic quality of a long-playing record. Dylan's seventh album, *Blonde on Blonde* was only the second whose title wasn't derived from a song on the album or didn't include "Bob Dylan" in the title—although it wasn't lost on savvier fans that the initial letters of the album title spelled out the name Bob, who, according to his mother, had beautiful blond curls as a child.

There are hints throughout the songs on *Blonde on Blonde* that Dylan had his background on his mind even when he was writing about the love and hate relationships that on the surface seem to preoccupy the singer's thoughts. Characters like the peddler and the fiddler from "Visions of Johanna" (Dylan's own immigrant grandfather, Zigman Zimmerman, was a peddler, and Dylan himself is a modern-day fiddler of sorts), the ragman of "Stuck Inside of Mobile with the Memphis Blues Again," the pawnbroker from "She's Your Lover Now" (recorded at the *Blonde on Blonde* sessions but not included on the final album), and the "saviors who are fast asleep" from "I Want You" collectively assert that deep inside his heart, Dylan knew he couldn't escape his Jewish immigrant heritage—and that in fact it provided him with a rich and colorful cast of characters upon which to draw.

Where *Highway 61 Revisited* was mostly loud, jittery, urgent, angry, and metallic, *Blonde on Blonde* was calmer, more reflective, less caffeinated, almost soothing at times. Where *Highway 61 Revisited* is all angles with knifelike, sharp edges, both musically and lyrically, *Blonde on Blonde* is curvier and more fluid, more wavelike. After "Rainy Day Women #12 & 35," the album continues with "Pledging My Time," a slow blues that, while beginning in the vein of an old-time blues lament, turns out to be something of a love song. Written and recorded in early 1966, the song concludes with a remarkable bit of foreshadowing:

Well, they sent for the ambulance
And one was sent.
Somebody got lucky
But it was an accident.

It's impossible to read these lines after the events of July 29, 1966, and not see in them portents of the motorcycle accident that brought Dylan's career as a performer and writer to a temporary halt and one from which he was lucky to escape with his life. These lines also introduce Dylan's alter ego, "Lucky" or "lucky," who will reappear in "Minstrel Boy" and "Idiot Wind," as well as in Dylan's pseudonym, Lucky Wilbury, as a member of the Traveling Wilburys supergroup in 1988.

"Visions of Johanna" is often thought to be yet another song addressed to Joan Baez (given the similarity between "Joan" and "Johanna," among other lyrical hints), this time around portraying her with much more compassion than in "Queen Jane Approximately." But the song could just as well be about Sara, especially when read as an illustration of what once was—a world of temptation, embodied by the character Louise, where "little boy lost . . . takes himself so seriously . . . brags of his misery [and] likes to live dangerously," and his conscience explodes—in contrast with what he now has with Johanna, who imparts a feeling, albeit unstated, of Zen-like quietude, now having conquered the narrator's mind. It is in visions, however, that Johanna causes the singer long nights of wakefulness, and that makes the false promise of fame in the end "seem so cruel." That Johanna's effects on the singer—the "fiddler" who "now steps to the road" also plays "skeleton keys" on a harmonica—come in night visions just lends her all the more of an ethereal, dreamlike quality.

The album concludes with the twelve-minute song, "Sad-Eyed Lady of the Lowlands," which took up the entirety of an LP side. Even if Dylan hadn't explicitly revealed in the 1975 song "Sara" that he wrote this song with his wife in mind (when he sang, "Stayin' up for days at the Chelsea Hotel / Writin' 'Sad-Eyed Lady of the Lowlands' for you"), he planted plenty of hints in the lyrics. There are references to her working-class background as the daughter of a scrap dealer—"With your sheet-metal memory of Cannery Row"—and several lines refer to her first husband, Hans Lownds, and their daughter, "With the child of a hoodlum wrapped up in your arms," "With . . . your magazine-husband who one day just had to go." The "sad-eyed lady" bears characteristics we have come to know as having belonged to Sara: "With . . . your eyes like smoke and your prayers like rhymes," "With . . . your gentleness now, which you just can't help but show," "With . . . your saintlike face and your ghostlike soul." Even the song's title seems to be an expansion of her previous name, Lownds, into "Lowlands."

Dylan puts himself in the song, presumably in the role of her protector. He's a pocket protector, in the sense that he offers her financial stability ("With your pockets well protected at last"), as well as her defender ("Oh, who among them do you think could destroy you?"), even as he describes himself as a thief—"Now you stand with your thief, you're on his parole." He is also a prophet, the "sad-eyed prophet" who "says that no man comes," now that she's his. The only question remaining is what to do with those damn drums.

Dylan wrapped up the recording of *Blonde on Blonde* in Nashville on March 10, 1966—the album was mixed in Los Angeles in early April and released in mid-May—and went back out on the road the very next day with the Hawks for more concerts in the southern and western United States, before heading off on the final leg of a world tour that would stop in Australasia, Europe, and the United Kingdom, for a series of shows including the famed "Judas" concert, for years incorrectly thought to have taken place at the Royal Albert Hall, but which in fact took place at the Free Trade Hall in Manchester. The notorious concert was finally officially documented with the release of *Live 1966: The "Royal Albert Hall" Concert (The Bootleg Series, Vol. 4)*, in 1998, after years of being widely bootlegged under various titles including *Zimmerman Looking Back* and *Guitars Kissing and the Contemporary Fix* (named after a poem in *Tarantula*, Dylan's book of prose poems), which perpetuated the myth of the concert having taken place in London. Regardless of the location, the live recording brilliantly captures the intensity of Dylan's forty-five-minute solo acoustic opening set, followed by the blistering rock 'n' roll tug-of-war between Dylan and the Hawks and the crowd, the latter seemingly divided into devotees and detractors. The dynamic performance, featuring some of the most dangerous rock 'n' roll ever captured on tape—Robbie Robertson's lead guitar rattling off an automatic weapon's worth of shattering fills in the spaces between Dylan's taunting sneers—is nearly matched by the dynamic heckling, which includes disruptive chanting and clapping, prompting Dylan to plead humorously, "If you only just wouldn't clap so hard." Finally, the showdown culminates with the legendary cry of betrayal, "JUDAS," to which Dylan responds, "I don't believe you; you're a liar!" before turning to the band and ordering them to "play fucking loud," which they do on a curtain-closing rendition of "Like a Rolling Stone." It hasn't gone unremarked-upon throughout the years that the epithet of choice, "Judas," was a cutting, if not dangerous, one to be cast upon a Jewish performer. Just who Dylan was supposedly betraying at this point defies any sort of logic or understanding, but soon enough it would all prove moot.

While in Britain, Dylan was accompanied by a film crew for a week, ostensibly to make a documentary concert film for ABC-TV, a sort of follow-up to the previous year's *Dont Look Back* (filmed almost exactly a year earlier to the day and publicly released a year later to the week). This time out, Dylan himself was hired to direct the film, although he did engage the services of *Dont Look Back*'s director D. A. Pennebaker, as chief cinematographer. The movie, *Eat the Document,* marked Dylan's first real effort as a filmmaker, his first attempt at capturing in the film medium that he grew up with and which was as close to his heart as music the same sort of expressionism he explored in song. The film combined concert footage with crowd scenes, backstage glimpses, rehearsal shots, travelogue, captured moments—this time with John Lennon playing the role of foil that Donovan played in *Dont Look Back*—as well as the sort of improvised scenes that Dylan would stage at much greater length and to much greater effect in his next film, the monumental four-hour epic *Renaldo and Clara.* In retrospect, *Eat the Document*— which wound up being rejected by ABC for the plain reason that it was technically unsuited for broadcast, to say nothing of being far too incoherent to be shown as a TV documentary (as opposed to an art film, which is in the end what it is), and was finally released theatrically in early 1971—reads like a dress rehearsal for *Renaldo and Clara,* hinting at several of the later film's themes, aspirations, and techniques.

The 1966 world tour—really the 1965–66 tour, as it was all of a piece with the Hawks backing him (although like some *Spinal Tap* joke, at least three different musicians, including Levon Helm, Sandy Konikoff, and Mickey Jones, would sit behind the drum kit during the course of the tour) and adhering to the same format— came to a rousing conclusion at London's Royal Albert Hall on May 27, three days after Dylan turned the ripe age of twenty-five. Plans were for a couple of months' respite before heading back out on the road, to allow Dylan to reunite with Sara and his children in Woodstock, as well as for wrapping up work on *Eat the Document* and his long-promised book of poems, *Tarantula.* He spent most of June and July in precisely this manner.

On July 29, 1966, something happened that derailed the course of Dylan's career, eventually setting him on a path very different from the one that seemed to flow logically from the one he was already on. That path probably would have seen more touring—Albert Grossman had allegedly made a deal for Dylan to play New York's Shea Stadium before heading for a tour behind the Iron Curtain in the Soviet Union—and presumably more recordings in the vein of what now and forever stands as a brilliant trilogy, *Bringing It All Back Home*, *Highway 61 Revisited*, and *Blonde on Blonde*. Hints of new songs are already evident in footage recorded in England in May included in *Eat the Document*.

Dylan's ambitions as a recording artist, however, were not matched by his ambitions as a touring artist. Although Dylan and the Hawks traveled the world in relative style and comfort, especially for that day, the touring was exhausting and the concerts were not especially lucrative. The sort of barnstorming worldwide rock tours that would become de rigueur years later were still a new phenomenon, and the financial kinks had yet to be worked out. While concerts did their part to help sell records, Dylan essentially subsidized the tours out of his own pocket, paying the musicians and road crew members a salary and dragging around the world a huge, state-of-the-art sound system at his own considerable expense.

But just two months after Dylan's European tour came to a close in London, news reports flashed around the world that Dylan was paralyzed, mad, a vegetable, or worse—hanging on for dear life. While the entire truth about what happened on July 29 may never be known, it's generally accepted as fact that Dylan had some sort of motorcycle mishap in Woodstock. He had a long history of crashing bikes going back to his teen years, but none that ever resulted in any serious injury. As the story goes, Dylan was taking his bike to a mechanic's shop for repairs when he came upon a sudden turn on a narrow, winding stretch. His brakes locked, and he flew over the handlebars. Sara was following in her car in order to drive him back from the shop, fortunately, and therefore was able to get him immediate medical attention. Dylan apparently injured his back (symptoms of lingering back problems became apparent in his strained onstage gait and his shedding of the electric guitar in favor of playing piano in the early 2000s) and his neck (visitors to his home soon after the accident reported that he wore a neck brace; other visitors at the time described him as confined to his bed).

Other reports have Dylan using this opportunity to recuperate from the accident to kick whatever drugs to which he had grown addicted at the time. It's widely assumed that in order to keep up the pace of his tour he made liberal use of amphetamines; some hear in his voice and demeanor of the time indications that he, as his own lyrics say, "started out on burgundy and soon hit the harder stuff." Some suggest that the entire story of the motorcycle accident was a ruse that Dylan concocted in part to get out of his responsibilities for continuing to tour and to go into private rehabilitation. Dylan supposedly resided at the home clinic of a doctor in Middletown, New York, for several weeks, where he may have undergone physical therapy or detoxification treatment.

Whatever the truth of the matter, the result was that the Dylan juggernaut came to a sudden halt. There were to be no more albums until *John Wesley Harding*, released just before the calendar page turned to 1968, and no more official public appearances, in concert or otherwise, until his one-off Isle of Wight concert in 1969. And it wouldn't be until eight years later that Dylan would hit the road once again for a sustained concert tour with the Hawks, by then known as the Band, a recording group in its own right, for the two-month tour of North America documented on the two-disk live album *Before the Flood.*

While the world may have lost Dylan for an extended period of time, this rolling stone gathered no moss. If Dylan retreated from the limelight and from the trajectory spinning him into worldwide rock 'n' roll stardom in favor of the reclusive country life in Woodstock, after a period of retrenchment and recovery he lost little time in getting back to creating new kinds of music, with and without the Hawks, and exploring other avenues of creativity, including completing work on *Eat the Document* and his book *Tarantula,* which finally saw publication in 1971.

In fact, the next year and a half proved to be one of the most remarkably creative and productive times in Dylan's life. During this "lost year," he wrote and informally recorded dozens of new songs with the Hawks—recordings that eventually became known as *The Basement Tapes,* although the official album released by that title in 1975 only scratches the surface of what went on in the basement— as well as the songs that would eventually comprise *John Wesley Harding.* To fill the gap in his official recording output after *Blonde on Blonde,* Columbia Records released *Bob Dylan's Greatest Hits,* a compilation of his best known songs and chart singles, including "Positively Fourth Street," insuring that fans who had already purchased all of his previous albums but hadn't gotten around to snagging a copy of the single version of that tune had to buy the whole collection just to get the one song—a strategic maneuver that would become common practice for many subsequent "greatest hits" packages and career retrospectives by Dylan and other recording artists.

In addition to his prolific songwriting and recording, the selfimposed seclusion among family and a small group of friends also prompted Dylan once again to open up the Bible, perhaps for solace during his recovery. As much as the songs Dylan wrote, rehearsed, and recorded with the Hawks drew upon, referenced, or updated the

"Old Weird America," in the critic Greil Marcus's term, the songs written during this period are also full of allusions, paraphrases, references to, and quotations from the Five Books of Moses and the Prophets, including Isaiah and Ezekiel.

Evidence of his Bible study crops up throughout the work of this period. After the birth of Dylan's daughter, Anna, in summer 1967, his parents visited him in Woodstock. Afterward, his mother told an interviewer that the Bible held a place of prominence in Dylan's home, permanently perched on a stand (in Hebrew called a *shtender*) so he could refer to it at any time (presumably in a standing position, easing the strain on his injured back).

By the spring of 1967, Garth Hudson, Rick Danko, and Richard Manuel had joined Robbie Robertson in the Woodstock area. By the summer, after Hudson had set up his Ampex reel-to-reel recorder in the basement of Big Pink, the house in Old Saugerties where Danko and Manuel lived, Dylan began a regular routine of coming by the house around noon each day. As Hudson cued up the tape to record, Dylan would begin to play, and the others—multi-instrumentalists, all of them—would join in, occasionally lending harmony vocals or trading phrases, as well as interjecting laughter or nonsensical lyrics. With Levon Helm still AWOL from his former bandmates, having left the world tour in late 1965 (the tough Arkansan apparently couldn't stand the booing), Manuel and Robertson, who typically played piano and electric guitar, respectively, did double duty on drums. In addition to bass, Danko lent his fiddle to some numbers, and in addition to making a universe of sounds with his organ, Hudson played a variety of horn instruments, including tuba and saxophone.

While many of the songs recorded at Big Pink were versions of old folk songs ("Come All Ye Fair"), novelty numbers ("See Ya Later, Alligator" rendered as "See Ya Later, Allen Ginsberg"), contemporary songs by other writers (Johnny Cash's "Folsom Prison Blues" and "Belshazzar"), nonsense tunes ("Million Dollar Bash"), and wholesale, often comic, improvisations ("Clothes Line Saga"), some of the most enduring songs of Dylan's career came out of this period, including "I Shall Be Released," "This Wheel's on Fire,"

"Tears of Rage," "You Ain't Goin' Nowhere," and "I'm Not There," which would eventually become the inspiration for the filmmaker Todd Haynes's loose meditation on Dylan, starring Cate Blanchett, Heath Ledger, and Richard Gere, by the same title.

While the official 1975 *Basement Tapes* release collects some of the best-known songs from these sessions (and made some of the obscurities better known)—and also tinkers with their sound after the fact—widely circulating unofficial recordings have made the original tracks readily available to collectors and even the mildly curious. The spirit of these sessions alternates between jovial and relaxed, but occasionally the musicians seem to know that they're on to something above average, such as on "I'm Not There," on which the musicians respectfully accompany Dylan's mystical investigation of identity.

In these sessions, Dylan sings about a world-altering calamity in "Down in the Flood" and a vision of G-d in "This Wheel's on Fire." In the former, like some latter-day Noah, Dylan warns:

> *If you go down in the flood*
> *It's gonna be your own fault . . .*
> *It's gonna be the meanest flood*
> *That anybody's seen.*

This is one of Dylan's classic, prophetic midrashes, turning a Bible story—one of prophetic doom and gloom—into a modern-day admonishment in vernacular language. So that the original, "G-d said to Noah, 'The earth is filled with robbery. . . . I am about to bring the flood-waters upon the earth to destroy all'" (Genesis 6:13, 17), and the subsequent story, becomes:

> *Crush on the levee, mama,*
> *Water's gonna overflow,*
> *Swamp's gonna rise,*
> *No boat's gonna row.*
> *Now, you can train on down*
> *To Williams Point,*

You can bust your feet,
You can rock this joint.
But oh mama, ain't you gonna miss your best friend now?
You're gonna have to find yourself
Another best friend, somehow.

The person delivering the warning seems to have a personal relationship with the person being warned, that of best friend, but in this case that best friend could be the Prophet himself, that is, Noah, or G-d speaking through the Prophet. And in the litany of options for escape, one is to "rock this joint," slang for getting the hell out of here, but also an allusion to Dylan himself, saying, in a sense, that not even being a rock star, or putting on a good show, will exempt anyone from the raging floodwaters of destruction.

In the second verse, Dylan digs deeper into the biblical story, making clear that the flood is meant as punishment for acts that can no longer be forgiven and not the act of some arbitrary, whimsical G-d:

Now, don't you try an' move me,
You're just gonna lose.
There's a crash on the levee
And, mama, you've been refused.
Well, it's sugar for sugar
And salt for salt,
If you go down in the flood,
It's gonna be your own fault.

In the final verse, however, the narrator seems to offer some hope for redemption to the individual (presumably an individual woman, but perhaps the entire female species, and by definition, the human race, because if no woman is spared from the flood, there can be no chance for repopulating the earth). So he tells her to pack her belongings quietly, perhaps to go along with him to some place of refuge, which we know as the ark, although the song makes no specific mention of or allusion to such a place:

Well, that high tide's risin',
Mama, don't you let me down.
Pack up your suitcase,
Mama, don't you make a sound.

Dylan has returned to this song time and again over the years, in different arrangements, and over time the song's apocalyptic nuances have slowly revealed themselves. The most dynamic versions include one he did in a guest stint with the Band at the Academy of Music on New Year's Eve, 1972 (a concert that was recorded for the Band's live album, *Rock of Ages,* which didn't include any of Dylan's tracks until it was rereleased as a two-CD package in 2001), and again in his own concerts in the late 1990s and early 2000s, when he often opened his shows with a raw, rocking version of the tune, which might have received its hardest-rocking treatment in the version included in his film *Masked and Anonymous.*

The narrator of "This Wheel's on Fire" could well be the same as, or rather cousin to, that of "Down in the Flood." The source for the imagery upon which the song is built is the book of Ezekiel, and in particular, his unique mystical experience—perhaps the most famous vision of G-d in all of Jewish scripture. Specifically, the imagery comes from chapter 1, verses 4, 5, and 16: "From the midst of the fire, in its midst there was a likeness of four creatures supporting the chariot. . . . Their appearance were as if there would be a wheel within a wheel." Ezekiel's vision of the chariot is understood to be a literal vision of G-d himself, riding through the heavens, revealing himself to Ezekiel in a blazing chariot supported by four winged beasts.

Dylan takes Ezekiel's story and, again, rather than recapitulate it, finds the human drama or tragedy inside it—in this case, one of the crestfallen G-d, or prophet, whose words of admonition have seemingly fallen on deaf ears, to the point that G-d ends prophecy here ("No man alive will come to you with another tale to tell"), until the point that His people prove their faith by remembering Him, which is in no small sense the single most important commandment and refrain running through the entire Bible. In fact, to invoke a comical Yiddish phrase, G-d veritably *hoks a tshaynik* throughout the book, constantly reminding (or, as the Yiddish translates literally, "bangs a teapot") Moses and the Jewish people to *remember*: Remember this, remember that, remember that I freed you from slavery, remember that I took you out of Egypt, remember that I led you to and gave you the Promised Land—remember everything, and while you're at it, don't forget! (This construction, too, is often used.) It is that commandment—to remember—that in some basic way comprises the covenant, or contract, between G-d and the Jewish people: the one that they would violate in every possible way (all boiling down to forgetting), leading to the need for G-d to send prophets to His people to *remind* them of their contract and its terms.

In "This Wheel's on Fire," Dylan sings about this memory and forgetting, in a haunting, plaintive, hurt, and pleading voice (as opposed to the stentorian warning of "Down in the Flood"):

> *If your mem'ry serves you well,*
> *We were goin' to meet again and wait,*
> *So I'm goin' to unpack all my things*
> *And sit before it gets too late.*

There is a gray area where it's unclear when G-d speaks directly through a Prophet or when a Prophet is paraphrasing G-d or just uttering divinely inspired sermons of his own creativity (hence the different themes and cadences favored by different Prophets, each of whom boasts his own personality and themes). In the preceding verse, it's not clear if the narrator is G-d, a Prophet, or specifically Ezekiel, although Ezekiel did go to a body of water to sit and wait for G-d to reveal himself.

> *This wheel's on fire,*
> *Rolling down the road,*

Best notify my next of kin,
This wheel shall explode!

G-d's appearance to Ezekiel in a chariot of fire (yes, that movie about a Jewish runner borrows its title from this same story) serves as a reminder, as proof, and as a warning. It's Ezekiel's duty now to spread the word to his "next of kin," meaning the Jewish people (a phrase, incidentally, that the Band impishly used to label a gatefold photo of their extended families on their debut album, *Music from Big Pink*, which included a rendition of "This Wheel's on Fire"), about his vision and its consequences. Again, what Dylan has done here is nothing less than extraordinary—he has written the tragic, human drama of Ezekiel and his impossible task in the form of a rock song.

Dylan continues:

If your mem'ry serves you well,
You'll remember you're the one
That called on me to call on them
To get you your favors done.

Here he captures Ezekiel at his wit's end, talking back to G-d and reminding *Him,* in a sense, giving him a taste of his own medicine, throwing His own words back at Him, that Ezekiel is only G-d's willing servant, powerless to effect a change among His people other than to "call on them" to change their ways, to *remember.* In his panicked state, Ezekiel refers to his role as interlocutor between G-d and the Israelites as one in which he is employed "to get You Your favors done," almost belittling the role of the Prophet, or having the Prophet talk to G-d as if he's some neighborhood gang leader—not entirely an inauthentic way to view the role of the Jewish G-d.

And after ev'ry plan had failed
And there was nothing more to tell,
You knew that we would meet again,
If your mem'ry served you well.

Ezekiel has the last word here, again, reminding G-d that, as the Omniscient Being, He knew full well that (a) the covenant, or the "plans," were destined to fail, (b) that the era of prophecy would come to an end without success ("There was nothing more to tell"), (c) that nevertheless, G-d knows full well that eventually His people *will* remember (although in doing so, Ezekiel almost pokes fun at G-d, challenging his own memory . . . farther on up the road).

Dylan will return to Ezekiel several times over the years, most notably in "Changing of the Guards," the opening track of the 1978 album *Street Legal,* in which he sings:

> *Peace will come*
> *With tranquility and splendor*
> *On the wheels of fire*

The chariot and wheels of fire are also mentioned in Daniel 7:9: "I watched as thrones were set up, and the One of Ancient Days sat. . . . His throne was tongues of flame, its wheels blazing fire."

That Dylan himself chose to use the form of the American folk and pop song similarly, to remind his listeners to uphold their end of the bargain (whatever bargain that may be—the promise of America, or morality, or humanism, or Judaism, or some other ethical or faith-based belief system), first explicitly as a protest singer and later as more of a prophet of abstraction, is in no small way what has powered his songs with their profound, abiding ability to move his listeners, many of whom would identify themselves as his followers and Dylan as their lowercase prophet (and not a few demented ones as their uppercase Prophet, much to Dylan's dismay).

For reasons known only to himself, when it came time for his next studio album, Dylan left behind the songs from the basement sessions and the musicians he'd been working with for the last two years and instead went to Nashville to record *John Wesley Harding,* which Dylan himself would call the "first biblical rock album." The all-acoustic, minimalist production—composed only of bass and drums, with pedal steel guitar on two numbers and Dylan handling all guitar, piano, and vocal chores—introduced an entirely new sound for Dylan. It marked a total break from the sound of the electric trilogy of the mid-1960s and is very unlike the music that was made in the basement with the Hawks.

The sound of *John Wesley Harding,* recorded in just four days and released in late 1967, is spare and laid-back, and even on darker, bluesy numbers, such as "The Wicked Messenger," somewhat swinging and comfortably reassuring. The music has an old-fashioned, folk-country lilt, more suggestive of an impromptu, back-porch picking session than any state-of-the-art, made-in-the-studio sound, be it rock, country, blues, or any other style. It's a sound that invites listeners to join in; the songs on *John Wesley Harding* are some of the easiest to play along with on guitar for anyone with a rudimentary command of the basic chords.

Yet behind the minimalist simplicity of the monochromatic arrangements lies a dark, visceral feel to some of the melodies and song structures, such that the legendary guitarist Jimi Hendrix listened to the minor-key strumming of "All Along the Watchtower," with its simple acoustic bass line and snare drum pattern, and heard the makings of a wild, acid-rock nightmare. And, indeed, it's there to be heard by anyone, in Dylan's harmonica line that pierces through the music like a siren sounding an alarm, and mostly in his vocal, full of panic and desperation.

The narratives, lyrics, and phrasing of the songs only add to the dark undertone that makes *John Wesley Harding* transcend its surface simplicity. The mix of outlaw ballads (the title track), Kafkaesque scenarios ("The Drifter's Escape"), desperadoes ("Where another man's life might begin that's exactly where mine ends"), hymnlike pleas ("Dear Landlord"), and archaic coinages ("I spied the fairest damsel") creates its own timeless universe. The writing here is shorn of the dazzling, expressionistic poetry of *Blonde on Blonde,* and bears none of the hallmarks of the psychedelia afflicting the greater culture of the time. There are no looking-glass pies or marshmallow skies on *John Wesley Harding*; rather, stories are told in clear expository language: "John Wesley Harding / Was a friend to the poor," "Frankie Lee and Judas Priest / They were the best of friends," and "There was a wicked messenger / From Eli he did come." Dylan also favors first-person narrative on the album, as can easily be ascertained from several of its song titles—"As I Went Out One Morning," "I Dreamed I Saw St. Augustine," "I Am a Lonesome Hobo," "I Pity the Poor Immigrant," and "I'll Be Your Baby Tonight."

Not only did this make for a discontinuity with Dylan's previous work, but it was in marked contrast to the music swirling around him, much of which had been inspired by *Highway 61 Revisited* and *Blonde on Blonde*. This quiet, rural, traditional-sounding collection of songs couldn't have been more unlike such studio-dependent psychedelic productions as the Beach Boys' *Pet Sounds,* the Beatles' *Sgt. Pepper's Lonely Hearts Club Band,* and the Rolling Stones' *Their Satanic Majesties Request,* all released in the eighteen months leading up to *John Wesley Harding*—although one could argue that the lyrics to "All Along the Watchtower," "I Dreamed I Saw St. Augustine," and "The Ballad of Frankie Lee and Judas Priest" were equally as psychedelic as anything on those other albums.

At a time when all eyes and ears were on Dylan and his first official "pronouncements" since his self-imposed retirement following the motorcycle accident, it's fair to say that *John Wesley Harding* was as stunning in its own impact—if only in its modesty and its apparent disregard of the cultural ferment and turmoil surrounding the Vietnam War and other political and social struggles facing the nation and the world at the height of the so-called Summer of Love. Instead, what listeners got on "Dear Landlord" was Dylan singing, "I'm not about to argue / I'm not about to move to no other place," in an easygoing, traditional country-jazz lilt, at the very time when it was all the fashion to talk about fleeing to Canada or the peace-loving nations of Scandinavia—or actually to emigrate, either in protest against U.S. policy or as a means to avoid being drafted into the military. It was hardly the stuff of political protest they could have been hoping for, and hardly the revolutionary context in which they might have hoped to hear it, in the wake of the aforementioned psychedelic rock settings of the moment.

The songs on *John Wesley Harding* capture Dylan at his most self-reflective. While we have seen he was no mere couch potato during his self-imposed seclusion, in fact writing and recording some of his most profound (and some of his least profound) works with the Band, the time between his last official recording, 1966's *Blonde on Blonde,* and the release of *John Wesley Harding* in 1968 allowed Dylan to present himself in an entirely new format and persona. While the difference in form may have been acciden-tal—some accounts claim that the stripped-down recordings were initially intended as demos that Dylan intended to give to the Band, with whom he would then rerecord the entire album, until Robbie Robertson heard them and suggested he just release them as is—the songs themselves were of a different style, although logical in evolution, from those of *Blonde on Blonde* and *The Base-ment Tapes.*

Much of the subject matter of the songs on *John Wesley Harding* directly confronts Dylan's role as prophet. For example, "I Dreamed I Saw St. Augustine" looks back on Dylan's role as a protest singer belonging to "the movement." The title character bears more than a passing resemblance to the folk-protest-era Dylan, "alive with fiery breath" and boasting "a voice without restraint"—a descrip-tion that could have been lifted wholesale from concert reviews of just a few years earlier. But in Dylan's dream, St. Augustine no longer roams the land, "Tearing through these quarters / In the utmost misery. . . . Searching for the very souls / Whom already have been sold."

Rather, now St. Augustine/Dylan declares, in archaic language that resembles classic English translations of the Bible, that "No martyr is among ye now / Whom you can call your own," renounc-ing the role of "savior" or "spokesman of a generation," not with bit-terness but with the suggestion that his followers "go on your way accordingly," while reassuring them that they're "not alone." Finally,

Dylan confesses that in actuality he bears responsibility for terminating St. Augustine's command: "I dreamed I was amongst the ones / That put him out to death." In other words, he had to bury the previous Dylan—the one who belonged to the Sixties—through a motorcycle accident and subsequent seclusion, in order to resurface with a new mission and a renewed sense of purpose. As if to underline this, in *Writings and Drawings,* the song is accompanied by a line drawing portraying a biblical, prophetlike figure with a blanket underneath his arm (as in the song) seemingly rising out of the cigarette smoke emanating from a prone, latter-day hipster, who could well have been Bob Dylan circa 1966.

In "The Wicked Messenger," Dylan portrays the plight of a prophet whose prophecies are unwanted by those who need to hear them. The protagonist of the title—the epithet attached to his name is ironic—is from a biblical-sounding place called Eli. He has "a mind that multiplied / The smallest matter" in the eyes of those who aren't receptive to his message. Like Moses before him, he is tongue-tied, impaired of speech, but also knows better than to utter G-d's name. So when asked who had sent for him, "He answered with his thumb / For his tongue it could not speak, but only flatter."

Also like Moses, who dwelled in a tent apart from the Israelite camp on the forty-year journey through the desert, our protagonist "stayed behind the assembly hall / It was there he made his bed / Oftentimes he could be seen returning." And just as Moses once returned from an absence with some literature that was met with ambivalence if not outright rejection, so, too, does the wicked messenger, who appears "With a note in his hand which read / 'The soles of my feet, I swear they're burning.'" Some read this to mean that the wicked messenger has returned from the fiery depths of hell, but given what has preceded and what follows, and given Dylan's penchant for drawing upon Ezekiel, it makes more sense to hear this as evidence that the messenger has returned from a mystical experience, as the latter described: "the soles of their feet . . . glittered with the color of burnished copper . . . their appearance was like fiery coals, burning like torches" (Ezekiel 1:7, 13). Moses' first mystical experience, too, occurred with bare feet; when G-d first spoke to Moses, he explicitly told him to remove his shoes (Exodus 3:5).

The song concludes in a scene right out of Exodus, where after having been liberated from Egyptian bondage through the miraculous hand of G-d working through Moses, the Israelites prove themselves time and again to be an ungrateful, stiff-necked bunch, thus casting the mold henceforward for the acrimonious relationship between the Prophets and the people:

> *Oh, the leaves began to fallin'*
> *And the seas began to part,*
> *And the people that confronted him were many.*
> *And he was told but these few words,*
> *Which opened up his heart,*
> *"If ye cannot bring good news, then don't bring any."*

One can only imagine that—in the aftermath of Newport, Manchester, and lingering accusations of having betrayed folk music, the political left, and even his own family and background—Dylan could find meaning, and perhaps even comfort, in the rejection of none other than Moses, who smashed the first version of the Ten Commandments upon descending Mount Sinai when he saw the Israelites partying it up around the Golden Calf, and in the rejection of the Prophets, whose testimonies and prophecies were often greeted with indifference or worse, including beating, imprisonment, and exile.

Dylan was clearly spending time reading the Bible and the Prophets before and during the writing of the songs on *John Wesley Harding*. "I Pity the Poor Immigrant" is another work of midrash, recasting phrases from the book of Leviticus and putting them into the mouth of a Prophet speaking on behalf of G-d himself:

Dylan: "I pity the poor immigrant . . ."
Leviticus 26:44: "Even when they are in their enemies' land, I will not reject them nor grow so tired of them that I would destroy them."

Dylan: "whose strength is spent in vain . . ."
Leviticus 26:20: "Your strength shall be spent in vain."

Dylan: "Whose heaven is like Ironsides"
Leviticus 26:19: "I will make your heaven like iron."

Dylan: "Who eats but is not satisfied"
Leviticus 26:26: "Though you eat, you shall not be satisfied"

Dylan: "Who hears but does not see."
Leviticus 26:16: "I shall make terror over you . . . that shall make your eyes fail."

Dylan does a similar thing with "All Along the Watchtower," building an ominous scene between two characters, the joker and the thief, out of a chapter from Isaiah. In the song, the thief tries to allay the joker's fears of impending doom, while in a moment of dramatic irony, we are privy to the approach of a real threat. The scene comes out of Isaiah, chapter 21, which begins, appropriately enough, as "A prophecy concerning the Wilderness of the West." Perhaps Dylan was attracted to that opening line, given the Old West orientation of *John Wesley Harding,* even though the biblical territory being referred to here is Babylonia, as Isaiah foretells its destruction, "Like windstorms sweeping through a desert," or, in Dylan, "the wind began to howl."

Isaiah continues:

My mind is confused, I shudder in panic. My night of pleasure has turned into terror. Setting the table to let the watchmen watch, eating and drinking, "Arise, officers, anoint the shield." For thus said my Lord to me: Go, station the lookout, and let him tell what he sees. He will see a pair of horsemen . . . and he will call out like a lion. My Lord, I stand on the lookout constantly during the day, and I am stationed at my post all the nights. Behold, it is coming: a chariot with a man, a pair of horsemen. Each says loudly, "It has fallen! Babylonia has fallen!" (Isaiah 21:4–9)

Which Dylan turns into:

There's too much confusion, I can't get no relief
Businessmen they drink my wine, plowmen dig my earth
None of them along the line, know what any of it is worth.
All along the watchtower, princes kept the view
While all the women came and went, barefoot servants, too.
Outside in the distance a wildcat did growl,
Two riders were approaching, the wind began to howl.

Beginning with songs on *The Basement Tapes*, Dylan's interests around this time shift from the merely prophetic toward the mystic. It's hard to separate the two, as the prophetic experience is at heart a mystical one—a Prophet, inspired by the divine, has undergone something of a mystical experience. And much of the basis of Jewish mysticism comes in the form of prophetic visions of the G-dhead, for example, Ezekiel's chariot, and in vivid descriptions of the end of days and the Messianic era. It is precisely this aspect of the prophetic tradition—call it prophetic mysticism—which now engages Bob Dylan intensely, more so than, say, that of societal criticism. This corresponds with a sense that with time and maturity Dylan has grown more concerned with personal matters and less with social critique, although as we shall see, the pendulum will swing back before settling somewhere in between the two polarities.

In spite of Dylan's conscious effort to construct an album of antipsychedelia, from the black-and-white cover photograph of himself with three Indians—members of the Bengali Bauls, a musical group that had been staying at Albert Grossman's place—to the earth tones of the album jacket to the monochromatic arrangements of the music, Columbia Records marketed *John Wesley Harding* in print advertisements featuring the colorful, pop-art-style drawing of Dylan by the renowned illustrator Milton Glaser that was originally packaged as a poster with *Bob Dylan's Greatest Hits*.

John Wesley Harding was recorded in three separate sessions in

Nashville in October and November, and was released around the New Year. In January, Dylan made his first public appearance since the end of his world tour in May 1966, performing at Carnegie Hall for the first Woody Guthrie Memorial Concert, honoring the folk music icon, who had died the previous October. Dylan was joined onstage by the Band for three Guthrie tunes. After the concert, Dylan continued to keep a low profile for more than a year, occupying his time in Woodstock working with Howard Alk on *Eat the Document* and generally living the life of a creative recluse. His year off was interrupted by the death of his father on June 5; Dylan returned to Hibbing for the funeral, stayed a few days, and rushed back to New York to be with Sara, who gave birth to their second son, Samuel, later that month.

Much has been made of how the death of his father affected Dylan. Some claim that the two were at odds over the last decade, although there is little indication of this in transcripts of interviews with Abe Zimmerman taken just a few weeks before his death, in which Abe comes across as nothing less than an incredibly proud, aware, and involved father, and, together with Beatty, a doting parent. While Dylan was obviously already studying Jewish texts, the concert promoter Harold Leventhal, who was Woody Guthrie's manager and had always been something of a mentor to Dylan, is said to have encouraged Bob to delve deeper into his religious heritage as a way to deal with the grief of losing his father and a means to gain closure surrounding any conflicts left unresolved.

In the fall, Dylan rekindled friendships with two musicians that would result in creative collaborations in both the short and long term, both of which would flavor his own work along the way. In October, Dylan hung out with Johnny Cash in New York City, after Cash played a concert at Carnegie Hall. And around Thanksgiving, George Harrison stayed at Dylan's place in Woodstock, during which time the two played and wrote music together, including the song "I'd Have You Anytime," which would appear on Harrison's first post-Beatles solo album, *All Things Must Pass*. Equally important, their time together cemented a friendship and creative partnership that would see the two collaborate several times over the next three decades, and they remained close friends until Harrison's death in 2001. When Dylan gave a concert in Liverpool, England, in May 2009, it was Harrison's "Something" that he chose to play as a tribute to the hometown heroes, the Beatles.

Dylan finally returned to Nashville to record the follow-up to *John Wesley Harding* more than a year after its release, in mid-February 1969. With Bob Johnston once again in the producer's chair, and reunited with the *John Wesley Harding* instrumental team of the bassist Charles McCoy, the drummer Kenny Buttrey, and the pedal steel guitarist Pete Drake—augmented by the guitarists Norman Blake and Charlie Daniels and the pianist Bob Wilson, among others— Dylan set to work laying down the tracks for his next album. In four days, he recorded *Nashville Skyline*, which, once again, introduced the world to another side of Bob Dylan.

Where *John Wesley Harding* wrapped biblical torment and angst in country-folk dressing, *Nashville Skyline* luxuriated in country corn. If *John Wesley Harding* was a renunciation of the musical values of the time, swapping recording studio psychedelics for organic verities, *Nashville Skyline* was an embrace, thematically and musically, of Southern country hospitality. That it came in the era of urban riots, violent antiwar demonstrations (culminating in the shooting of protestors by National Guard officers at Kent State University in 1970), and in the wake of political assassinations (Robert Kennedy and Martin Luther King, Jr., had been killed the previous year), and, as Dylan foretold, while death counts grew higher—to say nothing of the shadow of the ascendancy of Richard Nixon to the White House that January—was seen by some to be a reactionary slap in the face (contrast Dylan's lack of response to the violence swirling around him to that of his friend Neil Young, who immortalized the Kent State killings in "Ohio," a Top 20 hit for the group Crosby, Stills, Nash and Young). If rock music was the soundtrack to revolution, commercial country music was seen by the liberal intelligentsia and media elite as the domain of right-wing redneck culture. For Dylan to embrace this sound at this time was, well, once again, a sign of his idiosyncratic temperament at best or a perversity of political will at worst.

At least that was the party line. In retrospect and divorced from its particular sociocultural context, *Nashville Skyline* holds up as a good-natured tribute to an essential genre of American music. Over the years, Dylan would touch down in many genres of Americana, including folk and blues, but also R&B, reggae, jump blues, gospel, swing, and jazz. It was inevitable that he would at some point make a real, honest-to-goodness country album. And if the timing seemed a little off in terms of the political context and the dominant musical trends in rock, Dylan always answered to a higher power, be it his own muse or otherwise.

More logically, Dylan's attempt at making a pure country album was an outgrowth of all the time he had spent in Nashville over the past three years, since he first went south to record the bulk of *Blonde on Blonde*. Nashville was where his producer of choice at the time, Bob Johnston, preferred to work, and where his preferred studio musicians of the moment were located. It was also where his friend and collaborator Johnny Cash was based, and it was a lot easier for Dylan to go there to record—especially if the sound he was hearing was the Nashville sound—than to import everyone north to New York.

As surprising as his aesthetic choices for *Nashville Skyline* were— and everything about the album is surprising, from the music to the lyrics to the album art, featuring, for the first time, the face of a relaxed, happy, smiling singer, as far away from the would-be hobo, the fierce protestor, or the mod rocker as he could get—the biggest surprise on the album was Dylan's voice. While his vocals evolved subtly over time from the raw, coarse drawl of his early albums through the hazy, nasal whine of his mid-decade efforts, it all seemed part of a natural progression. The voice on *Nashville Sky-line* confronts the listener with a categorical leap; Dylan sounds like he's doing an Elvis Presley impersonation in a bathroom. In interviews at the time he attributed the qualitative change in his voice to having recently quit smoking, which was just more of his purposeful obfuscation. Quitting smoking wouldn't change anyone's voice to that extreme.

Rather, aided by some heavy-handed reverb courtesy of Bob Johnston, Dylan found a voice within that suited the material he was recording. If it wasn't his natural voice, if it was something of a put-on, so what? All singing is a put-on of sorts, and good singing tends to rely more on a purposeful put-on than not—just think of the sound of opera singers. Dylan was playing around with techniques of vocal control that he hadn't employed before, and in this case, it worked to good effect given the overall sound of the album, which gave Dylan his first Top 10 hit since 1966's "Rainy Day Women #12 & 35."

Dylan first wrote "Lay Lady Lay" on a commission from the producers of the Dustin Hoffman/Jon Voight film, *Midnight Cowboy*. Dylan was late in submitting the finished song, however, and in the meantime the filmmakers ran with Fred Neil's "Everybody's Talkin'" (in a Grammy Award–winning version sung by Harry Nilsson) for the movie's theme song. The song and the movie quickly became inextricably linked, so that Dylan's failure to meet his deadline turned out to be fortuitous for the film and for Fred Neil, who certainly deserved the break—especially given the fact that it was Neil who gave Dylan one of his earliest breaks, when in 1961 he employed the new arrival in Greenwich Village to accompany him on harmonica on several occasions.

On its own, nevertheless, "Lay Lady Lay" became a Dylan standard, one that he continued to refine in different live versions over the next forty years. *Nashville Skyline* contained other quiet gems— a duet version of "Girl of the North Country" with Johnny Cash; "I Threw It All Away," which became a showstopper on the Rolling Thunder Revue; and "Tonight I'll Be Staying Here with You," a funky, sensual idyll that was as much Southern soul as it was Southern country. "To Be Alone with You" is infectious rockabilly, and Dylan would revive the song as a lively concert opener in 2002.

Even with its apparent lack of cultural or musical relevance,

Dylan's laid-back crooning, and the reactionary implications of his having gone "country," *Nashville Skyline* was one of his most popular albums (or perhaps *because* of the foregoing), peaking at number 3 on the U.S. album charts and going all the way to number 1 in the U.K. It didn't hurt that it was one of his best-sounding albums, both in terms of the band arrangements and the professionalism of the recorded sound, which is not so much slick as it is well played. The album's vision of idyllic, rural domesticity undoubtedly appealed to a broad cross-section of the record-buying public that may have, up until this point, not been enthusiastic about Bob Dylan's sound or his difficult, puzzling songs.

Within two weeks of the April 9, 1969, release of *Nashville Skyline,* Dylan was back in Columbia Row Music Studios in Nashville with Johnston, recording a mixture of originals, folk, blues, pop, and country standards, including several Johnny Cash tunes, presumably in preparation for his appearance on Cash's new TV program. The tracks recorded in three sessions in Nashville then sat idle for nearly a year, until Dylan returned to a New York studio in March 1970 to record more cover tunes—including the work of contemporaries such as Paul Simon and Gordon Lightfoot—plus a few new compositions.

In the meantime, in summer 1969, Dylan took the first of what were to become annual summer trips for the next few years to Israel; little is known about these trips. When he returned to Woodstock in August, it was amid a swirl of preparations for what was planned to be a free outdoor music and arts festival the likes of which the world had never seen. While the festival promoters purposely chose Woodstock as the location for its connection with Dylan and in order to entice him to attend as a performer, Dylan declined repeated invitations to appear (although the Band did, along with Joan Baez, Santana, Janis Joplin, the Grateful Dead, Jefferson Airplane, Arlo Guthrie, and Jimi Hendrix, among others). As it turned out, the promoters realized that the original festival site was far too small for the potential audience, and the event was moved about forty miles southwest to Bethel.

Instead of performing at Woodstock, and in advance of the presumed thousands who'd be flocking to his rural outpost, Dylan left town for England after accepting an offer to headline the Isle of Wight Festival, which took place later in August. The Band joined him there, as would other by-then Woodstock veterans, including the Who, Richie Havens, and Joe Cocker. It was widely rumored that the Beatles would make an unannounced appearance on stage; John Lennon, George Harrison, and Ringo Starr were all present (hanging out backstage playing table tennis with Dylan), but they never made it to the stage. Dylan's performance with the Band was perfunctory at best, lasting only about an hour, and, from the evidence of live recordings of the show, it lacked the dynamism of his performances with the Hawks in 1965–66 and with the Band in 1974. Not until the latter tour would Dylan give another official headlining concert appearance.

Apparently disgusted by the manner in which Woodstock had become a magnet for hippies, stalkers, and obsessive fans—the most industrious of whom inevitably found their way onto his property or even inside his house—Dylan switched tack and in September moved his family to McDougal Street, into a townhouse just off Bleecker, in the heart of New York City's Greenwich Village. If he'd lost his privacy in rural upstate New York, perhaps, he presumably reasoned, he could enjoy relative anonymity in the heart of the Big Apple, where people are blasé about seeing celebrities around town and where the unwritten code is to leave them alone when they do. For a while at least, this seemed to work for the Dylans, and they simply became next-door neighbors to the Schapiros, sharing a communal backyard with them and the Cohens and other lawyers and doctors whose homes backed up on the enclosed garden behind the rectangle of brownstones and shops formed by Bleecker, McDougal, Sullivan, and Houston streets. (Sixth Avenue, which runs diagonally, right around the corner from where the Dylans lived, would be immortalized by Jakob Dylan in the 1996 song "6th Avenue Heartache," one of the biggest hits by his band, the Wallflowers, and one of his most "Dylanesque" numbers.)

Happily ensconced in New York with his wife and five children, Dylan didn't venture far when it came time to finish the work he had begun the previous April in Nashville. Three days of recording at Columbia Studio A in Manhattan with musicians including Al Kooper and the guitarist David Bromberg and a female gospel trio yielded more numbers for *Self Portrait* plus early versions of songs for what would be its follow-up album, *New Morning*. Around the same time, George Harrison would join Dylan in the studio for a few sessions with other musicians, the two running through a list of rock 'n' roll oldies, Dylan and Beatles numbers (including a touching vocal rendition by Dylan of "Yesterday"), and some new songs, including *New Morning*'s "If Not for You." The Dylan-Harrison version would eventually see official release on *The Bootleg Series, Vol. 1–3*, and Harrison rerecorded the tune for *All Things Must Pass*. Unofficial recordings of the Dylan-Harrison session circulate widely, and include the spectacle of these two brilliant singer-songwriters duetting on the Crystals' 1963 hit, "Da Doo Ron Ron." Even boys, apparently, just wanna have fun.

On June 8, after sessions stretching across nearly a year, Dylan's second double-album, *Self Portrait*, was finally released, to some of the worst critiques of his career. Writing in *Rolling Stone*, the critic Greil Marcus probably penned the most infamous opening line of a record review: "What is this shit?" With its syrupy string arrangements, songs on which Dylan doesn't even play or sing, female choir, and wacky juxtaposition of old folk and country tunes, pop standards, sloppy live numbers from the Isle of Wight concert, and covers of contemporary singer-songwriters, this seemed anything but a "self-portrait" of Bob Dylan, confounding critics and loyal listeners alike.

The title could have been merely referring to the album's cover, which featured an original oil painting by Dylan of himself. Or it could have been a cosmic joke by Dylan—his musical self-portrait being an album consisting of music that for the most part he didn't write, and for the making of which in substantial part he wasn't even in the studio (more sessions were devoted to overdubbing instrumental tracks without Dylan in attendance than those in which Dylan recorded his own contributions to the album).

More likely, by calling the album *Self Portrait*, Dylan was suggesting that it was an amalgam of musical influences—songs and styles that fed his own muse, that constituted the raw material that he turned into Bob Dylan music. Perhaps that's giving him too much credit, and the recording remains a novelty in his body of work (although no more so than mediocre mid-career albums including *Knocked Out Loaded* and *Down in the Groove*). Dylan's vocals veer from his smooth *Nashville Skyline* croon, minus the reverb, to the more organic sound to which he'd return on subsequent albums.

"Minstrel Boy," one of the few original songs on the album, recorded with the Band live at the Isle of Wight, is an overlooked gem that portrays a musician in need of money and spiritual salvation: "Who's gonna throw that minstrel boy a coin? / Who's gonna let it down easy to save his soul?" The song reintroduces one of Dylan's alter egos, Lucky, first mentioned in "Pledging My Time" on *Blonde on Blonde*. Other guilty pleasures from *Self Portrait* include Dylan's rendition of Paul Simon's "The Boxer," a rare instance of Dylan taking advantage of modern recording technology to overdub a second vocal behind the first, so that he harmonizes with himself as if he were both Simon *and* Garfunkel. Speculation as to why he chose to do this, as well as why he chose to record this song in the first place, ranges from a desire to mock Paul Simon, whom some saw as a would-be Dylan; to show that one Dylan was the equal of a pair of Simon and Garfunkel; or to send a message to Simon that he knew that the song was directed toward Dylan himself, as some suspected. Whatever Dylan's real intentions were, they undoubtedly included the simple desire to sing a good song, and, no less, one about one of his favorite topics: boxing.

Whereas the leaden Isle of Wight version of "Like a Rolling Stone" included on *Self Portrait* is so clunky it's almost embarrassing—Dylan can't even remember the words to his greatest hit— he and the Band turn in a funky, rocking version of "The Mighty Quinn (Quinn the Eskimo)," a song originally recorded during the basement sessions, which by this time had been a number 1 hit in Britain for the rock group Manfred Mann. The album also features a dreadful arrangement of "Blue Moon," with Dylan doing his best Elvis Presley impersonation, and a bizarre, wordless vocal tune called "Wigwam," featuring a mariachi-like instrumental accompaniment.

Perhaps fittingly, the album called *Self Portrait* opens with a track that doesn't even feature Dylan at all, but rather, a female choir repeatedly intoning the single phrase, "All the tired horses in the sun, how'm I s'posed to get any ridin' done," for longer than three minutes, underneath sweeping, syrupy strings. The phrase sounds suspiciously like "All the tired horses in the sun, how'm I s'posed to get any *writin'* done," perhaps Dylan's mischievous excuse for the skimpy number of original songs he's about to give the unwary listener.

After completing most of the recording for his next album, *New Morning,* in June, the same month he received an honorary doctorate in music from Princeton University, Dylan made another quiet visit to Israel. Upon his return, he seemed happy to opt out of the spotlight for a while, to, in the words of a song he wrote around this time, "sit down contentedly and watch the river flow." It was a good time to do so—in the fall of 1970, Jimi Hendrix and Janis Joplin, both of whom had performed at the previous year's Woodstock festival, died within a month of each other, both deaths linked to overdoses of drugs.

The way in which Dylan drew upon his knowledge of Jewish liturgy and themes—specifically those found in the daily *morning* prayer service—fuels the album *New Morning* and gives its songs their profound and powerful impact. It was one thing, after all, for Dylan to borrow themes or paraphrase the Bible and the Prophets in songs such as "I Pity the Poor Immigrant" and "All Along the Watchtower" on *John Wesley Harding*—drawing upon, in a sense, an important textual document widely available to all those well-versed in Western culture and literature. It's entirely another thing that by the time of *New Morning,* which was released in October 1970, Dylan appeared to be fluently conversant with the traditional morning liturgy, which none but the most religious Jews continued to make part of their ritual of observance (a ritual in which Dylan presumably witnessed his grandfather and other Jewish elders in Hibbing taking part), enough to have it inspire much of the imagery of the very suggestively titled *New Morning*.

A minyan, or group of at least ten men, traditionally assembles early in the morning at a synagogue, where they don *tallisim*, or prayer shawls, wrap tefillin, or "phylacteries"—leather straps with small leather boxes housing parchments—around arms and heads, and pray in Hebrew together, sometimes led by a *shaliach tzibbur*, a person skilled in the modes of prayer chant, or sometimes just praying alternately in unison and apart in what to an outsider might seem like organized chaos. The order of prayer begins with a litany of thanks to G-d for various gifts He provides each day. In the song "Father of Night" that concludes *New Morning*, Dylan seems to be offering an almost literal recounting of several of these gifts. The very first blessing of the morning service, in fact, thanks G-d for providing the understanding to distinguish between day and night; the very first line of the song is "Father of night, father of day," echoing that initial address to G-d. The blessing continues, "Blessed are you . . . who gives sight to the blind," just as Dylan continues, "Father, who taketh the darkness away."

The morning service continues with a recitation of a series of psalms, including psalm 147, reciting a litany of things G-d does, including

Who covers the sky with clouds
Who provides rain for the earth
Who makes mountains sprout with grass.

Dylan's lyrics, referring as they do to "Builder of rainbows up in the sky" and "Father, who build the mountain so high / Who shapeth the cloud up in the sky" allude to these same images from psalm 147, as well as adopting the verbal mannerisms of biblical translation. The recitation of the morning psalms begins with a blessing that concludes with the phrase "Blessed are you, O Lord, King extolled with hymns of praise," much as Dylan ends his song of thanks, "Father of whom we most solemnly praise."

The instrumentation of the prayer-song "Father of Night" features only Dylan on piano, and a female choir. Dylan plays a hard-driving, descending piano riff in a minor key, and the choir echoes the downward modulation of the chord progression. This is definitely *not* gospel music, and if it isn't quite classical synagogue music, it certainly could be a close cousin, or a popularized interpretation, of Jewish davening, or melodic chanting: to wit, the author Richard Williams calls the song "a ninety-second prayer . . . his first unobscured expression of faith, fast and direct, without a shred of irony or distance."

The song concludes the album by straightforwardly repeating themes that were more poetically rendered in the album's opening track, "If Not for You." Popularly thought of as a love song for a woman, probably his wife, Sara—and it certainly works as a love song and may very well have been intended as one—still, the lyrics draw upon some of the same imagery used in "Father of Night," and therefore those of the Jewish morning blessings:

Dylan sings:

> *If not for you,*
> *Babe, I couldn't find the door,*
> *Couldn't even see the floor,*

again, much in the same way that a Jew thanks G-d for restoring sight in the (new) morning after a night of "blindness": "Blessed are you . . . who gives sight to the blind." Dylan continues:

> *If not for you,*
> *Babe, I'd lay awake all night,*
> *Wait for the mornin' light*
> *To shine in through,*
> *But it would not be new,*
> *If not for you*

—seemingly paraphrasing an introductory blessing to the Shema, a prayer said several times a day, including in the morning service, acknowledging God's sovereignty and unity: "Blessed are You . . . He who illuminates the earth . . . and in His goodness renews the work of creation every day"—which really is a one-line summary of the theme of "If Not for You" (and, as we shall see, themes and imagery that are repeated throughout the title track). Dylan stresses that the "mornin' light . . . would not be new" if not for the "you" to whom the song is addressed, somehow imputing a spiritual aspect to every otherwise mundane dawn, in line with the Kabbalistic concept that the world is constantly created anew.

The song also repeats the line "If not for you my sky would fall" twice. The theme of God upholding the heavens is found throughout Jewish liturgy, most notably in Aleynu, the prayer concluding every worship service: "It is He who stretched forth the heavens and founded the earth." With every new morning, nothing is taken for granted; the restoration of one's senses after sleep and the marvel of Creation are given a transcendent aspect in Dylan's song in the same manner as in Jewish prayer. Whether or not Dylan consciously intended "If Not for You" to be for his wife, or a paean to G-d, the important point is that he draws upon the language of the traditional morning liturgy to write his ode to his beloved, or his Beloved, as the case may be.

The basic imagery that informs the morning prayer service also runs through the title track. A poetic expression of joy upon the new day, the song paints a scene full of sensual restoration and basks in the wonder of Creation: hearing, seeing, feeling the warmth of the morning sun, all images that are literally delineated in the morning blessings. Dylan kicks off this number with the crowing of a rooster. "Rooster" is the literal translation of *sekhvi,* the one who in the very first morning blessing is given understanding to distinguish between day and night (and subsequently, the one through whom G-d acts to wake us up to a new morning): "Blessed art Thou, Lord our G-d, King of the Universe, who gave the rooster intelligence to distinguish between day and night." Ultimately, the song "New Morning" is an elaboration of the litany of thanks a Jew gives to G-d upon wakening. The very first words an observant Jew mutters before getting out of bed are "I render thanks to Thee, everlasting King, for

You have restored my soul within me; great is your faithfulness." In other words, "So happy just to be alive . . ."

In his memoir, *Chronicles,* Dylan contextualizes the album *New Morning* as a response to his father's death in 1968. Chapter three of the book, called "New Morning," begins, "I had just returned to Woodstock from the Midwest—from my father's funeral." The death of Abe Zimmerman has often been delineated as a transition point in his son's relationship to Judaism, as earlier noted, attributed to the urgings of Harold Leventhal. Now living in the Village, Dylan was reputedly studying Judaism with a Hasidic rabbi in Brooklyn. Dylan also allegedly began flirting with support for the Jewish Defense League, an activist group mostly concerned at the time with the plight of Jews in the Soviet Union and led by the controversial Rabbi Meir Kahane (who, coincidentally, presided at the Brooklyn bar mitzvah of a young Arlo Guthrie in 1960). Kahane was eventually gunned down in 1990 by an Egyptian who was ultimately convicted as a coconspirator with the Al Qaeda terrorists who staged the first attack on the World Trade Center in 1993.

The author Stephen Pickering related to Dylan's biographer Robert Shelton a conversation Dylan had with a rabbi at the Mount Zion Yeshiva in Jerusalem on May 22, 1971—just two days shy of his thirtieth birthday: "I'm a Jew. It touches my poetry, my life, in ways I can't describe." It was on this trip that Dylan famously visited Kibbutz Givat Haim near Hadera and began the process of applying for guest residency with his family (a procedure that never went any further). A photojournalist captured Dylan on May 24, his birthday, bedecked in a yarmulke, at the Western Wall, in a photo that would soon flash around the world, feeding the belief that Dylan was a supporter of Zionism returning to the faith of his ancestors.

These days, *New Morning*—much of which was recorded in parallel with the sessions for *Self Portrait*—is generally considered a marginal work. In the early 1990s, Dylan opened concerts with the title track, and the 1998 Coen brothers' film, *The Big Lebowski,* made glorious use of another *New Morning* song, "The Man in Me," over the opening credits, giving that number something of a second life.

Otherwise, in the greater scheme of his career, the album is generally dismissed as middling Dylan at best.

In retrospect, *New Morning* merits another listen and perhaps a wholesale reevaluation. The title, for one, is quite pointed for a Dylan album, with its overt suggestion of renewal and rebirth, compared with more abstract Dylan album titles such as *Blonde on Blonde, Blood on the Tracks, Planet Waves, Street Legal,* and *Time Out of Mind.* The record also was one of the first of Dylan's to make extensive use of a female backup choir, which would reappear later in the decade beginning with *Street Legal* and continue through his gospel albums. It also was the first album to feature Dylan playing primarily piano, his first instrument, instead of guitar. The overall surface feel of the album lies somewhere in between *Nashville Skyline*'s laid-back country vibe and the folk-rock odes to domesticity that followed on Dylan's next album of new songs, 1974's *Planet Waves,* although lacking the latter's underlying sense of disquietude. The domestic focus was partly responsible for critical disappointment with the album (although after the disastrous *Self Portrait,* some greeted it as a full-fledged "comeback" and the album went gold); in 1970, at the height of the antiwar movement and the zenith of the counterculture, critics and critical fans didn't want reassurance from Bob Dylan that conventional, traditional familial arrangements were what life was all about.

But couched in Jewish imagery, that's exactly what Dylan was offering. In "Time Passes Slowly," he sings:

> *Time passes slowly up here in the daylight*
> *We stare straight ahead and try so hard to stay right.*

At a time when thousands or millions of his peers were indulging in overturning all aspects of everyday existence and doing everything they could to go *off* the straight and narrow path of righteousness, Dylan confounded listeners by pledging allegiance to the received morals and ethics of previous generations, practically thumbing his nose at the antiestablishment counterculture he in part, by no design of his own, helped to midwife into existence.

Dylan gave vent to these feelings in the song "Day of the Locusts," an elaboration of his unpleasant experience of being granted an honorary doctorate of music by Princeton University on June 9, 1970 ("As I stepped to the stage to pick up my degree"). Besides borrowing the title from Nathanael West's *The Day of the Locust*, a fictionalized portrayal of alienation in 1930s Hollywood (made into a terrific film by John Schlesinger in 1975), the song is bathed in biblical imagery. Dylan chooses the locust—the quintessential biblical insect best known as one of the ten plagues to hit Pharaoh's Egypt—to symbolize the award-givers, at first subversively describing the locusts (which can actually be heard chirping in the background on the recording) as innocuous or even pleasant:

> *And the locusts sang off in the distance*
> *Yeah, the locusts sang such a sweet melody,*
> *Oh, the locusts sang off in the distance*
> *Yeah, the locusts sang and they were singing for me.*

The song at this ceremony is superficially positive: the locusts sang "such a sweet melody." But the mere fact that the "sweet melody" is put in the mouths of locusts—best known for their destructive, swarming behavior that clouds the sky and strips fields of all vegetation—sets up a layer of irony. The "locusts" are presumably the academics who praised him upon presenting him his degree (his first academic honor since graduating high school), and they perhaps even symbolize others—those "off in the distance," including critics and fans, who excessively honored Dylan at a time when, at least according to the lyrics of the rest of the album's songs, all he wanted was to be left at home alone with his family.

In *Chronicles*, Dylan mocks the Princeton professor who spoke in support of his award, who claimed that while Dylan "prefer[s] the solidarity of his family and isolation from the world . . . he remains the authentic expression of the disturbed and concerned conscience of Young America," prompting Dylan's retort: ". . . it was like he told them that I preferred being in an iron tomb with my food shoved in on a tray."

As if to drive the point home that this wasn't a *pleasant* experience, toward the end of the song Dylan sings, "Sure was glad to get out of there alive." Like a swarm of biblical locusts, this wasn't merely the annoying chirping of ass-kissers and sycophants, but truly a life-threatening, or at least soul-deadening, experience. Or, as Dylan himself put it in *Chronicles*:

> The events of the day, all the cultural mumbo jumbo were imprisoning my soul—nauseating me. . . . I was determined to put myself beyond the reach of it all. I was a family man now, didn't want to be in that group portrait.

Dylan notes that while the initial impetus for the songs on *New Morning* grew out of a projected collaboration with the poet Archibald MacLeish, who wanted Dylan to write new songs for a musical MacLeish was writing based on Stephen Vincent Benét's short story "The Devil and Daniel Webster," he felt disconnected from MacLeish's "world of paranoia, guilt and fear—it . . . reeked of foul play. . . . The play was up to something and I didn't think I wanted to know."

New Morning has its share of fluff, for example, the icy waltz "Winterlude" and the jazzy nursery rhyme "If Dogs Run Free." But the domesticity Dylan embraces, linked to the Jewish liturgy and imagery upon which he draws, points to a burgeoning spirituality far beyond the obvious invocation, "Father of Night," that concludes the album.

In one of few explicitly autobiographical references in his corpus of songs, Dylan ties this song cycle back to his roots in Hibbing. "Went to See the Gypsy" has commonly been thought to have been based upon a meeting with Elvis Presley, but such a tête-à-tête has never been documented, and in a 2009 interview in *Rolling Stone*, Dylan said he never met Presley. The song could just as easily recount Dylan's oft-told experience of seeing Buddy Holly in Duluth when he was seventeen, at a concert where he has said he locked eyes with Holly, saw an aura around him, and felt a jolt of inspiration.

In the song, after the concert is over and everyone has left, he "watched that sun come rising / From that little Minnesota town." Once again Dylan draws on the imagery of dawn to suggest a new beginning, but in this case he does it with a pun: the "sun come rising" can also be heard as the "son come rising," as in the favorite son, the son of Hibbing. Perhaps in a prophetic vision, a teenage Robert Zimmerman saw his destiny in the very moment when he locked eyes with Buddy Holly (as Dylan recounted upon receiving the Grammy Award for best album for *Time Out of Mind* in 1998), who died tragically just three days later in a plane crash. It's back home in "that little Minnesota town," in the observant Jewish household where he grew up the son of Abe and Beatty Zimmerman, a house shared with his immigrant grandmother, in a town full of uncles, aunts, and cousins, where Dylan ultimately finds the contentment and inspiration of a "new morning."

A three-year interval separated *New Morning* from Dylan's next official studio album, *Planet Waves*—an album that, as we shall see, was no less infused with Jewish themes and imagery. But in the meantime, Dylan was no slouch. After an aborted stab at forming a road band to take on tour in the wake of the release of *New Morning,* Dylan became active in several collaborations and side projects.

Just a few weeks after the release of *New Morning,* Dylan's long-promised book of surrealistic poetry and prose, *Tarantula,* was published by Macmillan. Mostly written in 1966, the book was originally scheduled for publication that year, but Dylan apparently got cold feet and insisted that it be withdrawn. In fits and starts he tinkered with it over the next few years, while manuscripts leaked out—not only were his recordings bootlegged, but so was his "fragmentary novel." *Tarantula* calls itself a book of poems, and the writing in it is a cross between some of Dylan's more poetic, abstract lyrics from the mid-1960s and his more free-associative liner notes. Those familiar with his song lyrics recognize words (*Neptune, paranoia, diplomats, corpse*) and phrases (*charity organizations, the good samaritan, can't buy a thrill*) used in both. There is a lot of riffing about music: the book opens, "aretha/crystal jukebox queen of hymn," and continues talking about Aretha—"she owns this melody"—and her "religious thighs," presumably referring to or at least inspired by the soul singer Aretha Franklin.

Tarantula also evinces Dylan's obsession with G-d, the Prophets, and religious figures. The fourth line refers to "ye battered personal god," on the second page someone is "prophesying blind allegiance," and by page eight he has already name-checked Allah, Mohammed, and Jesus. The juxtapositions can be shocking or comical—"you who know that everybody's not a Job or a Nero nor a J.C. Penney"—and some poems seem to be alternative versions of songs. For example, "(Pointless Like a Witch)" begins:

> trip into the light here abraham . . . what about this boss of yours?
> & dont tell me that you just do what youre told! . . . just dont try &
> touch my kid [second ellipsis mine]

—which is really just a variant version of "Highway 61 Revisited," another midrash on the Abraham and Isaac story, if you will. (N.B.: With some exceptions, Dylan eschews most punctuation and upper-case letters in *Tarantula*.)

Tarantula has moments of sophisticated social and cultural criticism disguised as doggerel:

> i gave my love a cherry. sure you did. did she tell you how it tasted?
> what? you also gave her a chicken? fool! no wonder you want to
> start a revolution.

That first sentence, "I gave my love a cherry," is a line from an old English lullaby called "The Riddle Song," recorded by Pete Seeger, Joan Baez, and Doc Watson, among many others. In the next few phrases, Dylan tenderly mocks the literal meaning of the phrase before deftly connecting it to the folk-protest movement and, with one simple rhetorical flourish—"you also gave her a chicken? fool! no wonder you want to start a revolution"—takes the piss out of the entire movement.

Amid the surrealistic jive and the Beatnik poetry, Dylan drops in some of his most plainspoken political and philosophical observations, such as in a passage about the "great man" theory of history, as applied to Adolf Hitler: "hitler did not change / history. hitler WAS history."

"The Horse Race" is a dizzying bit of biblical midrash that in one long paragraph retells the story of Creation, Cain and Abel, the Flood, and Moses, recast as hipster jive. In it, Dylan pays close attention to detail in his rendering of the Creation. He notes that by the seventh day, the heavens were already formed, and his description of the sky, "already strung up shivered like the top of a tent," is a beautifully rendered poetic version of the original biblical account. The character Gonzalas, the Cain-like figure in this midrash, gets his role wrong in the story at first, believing that it's his job to unleash the torrential downpour that will bring about the great Flood. The Lord then has him, Noah-like, building an ark. Dylan then gives a comic, Freudian account of the struggle between Cain/Gonzalas and his parents—the original "generation gap," if you will—before recycling the cane/Cain pun he first employed in "The Lonesome Death of Hattie Carroll." The G-d portrayed here is a lot like the one in "Highway 61 Revisited"—He has a sense of humor, but He doesn't put up with any nonsense. Hence, when Edgar Allan Poe, in the role of Moses, wanders into the story, G-d tells him, "it's not your time yet" and turns out his lights.

Tarantula is also a wellspring of themes and characters that would later reappear in Dylan songs, including Claudette from "Groom's Still Waiting at the Altar" and Angelina, in her eponymous song—both, incidentally, recorded for the *Shot of Love* album in 1981 but not included in the first official release of the album. (Before bringing her back in *Tarantula*, Dylan had said farewell to Angelina in "Farewell Angelina," a *Bringing It All Back Home*–era number that finally saw release on the original *Bootleg Series* compilation; after existing only on the B side of the single version of "Heart of Mine," Claudette made her first official album appearance on a mid-1980s reconfiguration of *Shot of Love* that added "Groom's Still Waiting at the Altar" to the program, and on the *Biograph* compilation in

1985.) Numerous discoveries and delights await readers of *Tarantula*, including more mockery of Hitler; references to biblical figures such as Daniel, Delilah, and Babylon; and, in one salutation at the end of one of the many short letters that serve as comic relief to the longer poems, a self-reference to "a rabble rouser from the mountains," as apt a description of Dylan or of any of the biblical Prophets as one might offer.

In the meantime, in the fall and winter of 1970–71, Dylan plunged into city life, attending back-to-back concerts by Elton John with members of the Band and his wife, Sara, at Bill Graham's legendary rock palace, the Fillmore East, where he'd seen Dr. John the previous October. Later in 1971, he'd return to the Fillmore to take in a show by Frank Zappa, just a few days after seeing Crosby and Nash at Carnegie Hall (at a concert featuring surprise appearances by Stephen Stills and Neil Young, making for a reunion of the supergroup Crosby, Stills, Nash and Young), and toward the end of the year he caught a show by the Staple Singers at the Apollo Theater in Harlem. Dylan lent his harmonica and guitar to a documentary paying tribute to the bluegrass pioneer Earl Scruggs in December, and reportedly met with Huey Newton and David Hilliard of the Black Panthers, an activist organization, in an aborted attempt at finding common ground (an attempt that was apparently derailed by his interlocutors' rabid anti-Israel posturing that bordered on anti-Semitism).

After years of prodding, Dylan finally agreed to sit for interviews with Anthony Scaduto, whose *Bob Dylan: An Intimate Biography*, published by Grossett & Dunlap in 1971, was the first major, full-length biography of the musician. Over a period of months, Dylan was spotted around the Village ducking into nightclubs to take in shows by old folk-music friends such as Bob Neuwirth, Tony Joe White, and Steve Goodman. All in all, city life seemed to suit him, save for the pestering intrusions into his privacy by self-styled "garbologist" and "Dylanologist" A. J. Weberman, a renegade journalist who picked through Dylan's garbage looking for signs of drug use and went on to wage a lifelong campaign of wild theories aimed at proving that Dylan was a capitalist, a fraud, and a junkie, and that his songs were mostly written to and about Weberman himself. (By the late-1990s, a mostly and justly forgotten Weberman was claiming on his website that the songs on Dylan's album *Time Out of Mind* embedded hidden messages that Dylan suffered from AIDS.)

In March 1971, Dylan spent a few days in a New York recording studio with Leon Russell and other musicians laying down several one-off tracks, including "Watching the River Flow" and "When I Paint My Masterpiece." The former offered keen insight into Dylan's state of mind at the time, and the latter would eventually serve as the striking prelude under the opening credits of *Renaldo and Clara*. Not recorded for any particular studio album, both numbers would find a home on *Bob Dylan's Greatest Hits, Vol. 2,* released in November 1971. And thus a world eager for the latest prophecy from Dylan's pen got this from "Watching the River Flow," which held the opening slot on that double LP set:

> *What's the matter with me,*
> *I don't have much to say . . .*

Again, Dylan turns his back on the political and culture wars, preferring to "read a book" (perhaps *the* book, the Bible?) and sit back to watch the disagreements play themselves out: watch the river flow. Listeners also got hints of an artist still hoping to make his greatest mark, in "When I Paint My Masterpiece"—which made its debut two months earlier in a version by the Band on the album *Cahoots*—in which Dylan sang, "Someday, everything is gonna be diff'rent / When I paint my masterpiece."

On August 1, nearly two years since his last official public performance, Dylan made a surprise, unbilled appearance at George Harrison's Concert for Bangladesh. The first superstar benefit concert (there were actually two concerts—one in the afternoon and one in the evening), the show was intended to aid the cause of starving refugees fleeing what was then East Pakistan (now Bangladesh) to avoid floods amid the strife of war between India and Pakistan (which then ruled the mostly Muslim nation).

Dylan and Harrison had grown close over the past few years, sharing a spiritual kinship that allowed their enormous talents to coexist humbly (as opposed to Dylan and John Lennon, who despite several attempts, ultimately failed to bond, presumably because of Lennon's sense of insecurity toward and competitiveness with Dylan). While the Bangladesh concert included appearances by Harrison, Ringo Starr, Eric Clapton, Billy Preston, and the famed Indian sitarist Ravi Shankar, Dylan's participation was the highlight of the event, both for its rare glimpse of the elusive star and for his intense renditions of five numbers at each show, including "Blowin' in the Wind," "Just Like a Woman," and "A Hard Rain's a-Gonna Fall," accompanied by Harrison on guitar, Leon Russell on bass, and Starr on percussion. Much as the Band's 1976 farewell concert film, *The Last Waltz*, would culminate in Dylan's appearance, so, too, did the film *The Concert for Bangladesh* build to a climax featuring Dylan's set of songs.

The event was a financial success reportedly to the tune of a quarter-million dollars, undoubtedly helped by rumors that it would feature appearances by John Lennon (who in fact was slated to appear but who pulled out at the last minute) and Paul McCartney, which would have made for the full-fledged Beatles reunion that never did take place after the group split for good in 1970. Dylan's agreement to allow his performances to be used in the subsequent live album and film of the concert undoubtedly helped those souvenirs of the event net several million more for the cause, which set the bar for subsequent rock superstar charity benefits, such as 1979's No Nukes and 1985's Live Aid. Mostly, though, Dylan's participation in *Bangladesh* sparked excitement about his return to the concert stage, whetting the audience's appetite for a full-fledged Dylan concert and undoubtedly fueling his own desire to return to live performance, which he would do in earnest finally in early 1974 on his nationwide comeback tour with the Band.

All this urban activity also fueled Dylan's desire to collaborate with other musicians and artists, which would find its ultimate realization in the barnstorming Rolling Thunder Revue tour of 1975–76. Much of the fall of 1971 was taken up with jam sessions, rehearsals, and recording sessions with Allen Ginsberg and other poets, including Ginsberg's lover Peter Orlovsky, Gerard Malanga, and Anne Waldman, with musical participation by the composer/multi-instrumentalist David Amram and the musical brothers Happy and Artie Traum, whom Dylan knew from Woodstock. After reading *Soledad Brother,* a prison memoir by the recently slain black activist George Jackson, Dylan wrote an ode to Jackson that he recorded immediately and released as a single. *Bob Dylan's Greatest Hits, Vol. 2* was released in mid-November and included several previously unavailable tracks, such as "Tomorrow Is a Long Time" and "I Shall Be Released," originally recorded with the Band during the *Basement Tapes* sessions but heard here in a new, laid-back version accompanied only by Happy Traum.

In a hint of things to come, Dylan would ring out the old and ring in the new on New Year's Eve, 1972, by taking the stage at New York's Academy of Music, where the Band was completing a four-night stand. On the final night, Dylan played guitar and sang four songs with the group, "When I Paint My Masterpiece," "Like a Rolling Stone," and two *Basement Tapes*–era songs, "Down in the Flood" and "Don't Ya Tell Henry." The concert was recorded for ultimate release on the Band's live double album, *Rock of Ages,* but the Dylan numbers weren't included on the LP when it was first released. They did circulate, however, through unofficial channels, and eventually wound up being included in the 2001 two-CD rerelease of *Rock of Ages.*

Still living in New York, Dylan spent much of the next year as he had the last—attending performances at folk clubs, theaters, and arenas (including Jackson Browne at the Bitter End, Link Wray at Max's Kansas City, and Elvis Presley at Madison Square Garden), making low-key guest appearances on friends' recordings (including ones by Steve Goodman and Doug Sahm), but presumably mostly attending to the busy home front, with five children in the nest. His lack of recorded output during this time may have been due to his tangled business arrangements: his management deal with Albert

Grossman had expired a few years earlier, but Grossman still would receive a significant percentage of any sales owed to him under a publishing deal. Dylan's five-year contract with Columbia Records, negotiated by Grossman under terms Dylan deemed unfavorable, expired the previous year. In part to get away from it all, Dylan reportedly spent time on a ranch in Arizona, assembling the lyrical content and illustrations that would become *Writings and Drawings*, his first official book of lyrics, published in 1973, and sketching out the beginnings of a song that would become nearly as much of an anthem as "Blowin' in the Wind" had been. The song wasn't to surface until the 1974 release of *Planet Waves*, but it would prove the centerpiece, both musically and thematically, of Dylan's next "comeback album," as well as his next great statement of Jewish themes. The song, of course, was "Forever Young."

For two weeks in October 1972, Dylan joined something of a roots-rock supergroup at Atlantic Recording Studios in New York in the service of Doug Sahm, leader of the legendary mid-1960s group the Sir Douglas Quintet, whose hits included "Mendocino" and "She's About a Mover." Dylan wound up as something of a phantom presence on the resulting album, *Doug Sahm and Band*, which was released in January 1973. On the album's back cover photograph, Dylan hides behind Sahm, and in addition to several members of the Quintet, the musicians in the photo include the New Orleans pianist Dr. John, the guitarist David Bromberg, the accordionist Flaco Jimenez, the guitarist/keyboardist Augie Meyers, the jazz saxophonist David "Fathead" Newman, and the newgrass mandolinist Andy Statman (who would go on to pioneer the klezmer revival of the late-1970s, along the way returning to the Orthodox Judaism of his ancestors). On the album, which has the easygoing, laid-back feel of a jam session, Dylan's harmony vocals dominate "(Is Anybody Going to) San Antone" and "Blues Stay Away from Me," and he takes the lead in singing his own composition "Wallflower" (a little-known tune that Dylan's son Jakob would eventually adopt for the name of his rock band, the Wallflowers—a band in which he initially had hoped to hide his own identity as Bob Dylan's son, much like a wallflower). The album also marked Dylan's first studio work with the producer Jerry Wexler, with whom Dylan would reunite for 1979's *Slow Train Coming*.

Around the same time, at the urging of the country music singer Kris Kristofferson, Rudy Wurlitzer sent Dylan his screenplay for *Pat Garrett and Billy the Kid* in the hope of luring him to write a song for the Sam Peckinpah–directed film, set to star James Coburn, Jason Robards, and Dylan's longtime pal Kristofferson as Billy. As it turned out, Wurlitzer and Peckinpah, who by then had established a reputation for his brilliant, graphically violent deconstructions of the Western genre (most notably in 1969's *The Wild Bunch*) as well as for his irascible, alcohol-fueled temperament, got more Dylan than they had originally bargained for. On the basis of his ballad, "Billy," Dylan was invited to the set in Durango, Mexico, to discuss his involvement in the film. After meeting with Peckinpah, playing his song, and discussing the film's revisionist take on the legendary outlaw and sheriff (much in keeping with Dylan's portrayal of the historical John Wesley Hardin as something of a hero in his song "John Wesley Harding" on the album of the same name), Dylan signed on to score the entire film and to play a supporting role as an enigmatic character—a Western version of a Shakespearean fool—named, aptly enough, Alias.

Dylan brought Sara and their children back to Durango in late November, and with only a few breaks (including quick trips to London and Israel), he participated in the filming and did several recording sessions (in Mexico City and Los Angeles) that resulted in music for the film as well as for a mostly instrumental soundtrack album, *Pat Garrett and Billy the Kid*, which yielded one of Dylan's greatest, most-beloved and oft-recorded anthems, "Knockin' on Heaven's Door." The film, however, didn't fare as well. Throughout the shoot Peckinpah fought with the MGM studio honchos, who argued against his ballooning budget and his multiple setups and takes, eventually taking the film away from him, releasing a shortened version that met with a considerable critical drubbing. Peckinpah, however, kept a copy of his own, longer version of the film, and his director's cut is now widely recognized as a classic of the revisionist Western genre.

As for Dylan, he got several things out of the experience (besides a herd of children run down by a flu that swept through the cast and crew): his first extensive participation in a feature film (which presumably held him in good stead for future self-driven projects, including *Renaldo and Clara* and *Masked and Anonymous*); a hit song that would become a signature tune; and a relationship with Mexico that would resurface several times in song, most notably in "Romance in Durango" on the 1976 album *Desire,* and in much of 2009's *Together Through Life.*

The simple, mournful "Knockin' on Heaven's Door" immediately transcended its functional role in the film, as the dying thoughts of Sheriff Baker addressed to his wife, whom he calls "Mama." In its original version as recorded for the soundtrack, the song had only two verses. But in subsequent years, in concert versions, Dylan would often add new verses. He'd frequently sing, "Mama, wipe these tears off-a my face / I can't see through them anymore," tying the song's theme of reconciliation with death to this verse in Isaiah: "He will eliminate death forever, and my Lord G-d will wipe the tears away from all faces" (25:8). Dylan often returns to this chapter, from which he also derived the title image for "Shelter from the Storm" from *Blood on the Tracks*—"For You were . . . a shelter from the storm" (25:4)—and his numerous mentions of and allusions to masks, such as "On this mountain He will eliminate the veiled faces . . . and the masks that mask all nations" (25:7).

Filming in Mexico also seems to have propelled Dylan's inevitable move from New York to California. Life in Greenwich Village had simply become untenable: too many people knew exactly where Dylan and his family lived, and any sense of privacy or anonymity Dylan thought he might gain by living in the teeming metropolis soon proved elusive. Plus, the music business, at one time based in New York, had for the most part gravitated to Los Angeles, where nearly all the record companies' main offices were now located. The creative axis had also shifted in large part to Los Angeles, where folk clubs such as the Troubadour eclipsed New York venues such as Folk City and the Kettle of Fish. When his children fell ill in Mexico, he flew them to Los Angeles for treatment, wound up renting a house in Malibu, and in short order began construction on his controversial multimillion-dollar seaside mansion, replete with a mosquelike onion dome and a living room large enough to ride a horse through.

Dylan wasn't the only one making the transition to the West down from the East. The Band's Robbie Robertson had tired of the scene in Woodstock and also made the trek westward, where he started hanging out with Dylan and nudging him toward reuniting with his former Band-mates for a concert tour—in a sense, completing the 1966 tour that was cut short by Dylan's motorcycle accident. By the end of the summer, Dylan and the members of the Band were getting together to play through approximately six dozen tunes, presumably looking for ones they were comfortable enough to bring back to the stage.

At the same time, Dylan had fallen in with the artist manager and Asylum Records label head David Geffen, whose clients included Joni Mitchell, the Eagles, Jackson Browne, and Linda Ronstadt. While Columbia Records continued to dither over a new contract for Dylan, with a final agreement falling by the wayside when the label's head, Clive Davis, who led the negotiations all but to completion, left the company amid allegations of financial improprieties, Geffen waited in the wings for the right time to ink Dylan to a deal on his own incipient label. With the promoter Bill Graham lining up a nationwide tour of forty shows in twenty-one cities, and with Geffen whispering in his ear that he could have any deal he wanted with Asylum—including the best possible deal, which was no deal at all, but just an album-to-album understanding—Dylan realized it made financial sense to tour behind a new recording.

The January 1974 release of *Planet Waves*, Dylan's first studio album of original songs since *New Morning* in the fall of 1970, marked the beginning of his most fertile and prolific creative period since the mid-1960s. Whereas the previous eight years saw only three officially released studio albums of all original material (supplemented by two *Greatest Hits* packages, the *Self Portrait* sampler, the *Pat Garrett* movie soundtrack, and Columbia Records' vindictive release of outtakes from the *Self Portrait* and *New Morning* sessions packaged as *Dylan* upon the news of his jumping to Asylum), beginning with *Planet Waves*, Dylan would release a new studio album almost without fail every year through 1981.

Given the casual, off-the-cuff origins of *Planet Waves*, it's remarkable how the album has stood up over the years. It contains one full-fledged classic, the aforementioned "Forever Young," which has gone on to have a life far beyond Dylan himself, with versions by the likes of the Pretenders, Meat Loaf, Diana Ross, Kitty Wells, Joan Baez, Johnny Cash, Sandy Denny, and Jerry Garcia. But *Planet Waves* is also a remarkable document for how it sits halfway between the cozy domestic platitudes of *New Morning* and the bitter odes of betrayal and disappointment on its follow-up, *Blood on the Tracks*, recorded within a year of *Planet Waves*, and the seeds of which can be found hidden not too deep in the grooves of this album.

Dylan recorded *Planet Waves* in four quick sessions in Los Angeles over the course of a week. He enlisted the members of the Band to play with him—the first (and only) time that the group solely and entirely backed him on a studio album. The musicians came into the sessions cold, never having heard the songs before, and consequently the resulting recording boasts a relaxed, improvised feel. Still, the affinity the musicians had for playing with one another and with Dylan is readily apparent. Although they don't lend any vocal support, they sing along with Dylan through their instruments, with Robertson punctuating Dylan's phrases with the same astute perception as he did on the 1966 tour. Garth Hudson colored several of the numbers with his ethereal organ, and Richard Manuel contributed both piano and drums to the album until the Band's regular drummer, Levon Helm, returned from a vacation.

The songs alternated from straightforward love songs ("Something There Is About You," "You Angel You") to songs of unease ("Dirge," "Going Going Gone"), to songs that blended both emotions ("Wedding Song," "Hazel"). But before one even played the record, the LP's cover and liner notes arrived as a highly suggestive message that things had changed. For one, the album marked the first publication of songs under Dylan's new publishing company, Ram's Horn Music, a reference to the shofar, a trumpetlike instrument made out of a ram's horn used most auspiciously on the days leading up to and including the Jewish holidays of Rosh Hashanah and Yom Kippur, reminding and calling upon Jews to take stock of their behavior and do whatever they can to return to the ways of the Lord—a metaphor, really, for the work of the Prophets, aptly used here to describe Dylan's songs.

Second, Dylan's liner notes cast a sweeping net summarizing his entire life until that point, and are remarkable for the overt Jewish references they contain. "Back to the starting point!" he wrote. "The kickoff, Hebrew letters on the wall. . . ." Was Dylan referring to his childhood, to attending Hebrew school (in keeping with several mentions of or allusions to his Minnesota youth in the songs on *Planet Waves*)? Or was he referring to his recent trips to Israel, the "Hebrew letters on the wall" being the letters that people write to G-d and tuck into the crevices of the stones in the Western Wall in the Old City of Jerusalem? And just what does he mean by terming this "the starting point" and "the kickoff"?

The liner notes go on in just a few lines outlining an impressionistic autobiography, starting back in Hibbing: "beer halls & pin balls . . . headwinds & snowstorms, family outings with strangers . . . All wired up & voting for Eisenhower, waving flags . . . getting killed on motorcycles," an ironic confession of his lousy luck when it came to bike riding. (Those following the "mask" theme throughout Dylan's career should note that he also wrote, "We sensed each other beneath the mask.") In just a few more lines he summarizes the Sixties and his ultimate disappointment with the counterculture (". . . pitched a tent in the street and joined the traveling circus, Love at first sight! History became a lie! The sideshow took over—what a sight . . . the threshold of the Modern Bomb . . . I lit out for parts unknown"), and then says he "found Jacob's ladder up against an adobe wall & bought a serpant [*sic*] from a passing Angel . . ."

"Jacob's ladder" refers to the biblical story in which Jacob has a vision of angels ascending and descending a ladder reaching into the heavens. Mystics believe that the angels and the ladder were always with Jacob, granting him G-d's protection. Jacob is also a reference to Dylan's son Jakob, and the reference to Jacob's ladder also ties in with the song "Forever Young," widely acknowledged to have been written for Jakob, his youngest, and in which Dylan sings, "May you build a ladder to the stars / And climb on every rung."

The liner notes continue, "Yeah the old days are gone forever and the new ones ain't far behind, the laughter is fading away, echos [*sic*] of a star, or energy vampires in the gone world going wild!"—as apt a poetic description of the post-Sixties hangover as any. Dylan goes on to evoke a litany of Midwestern cities, placing them in a prophetic context of biblical destruction, figuratively and literally, and concluding with an invocation to his birthplace, Duluth (to which he also refers in the song "Something There Is About You"), with a specific biblical reference to the figure of Joshua (a musician who literally "killed" his audience with music—in his case, the trumpets that brought down the walls of Jericho):

Innocent lambs! The wretched of the Earth, My brothers of the flood, cities of the flesh—Milwaukee, Ann Arbour [*sic*], Chicago, Bismarck, South Dakota, Duluth! Duluth—where Baudelaire lived and Goya cashed in his chips, where Joshua brought the house down!

As it turned out, this was a bit of secular prophecy on Dylan's part, foreshadowing the impact his performance—as documented on the two-LP live recording, *Before the Flood,* issued later in 1974—would have on audiences. Where Dylan's concerts with the Band (then the Hawks) in 1966 were revolutionary in their impact, throwing down an anarchic gauntlet of wild poetic energy and electricity that had never before and has never since been equaled, his concerts with the Band in 1974, reportedly equally as loud as those in 1966, took that energy, organized it, and channeled it into the fiercest performances of his career. This was Dylan in command, a veritable Joshua leading his troops (the Band) into battle fully confident of the outcome. Dylan never sounded as authoritative or as downright angry and impassioned as he does on *Before the Flood*, released in the summer of 1974, on which he gives a performance often called "stentorian," which simply means "loud" but insinuates something of a martial aspect (perhaps owing to the word's root in Stentor, a herald in the *Iliad*, noted for his loud voice, "as powerful as fifty voices of other men," according to Homer, and as good a description as any for Dylan's sound on the album).

Dylan's song choices on that tour matched his stentorian or martial approach, with anthems such as "Rainy Day Women #12 and 35," "Highway 61 Revisited," "Knockin' on Heaven's Door," "All Along the Watchtower" (which, if they weren't martial or biblical to begin with, sure came out sounding that way after Dylan and the Band rearranged them for the tour; many are recast literally in march time, and Dylan sings/shouts a lot of the key phrases). "This is the craziest and strongest rock and roll ever recorded," wrote the *Village Voice* rock critic Robert Christgau. Even the album title itself hinted at Dylan's purpose: it can be read simply as a reference to the biblical Flood, by which its meaning would be to portend or warn of an oncoming flood—a theme that runs throughout Dylan's work, most overtly in the *Basement Tapes*-era number "Down in the Flood"—and thereby goes to some lengths to explain why Dylan is shouting so much. Or it could also have been a reference to a trilogy of novels so named by the Yiddish writer Sholem Asch, father of Moe Asch, the founder of Folkways Records, the label that recorded Woody Guthrie, Lead Belly, and many more of Dylan's favorite folk and blues artists.

Among the *Planet Waves* numbers that were included on the tour was the aforementioned "Forever Young." On its surface a simple ode to a child, bestowing on him the wish that he remain youthful and blessed, in fact the song bears a remarkable similarity to the blessing of the Kohanim, or the priestly blessing, recited in every synagogue service, but more important, on every Friday night, in slightly different form, delivered expressly by a father to his children, with the placing of his hands on the child's head.

Dylan opens the song singing, "May God bless and keep you always," just as a father blesses his child: "May God bless you and protect you."

Dylan goes on to wish that his child will ". . . always know the truth / And see the light surrounding you," paraphrasing the next line of the blessing: "May God illuminate His countenance for you and be gracious to you."

Aside from the inspiration this gains from the blessing of the children, there is a sophisticated code built into the song—one that Dylan had labored over, on and off, for several years—that mirrors the Kabbalistic concept of the *sefirot,* or the channels of spirituality through which G-d interacts with man. These channels are illustrated in many ways, sometimes likened to the rungs of a ladder ("May you build a ladder to the stars / And climb on every rung"). The characteristics he wishes upon his son line up approximately with these ten manifestations of godliness on earth, including *hesed,* or kindness ("may you always do for others"), *da'at,* or knowledge ("may you always know the truth"), *gevurah,* or strength ("stand upright and be strong"), and *yesod,* or foundation ("may you have a strong foundation").

"Something There Is About You" refers back to Dylan's liner notes (or vice versa) in looking back to his origins and taking stock of where he's been and how far he's come. At first his nostalgia seems to be initiated by a person, probably a woman, most likely Sara:

Something there is about you that strikes a match in me
Is it the way your body moves or is it the way your hair blows free?
Or is it because you remind me of something that used to be
Somethin' that crossed over from another century?

Dylan goes back in time even beyond his birth and childhood in Duluth and Hibbing—which he invokes in the next stanza—and hints at a deeper pull, literally to the Old World or figuratively to the ancients.

But then he is transformed by this reverie, by this lure back in time, on a spiritual journey, and his joy and love for a woman overlaps with that of his love for G-d. Or at least the two are equated; in the love of a woman, he finds G-d, or in his love for G-d, he finds romance:

Suddenly I found you and the spirit in me sings
Don't have to look no further, you're the soul of many things. . . .
I was in a whirlwind, now I'm in some better place.

In the Sefer Yetzirah, the mystical book of Creation, the *sefirot* are described as running and returning like flashes of lightning whenever G-d speaks. This action is understood to be carried out on the human plane by the Prophets, who ordinarily attend to G-d's speech, his "word" (in Hebrew, *Davar*), by running and returning—"in a flash," so to speak. But whenever G-d issues a saying or an edict, a *Ma'amar*, above and beyond generic speech, the *sefirot*, or Prophets, rush to hear it like a *Sufah*, a hurricane or a whirlwind. The means toward attaining the mystical experience, the meeting with G-d, is via the *Merkavah*, or the Chariot. Thus Isaiah notes that G-d's chariot arrives "like the whirlwind" [*chasufah*, 66:15], implying that the mystic is drawn to G-d in a whirlwind, presumably leaving him, afterward, "in some better place."

The album closes with "Wedding Song," a last-minute addition that Dylan recorded alone in one take, replete with his jacket buttons clicking against his guitar. After the first run-through, the recording engineer Rob Fraboni asked Dylan if he'd like to take off his jacket and rerecord it without the sounds made by his buttons. Dylan uttered a simple "no," and to this day, if you listen closely you can hear the buttons on this amazingly deep, dark, ironically titled love song—hinting at the direction he was headed toward on his next album—a song full of suggestive imagery, using the prophetic mode in an ostensible love song:

. . . You breathed on me and made my life a richer one to live,
When I was deep in poverty you taught me how to give,
Dried the tears up from my dreams and pulled me from the hole,
Quenched my thirst and satisfied the burning in my soul.

Jewish belief has it that Adam, the first human, was given life when, after being molded out of the earth by G-d, he was literally inspired—on the receiving end of G-d's breath, which equaled life: "G-d formed man out of dust of the ground, and breathed into his nostrils a breath of life. Man thus became a living creature" (Genesis 2:7). Many biblical figures, among them Joseph (Genesis 37:28) and Jeremiah (Jeremiah 38:5–13), were rescued from wells, pits, or holes.

In an odd construction, Dylan compares his object's love to that of biblical justice, "Eye for eye and tooth for tooth, your love cuts like a knife . . ." resonant of Exodus 21:23–24: "If there shall be other damage, then you shall award life for life; eye for eye, tooth for tooth." And his obsession with flood imagery recurs in the line "What's lost is lost, we can't regain what went down in the flood . . ."

Dylan backs away from the role with which he was deputized in the next verse:

> *It's never been my duty to remake the world at large,*
> *Nor is it my intention to sound a battle charge,*

here playing the role of reluctant prophet, like the biblical Prophets. Prophets are often unwilling at best—even cursing their fate at worst—as in Jeremiah 20:7, 14: "I have become a laughingstock. . . . Accursed be the day on which I was born." In Dylan's case, he is probably referring to his lack of overt political intent rather than totally denying his more subtle work as a poet of spirituality. In the end, he declares his belief in the Jewish idea of *bashert*, or romantic destiny, which posits that lovers or soulmates are foreordained at the moment of birth and that they find each other in order to form a more complete, unified being:

> *Oh, can't you see that you were born to stand by my side*
> *And I was born to be with you, you were born to be my bride,*
> *You're the other half of what I am, you're the missing piece*
> *And I love you more than ever with that love that doesn't cease.*

These lyrics would gain all the more poignancy when it became clear in late 1974 that, regardless of the sentiments expressed herein, Dylan's marriage to Sara was falling apart, which would be the main subject of his next album of new material, 1975's *Blood on the Tracks,* widely considered to be one of the greatest albums of the rock era.

SEVEN

LAMENTATIONS

After the rigors of the winter tour, Dylan returned to New York City and, in the spring of 1974, enrolled in a painting class taught by Norman Raeben. Dylan had always had a strong attraction to the visual arts, which wasn't just limited to film. He had drawn ever since he was a child, and when his first collection of lyrics was published in 1973, it was under the title *Writings and Drawings*, and included line drawings he had done over the years. Since that time, several collections of his drawings and paintings have been published, including *Drawn Blank*, and his artwork has been exhibited in gallery and museum shows.

Much has been made about how Dylan's two-month course of studies with Raeben, which took place in the latter's private studio on the eleventh floor of Carnegie Hall, opened up his mind to a new way of songwriting. In subsequent interviews, Dylan credited Raeben specifically with encouraging an intuitive, expressionistic approach to creating art that allowed him to play with a sense of fluidity, accounting for the shifts in perspective—of time, space, and scenes—that characterized many of the best songs on *Blood on the Tracks* and subsequent albums, and, especially, in Dylan's film *Renaldo and Clara*. Dylan felt he was now able to do consciously what he had done in the

159

1960s, up through *Blonde on Blonde,* unconsciously. He had always seen songwriting in terms of painting, expressing this very idea in his 1971 song "When I Paint My Masterpiece." Little did he know that just a few years later, with the help of a painting teacher, he would paint—or craft—what many came to regard as his masterpiece.

The Russian-born Raeben was seventy-three years old when Dylan studied with him, and neither apparently knew much about the other. Raeben apparently had no idea who Bob Dylan was, and it's not clear if Dylan knew that Raeben was the youngest son of the most famous Yiddish author, Sholem Aleichem, whose stories about Tevye the Milkman were adapted for the hit Broadway musical *Fiddler on the Roof.* Sholem Aleichem was a pen name; the family name was Rabinowitz, which Raeben apparently modified.

Although their time together was short, it had a lasting effect on Dylan, who even told an interviewer that once he left Raeben with his newfound point of view, his wife, Sara, never really understood him again. The two had already been having marital difficulties after a period of domestic harmony, which, as we've seen, Dylan hinted at in some of the songs on *Planet Waves.* Dylan apparently fell into some old, long-abandoned habits while he was out on tour with the Band, and Sara didn't appreciate the fact that he was cheating on her. Most biographies link Dylan at this time to Ellen Bernstein, a record company staffer in her mid-twenties whom he met on the tour and with whom he began spending time.

In the meantime, Dylan stayed in New York while Sara was in California dealing with the construction of the Malibu mansion. Dylan was enjoying being back in the Village again, palling around with old friends including Phil Ochs, Dave Van Ronk, and Jacques Levy. He joined Ochs and company, including Pete Seeger and Arlo Guthrie, at a wine-besotted Friends of Chile benefit concert at Madison Square Garden's Felt Forum in early May, which apparently was more of a party than a concert. His last-minute addition to the bill salvaged what looked to be a financial disaster; as soon as his participation was announced, the event sold out.

By early summer, news stories began to report that Dylan and Sara had split up, although there hadn't been any formal separation at this time. Stories linked Dylan to various women, including Bernstein, who visited Dylan at his farm in Minnesota in July, where he stayed with his children and began writing songs at a lightning pace, many of which would find their way onto his next album. In August, Dylan re-signed with Columbia Records, and in mid-September, he returned to New York to begin recording *Blood on the Tracks*.

Dylan laid down the original tracks for the album over a nine-day period in mid- to late September. Ellen Bernstein was in attendance for most of the sessions, which were engineered by Phil Ramone, best known as a hit producer with a closetful of Grammy Awards, whose production credits include albums for Billy Joel, Frank Sinatra, Rod Stewart, Paul Simon, and Tony Bennett. These sessions, however, didn't require much production; they were mostly stripped-down, acoustic affairs, with Dylan variously accompanied by Eric Weissberg and members of his string band, Deliverance, the organist Paul Griffin, who played piano on sessions for *Bringing It All Back Home*, *Highway 61 Revisited*, and *Blonde on Blonde*, and Buddy Cage, who played pedal steel guitar for the Grateful Dead offshoot band New Riders of the Purple Sage.

The album was pressed by the record company and all set to be released when Dylan pulled the plug. In December, he went back to Minnesota, where he played the finished album for his brother, who convinced him that the recording needed more work. For the first and only time, David Zimmerman played a role in his brother's artistic career. Heavily involved in the Minneapolis music scene himself, Zimmerman brought Dylan into a recording studio where he teamed him with local musicians, and as a result they recut half of the album—including the final versions of "You're a Big Girl Now," "Lily, Rosemary and the Jack of Hearts," "If You See Her, Say Hello," "Idiot Wind," and "Tangled Up in Blue"—in just two days between Christmas and New Year's Day.

Released on January 17, 1975, just a few weeks after the completion of the recording, *Blood on the Tracks* was greeted as an instant classic—a masterpiece—and its status in Dylan's canon and the greater rock music canon has never dipped. It's widely accepted as Dylan's greatest album of the seventies, and often called *the* greatest album of the decade. It's ranked with the best of Dylan's work—*Highway 61 Revisited* and *Blonde on Blonde*—and, although highly idiosyncratic (as are all Dylan's albums), considered to be the crowning achievement of the confessional singer-songwriter genre, whose impact continues to be felt to this day in the new-folk songwriting by the likes of Shawn Colvin, Richard Shindell, and Greg Brown.

Early on, Dylan publicly puzzled over the album's critical acclaim and commercial success, commenting to Mary Travers, then the host of a radio program, that he couldn't understand how so many people could enjoy so much pain. The album as a whole constitutes a searing portrait of the breakup of a marriage; *Blood on the Tracks* is widely known as Dylan's "divorce album," even though it would be several years before he and Sara were officially divorced.

Nevertheless, to most ears, the songs on *Blood on the Tracks* rang true as nakedly autobiographical. Not in any way relating to the music on the pop charts at the time, and with no hit single, the album must have struck a chord with listeners on its own merits in order for it to have done so well commercially. And while it may not have been spun on hit radio, the album was perfectly timed for the height of free-form FM radio, where on stations like New York's WNEW-FM, DJs were free to play album tracks as opposed to singles—when *Blood on the Tracks* arrived at WNEW, all regular programming ceased and the station just played the entire album from beginning to end.

The opening number and its signature tune, "Tangled Up in Blue," tells a story—or many stories—about the course of a marriage, or several relationships, against the greater context of the popular culture. The first verse finds the narrator alone in bed recalling an old love from out west. Dylan mixes some autobiography with some fantasy here, placing himself—or the first-person narrator, if it's not Dylan himself—in the Midwest (or the West) before coming to New York City. There are hints of his ill-fated high school relationship with Echo Helstrom, but here the socioeconomic tables are reversed—it's the woman's family that looks down on the man's family as not suitable for their daughter.

But there's no clear autobiographical narrative running through the song; rather, Dylan offers up a collage of images, some that come right out of his biography, others that are twisted, and presumably most of which are invented out of whole cloth. Thus, the second verse begins with a clear reference to Sara: "She was married when we first met / Soon to be divorced." In six couplets of the verse, he spells out the entire course of the relationship, boiling it down to its essence:

> We drove that car as far as we could
> Abandoned it out West

The car is a symbol of the relationship, and the abandonment of the stalled vehicle "out West" coincides with the fact that Sara stayed in Los Angeles while Dylan moved back to New York City, using his Minnesota farm as a place to reunite with his family.

The next few verses diverge from any biographical facts for the most part—although the teenage Dylan did "have a job in the great North woods working as a cook for a spell," or at least as a dishwasher or waiter, in the North Dakota restaurant where he first hooked up with Bobby Vee for his short-lived stint as the teen idol's piano player. While Dylan never worked on a fishing boat in Louisiana, that's a mere detail in order to locate someone who, in very Dylanesque fashion, could claim:

> But all the while I was alone
> The past was close behind,
> I seen a lot of women
> But she never escaped my mind, and I just grew
> Tangled up in blue.

Part of the genius of this song is the manner in which the meaning of the refrain phrase, "Tangled up in blue," changes each time it gets used, depending on what's come before. In this case, for example, the singer "just grew tangled up in blue," the emphasis here being on finding oneself in a life situation akin to being "tangled up." Contrast this with the next verse, where it ends almost as a joke, where a dancer in a topless bar inexplicably bends down to tie the laces of his shoe, laces that are "tangled."

The woman who brings him back to her place in the next verse could be the woman from the "topless place" or a different woman; she seems to be the same woman, as there's a sense in both verses that they have met before (and that she even could be the woman from the very first verse, years later). Dylan ingeniously has the narrator dropping into the topless joint just for a beer—he's not interested in seeing topless women, in other words—and when he recognizes her he just looks "at the side of her face," a clever play on "at the sight of her face."

The penultimate verse opens up the song with the introduction of another couple "on Montague Street," which is in Brooklyn, New York. The narrator gets involved with them at a time of great upheaval, a time that sounds very much like the Sixties—"There was music in the cafés at night and revolution in the air"—but over time they seem to lose their way, or their ideals: "He started into dealing with slaves, something inside of him died; she had to sell everything she owned and froze up inside." The narrator cuts his losses and heads on out—"The only thing I knew how to do was to keep on keepin' on like a bird that flew." In just a few lines, Dylan turns this impressionistic song of relationships into a sociocultural saga, tracing his own odyssey as well as that of his generation through the triumphs of the idealistic 1960s to the disappointments of the 1970s—the "Me Decade."

"Simple Twist of Fate," "If You See Her, Say Hello," "Shelter from the Storm," and "You're Gonna Make Me Lonesome When You Go" constitute the core of *Blood on the Tracks*: songs that recount and examine relationships gone bad, often in an effort to make sense of what happened and why. In "Simple Twist of Fate," for example, after five verses that could be scenes from a film, the narrator, feeling lost and empty, concludes:

> *People tell me it's a sin*
> *To know and feel too much within*

I still believe she was my twin, but I lost the ring.
She was born in spring, but I was born too late
Blame it on a simple twist of fate.

Of course, the narrator doesn't really blame it on "a simple twist of fate," but in the end, he might as well, since he's powerless to effect change. Dylan drops a few autobiographical elements into these lines to tantalize listeners, referring to the woman as his "twin"—an allusion to his being a Gemini—and losing the ring as a symbol of the end of a marriage.

The narrator isn't as wistful on "Shelter from the Storm," which veers recklessly back and forth through time, to when he came from a battlefield ("a world of steel-eyed death, and men who are fighting to be warm") to when they met ("suddenly I turned around and she was standing there / With silver bracelets on her wrists and flowers in her hair") to when she provided him a place of refuge ("Try imagining a place where it's always safe and warm") to the forsaken present, when "there's a wall between us, something there's been lost." It doesn't play out precisely in order, but rather like someone thinking back over the past, jumping from then to now, which is what gives the song its powerful realism and its searing hopelessness.

"You're a Big Girl Now" is a more direct, emotional appeal to a former lover in which the third line of each verse ends in a painful howl. Dylan only slightly tempers what is a desperate appeal to Sara to reconsider their split with some poetic observations like, "Time is a jet plane, it moves too fast," but for the most part, every line is like the opening of a raw wound or a bleeding heart. On the page, the lyrics are almost overwrought, but Dylan pulls them off through the sense of risk and vulnerability he imparts in the performances on the album and later on in concert during the Rolling Thunder tour.

The album's epic tune is "Idiot Wind," a song that at base may be just another divorce song, but which embraces a much wider and deeper sense of disappointment mixed with anger. When Dylan took to the concert stage later in the year and began performing the song on the Rolling Thunder Revue, he spit out venom and sparks in a veritable rage. On the album version, drenched with some Al

Kooper–style organ, Dylan combines disgust with heartbreak. Some of it is personal—

It was gravity which pulled us down and destiny which broke us apart
You tamed the lion in my cage but it just wasn't enough to change my
heart

—but nearly as much of it is directed outward, as in the next lines:

Now everything's a little upside down, as a matter of fact the wheels
have stopped,
What's good is bad, what's bad is good, you'll find out when you reach the
top
You're on the bottom.

When a relationship ends, people go through several stages of mourning, including grief and anger. Whereas "You're a Big Girl Now" is grief, it's followed directly by "Idiot Wind," which is anger tempered with empathy, a fervent desire to understand.

You'll never know the hurt I suffered nor the pain I rise above
And I'll never know the same about you, your holiness or your kind of
love,
And it makes me feel so sorry.

The refrain is vicious: "You're an idiot, babe, it's a wonder that you still know how to breathe." But just what is this "idiot wind" that blows through one's mouth, through flowers, through curtains, through teeth, through buttons, through letters, and through dust? I've searched far and wide and never found a literary antecedent for the term. I sat across a dinner table from the renowned literary scholar Christopher Ricks, who is as familiar with John Donne and John Keats as he is with Bob Dylan (having written the best book on Dylan's writing as poetry, *Dylan's Visions of Sin*), and asked him if he knew of any literary precedent for this odd, idiomatic expression. He drew a blank.

This is why I was startled when stumbling upon these words from the Talmud (Tractate Sotah 3a): "Reysh Lakish said, *Eyn adam over aveyre ela im keyn nikhnas bo* ruach shtus" (emphasis mine). In translation: "No one commits a sin unless the *wind of idiocy* enters into him." The *ruach shtus* is the breath of idiocy, or wind of idiocy. Dylan uses both terms: "Idiot *wind,* it's a wonder that you still know how to *breathe.*" The use of the term also implies an equation between idiocy and sin—that the acts of stupidity recounted in the song, acts surpassing the ill-fated maneuvers of the object of scorn in "Like a Rolling Stone," can only be explained as the wages of sin. And in its use of the central image of wind, the song also echoes that earlier anthem that addresses sin and idiocy of a sort—the kind that was "blowin' in the wind."

"Idiot Wind" is one long vituperative accusation ("Someone's got it in for me, they're planting stories in the press," "You hurt the ones that I love best and cover up the truth with lies") and threat ("One day you'll be in the ditch, flies buzzin' around your eyes," "You'll find out when you reach the top / You're on the bottom"). The fact that the "wind of idiocy" is to blame lessens some of the responsibility on the part of the accused (whoever he, she, or they may be); the fact that, in the end, Dylan includes himself in this group—"We're idiots, babe / It's a wonder we can even feed ourselves"—is simply a stroke of genius on his part, resolving the nearly impossible tension that he has built up by releasing it with a dig at himself and a hint of humor, or at least ironic self-reflection.

Apparently the emotional distress expressed on *Blood on the Tracks,* along with the sense of shared responsibility for the breakdown of the marriage—to say nothing of the protestations of eternal love (which will continue throughout his career, long after they are officially divorced)—had their achieved effect on Sara, at least for a few days in March 1975, when she accompanied him to a benefit concert in San Francisco and a postconcert dinner whose guests included Bill Graham and Marlon Brando. The two also reportedly attended a party that month given by rock 'n' roll's reigning lovebirds, Paul and Linda McCartney.

The Dylans split company, if not affections, soon afterward, with

Dylan spending six weeks in the spring in France with his friend the painter David Oppenheim (whose work graced the album jacket of *Blood on the Tracks*). Dylan returned to New York City in the summer, becoming a denizen of what little remained of the Greenwich Village folk music scene, hanging out at clubs including the Bottom Line and the Other End (formerly the Bitter End, newly reopened that June), attending shows by the likes of Victoria Spivey, Patti Smith, Muddy Waters, and old friends Ramblin' Jack Elliott and Bob Neuwirth. Energized by the scene, Dylan began writing songs for his next album and reestablishing a coterie of musician friends, planting the seeds for what would become the Rolling Thunder Revue, a kind of Village-on-the-road barnstorming tour.

On the heels of the critical and commercial success of *Blood on the Tracks,* Columbia Records finally issued an official release of *The Basement Tapes* in June. Compiled, produced, and remixed by Robbie Robertson, the two-LP set included cleaned-up versions of numbers featuring Dylan backed by the Band as well as several numbers by the Band alone. It offered just a small taste of what went down at Big Pink nearly a decade earlier, but the album was widely hailed as a long-awaited masterpiece, just adding to the overall impression at the time that Bob Dylan—once counted out as a Sixties has-been—had returned as a vital, creative force on the music scene.

In July, Dylan began spending time with the theater director Jacques Levy, who had been cowriting songs with Roger McGuinn—including one of McGuinn's signature tunes, "Chestnut Mare"—for years. Levy was an early champion of the work of the playwright Sam Shepard, who would also soon join Dylan's orbit, and was best known as the director of the groundbreaking erotic revue *Oh! Calcutta!* created by Kenneth Tynan and featuring sketches written by Samuel Beckett, John Lennon, the cartoonist Jules Feiffer, Shepard, and others. (The polymathic Levy was also a trained psychoanalyst and clinical psychologist, and went on to become an English professor at Colgate University.) In one of the few such times in his career, Dylan would collaborate with someone on songwriting, and when *Desire* was released, Levy was cocredited with writing seven of the nine songs on the album.

Recorded little more than half a year after *Blood on the Tracks,* the follow-up, *Desire,* had an entirely different sound and feel. Dylan's musicians were again mostly anonymous ones, this time picked up during his days and nights in the Village. The bassist Rob Stoner would anchor the band—a role that Dylan's bassists had played at least since Rick Danko of the Hawks and the Band, through Tony Brown's understated yet intuitive accompaniment on *Blood on the Tracks,* through Tim Drummond's work during the gospel period, and then for the two decades of the 1990s and 2000s, when Tony Garnier would basically run the show for Dylan. Stoner brought along his drummer, Howie Wyeth, whose crisp, characteristic playing, full of rim-shots, would give *Desire* and Rolling Thunder a boost all its own. On record, Emmylou Harris's colorful, twang-laden harmony vocals would achieve an organic blend with Dylan that always eluded Joan Baez's crystalline, arch soprano. And finally, Scarlet Rivera's fiddle would give *Desire* its haunting, gypsylike overtones, which, with support from Allen Ginsberg's liner notes, titled "Songs of Redemption," some heard as an Eastern European, Jewish influence.

The album opens with "Hurricane," which recounts the story of the boxer Rubin "Hurricane" Carter, who was convicted of a triple murder committed in the course of an armed robbery of a Paterson, New Jersey, bar in 1966. Dylan had read Carter's memoir, *The Sixteenth Round,* earlier in the summer, and with Levy, constructed a narrative that simultaneously told the story of the night in question and the subsequent trial and guilty verdict (with some poetic license) while making the case for Carter's innocence and tying his conviction to racism. The eight-and-a-half-minute song was released as a single in November 1975, a couple of months before the album came out. Coming as Dylan's first topical song since his 1971 ode to George Jackson, about the Black Panther–cum–prison activist and author of *Soledad Brother,* who was killed by prison guards during an alleged escape attempt, "Hurricane" was greeted by some as a "return" to protest music for Dylan. The song wasn't so much an act of protest as it was part of a campaign of political action, which, along with the intervention of other celebrities including Muhammad Ali, succeeded in bringing enough attention to Carter's claims of innocence to provoke a retrial. (Denzel Washington received an Oscar nomination for Best Actor for his portrayal of Carter in the 1999 film *The Hurricane*, which employed Dylan's song in its soundtrack.)

If "Hurricane" was an attempt to glorify someone who was falsely accused, its mirror or twin, "Joey," was an attempt at finding the human story beneath the tale of a vicious gangster. Dylan and Levy had spent an evening over dinner with the actor Jerry Orbach, a longtime friend of the slain gangster Joey Gallo, who regaled the guests with stories of "Crazy Joe." It's easy to see why Dylan would be empathic toward this temperamental killer, who used his time in prison to study painting, the French existentialists, and German nihilists. Gallo also stood apart from his fellow Italian mobsters in his good relations with African Americans, both before entering prison and while in stir. As Dylan sang, "His closest friends were black men 'cause they seemed to understand / What it's like to be in society with a shackle on your hand." It's an odd song, but Rivera's fiddle and accordion by Dom Cortese give it the musical flavor of Little Italy, making it fit well within the overall urban-folk program of *Desire*. While Dylan would often, perhaps bafflingly, return to "Joey" in concert throughout his career, *Desire*'s more memorable songs include "Isis," "Oh, Sister," and "One More Cup of Coffee."

In his liner notes, referring to "One More Cup of Coffee," Allen Ginsberg wrote, "voice lifts in Hebraic cantillation never before heard in U.S. song, ancient blood singing." Dylan uses techniques characteristic of cantorial singing on this song: the trademark bends, trills, and breaks in notes that are unique to Jewish music, and the polar opposite of so many other American traditions, for example, the smooth, sweeping melismas of gospel, the moaning of the blues, the full-throated hollers of Appalachian folk, and the soaring swells of country singing. On "One More Cup of Coffee," for the first and only time on record, Dylan seemingly channels, as Ginsberg aptly puts it, the sound of his forefathers—perhaps sounds he had heard more recently in the Brooklyn synagogues he is said to have visited, or sounds he remembered from synagogue visits of his childhood.

Specifically, in each couplet, Dylan takes one syllable in the last word of the first phrase and stretches it out over three or four separate notes, bouncing it up and down through fleet microtones—notes in between the ones on a piano keyboard. He had never done this sort of singing before and has never done it since; there was just something in the sound of the song, or the effect he was trying to put forth, that made him sing in this entirely singular manner. Scarlet Rivera plays fiddle in a similar fashion on this song. She wasn't really the gypsy fiddler she was so often said to be, but she also nailed the sound, so that no less an authority than the music critic Nat Hentoff, writing at the time, called this klezmer music, using a descriptor that hadn't yet even gained currency in the Jewish music world, it being still a few years before the klezmer revival would properly begin (with an album called *Jewish Klezmer Music* by the mandolinist and clarinetist Andy Statman, who played with Dylan back in 1972 on the sessions for *Doug Sahm and Band*).

As a sixteen-year-old, I was so struck by the sound of this number that I sat my grandfather down in front of my stereo and, without telling him what he was about to hear, asked him to listen to one song. My grandfather Bernard Peretz, who immigrated to America from Russia in the 1920s, had been a cantor. I figured if anyone could appreciate Dylan's singing on this number, he could, even though he had virtually no exposure to or understanding of rock music or American folk music (although he was acquainted with classical music, opera, and Broadway show tunes—particularly the score from *Fiddler on the Roof*). Before the end of the three-verse, four-minute song, tears were streaming down my grandfather's face—neither a response I expected nor one I had intended to elicit. "What is this?" my grandfather asked. "Who is this?" He left my house with my copy of *Desire,* the Anthony Scaduto biography, and my copy of Stephen Pickering's self-styled "midrash," *Bob Dylan Approximately.* He read the books and returned them, but *Desire* stayed in his record collection until the day he died in 1981. (I bought another copy of *Desire* in the meantime.)

Dylan recorded the last of the album's nine songs on the final day of July. With his estranged wife standing in the control booth, he launched into a new song that she hadn't yet heard. If Dylan could put distance between himself and the songs on *Blood on the Tracks*, if he could claim they were not necessarily autobiographical nor about his marriage, he dropped all pretense on this number, which he loaded with specific details from his life and marriage and called "Sara." Thus, there was no doubt who the song was about, nor who he was addressing in the refrain:

> *Sara, Sara*
> *Whatever made you want to change your mind?*

The song continues in this vein, with images of their children at play and reading them fairy tales (the cheapest of shots, really, to invoke memories of blissful parenthood when the issues that separated the two of them presumably had nothing to do with their kids), references to romantic European vacations, addresses of homes they shared ("on Lily Pond Lane"), and, in the ultimate reveal, an unprecedented bit of autobiography-in-song, confessing that he had written "Sad-Eyed Lady of the Lowlands" for her.

The song's six choruses are all different, but they all are direct invocations of love and apology. Dylan ends the song on the bleakest of notes, with a picture of a deserted beach—no more children playing, no more happy family—and then simply begs Sara to stay with him. If Dylan's performance weren't so sincere, if the emotions weren't so naked and so raw, this would have been the most maudlin song ever written. Instead, it succeeds as a magnificent love song, one that successfully transcends the specifics of his situation and relationship, one that speaks to and of the pain and anguish of heartbreak and separation in a universal manner.

Sara was apparently moved enough by the studio performance to accompany her husband to Minnesota a couple of days later, where Dylan attended the marriage of a cousin and visited other friends in the area. Just a few weeks later, he flew to Chicago, where he and Rivera, Stoner, and Wyeth performed three songs for a PBS-TV tribute to John Hammond. Dylan played "Simple Twist of Fate," which the musicians had never played with him before, and debuted "Hurricane" and "Oh, Sister" from his upcoming album. After a short stay in Malibu with Sara, Dylan returned to New York, where he put the finishing touches on *Desire* and began recruiting musicians to join him on the Rolling Thunder Revue, which left New York with several busloads of musicians, a film crew, and stagehands on October 27, headed for a motel in North Falmouth, Massachusetts.

The Rolling Thunder Revue, which actually consisted of two distinct concert tours, was many things: a guerrilla-style road show influenced by 1960s street theater; a movable feast and party; an attempt to recapture the hootenanny spirit of Greenwich Village in its folk heyday by reuniting many of the key figures from that era and putting them all on a traveling stage; an expression of bicentennial fervor; a setting for Dylan's attempt to make his great film masterpiece and a means to bankroll the film; an effort to spread awareness of and raise funds for Hurricane Carter's defense fund; an attempt to capitalize on the popularity of two of Dylan's most successful albums by touring behind *Blood on the Tracks* and *Desire*; an escape from the painful reality of a marriage that was dissolving; an attempt to salvage that marriage through performances almost wholly dedicated to winning back his wife through song; and an attempt to create a new kind of never-ending concert tour in which musicians would just drop in and drop out as their schedules allowed.

Overall, the balance sheet wound up in Dylan's favor, despite several setbacks along the way. His dream that a phone line would be set up which superstar rockers like Neil Young, Eric Clapton, and Keith Richards could call to find out where the next show was taking place (many of the concerts on the first leg of the tour were announced only a day or two in advance) and drop in to perform never materialized. While he was successful in making Hurricane Carter's case a cause célèbre, culminating in a sold-out, star-studded Night of the Hurricane benefit concert at Madison Square Garden, the victory seemed pyrrhic when Carter was reconvicted after a retrial (the conviction was eventually thrown out by a federal appeals court). The good feelings initially created by Dylan's inviting a host of Greenwich Village folkies, who had been somewhat left in the dust by his rise to pop star heights, to share in his spotlight—including Ramblin' Jack Elliott, Bob Neuwirth, and David Blue—soon devolved, as these things almost always do, into bitterness and back-stabbing, as egotism replaced harmony, bringing old resentments to the surface, as Dylan remained aloof from many of these people (although not all). Elliott found himself uninvited to the second leg of the tour merely by omission, his place in the roster taken by the Texas singer-songwriter Kinky Friedman (who led a group called the Texas Jewboys). Phil Ochs, who always had a troubled, competitive relationship with Dylan, was plagued by manic depression, personality disorders and drug and alcohol addiction; in no shape to take part in the tour, he committed suicide at his sister's home in April 1976, casting a pall on the proceedings.

The tour did, however, reunite Dylan with his erstwhile duet partner and former lover, Joan Baez. Given their tormented history, it was a questionable move on their part personally—especially at a time when Dylan was presumably trying to salvage his marriage. Why invite the woman with whom he was publicly identified as a lover—one who thought she *was* his lover, when out of the blue she discovered that Dylan had married someone named Sara? Artistically, though, it made huge sense for the two to reunite, especially in the wake of Baez's career-topping album, *Diamonds and Rust,* the title track of which was clearly addressed to Dylan. Baez's participation in the tour also figured largely in *Renaldo and Clara,* including her role in several remarkably intimate scenes with Dylan and Sara that seemed wholly lifted from real life.

Other longtime friends and acquaintances who came along on the tour included Roger McGuinn, whose career got a boost from his renewed identification with Dylan. McGuinn went on to make several albums with members of the Rolling Thunder band, including one called *ThunderByrd.* Allen Ginsberg was brought along in large part for comic relief and for blessing the tour with his Beatific presence; he also wound up playing in several key scenes of *Renaldo and Clara.* Sam Shepard was drafted to write scenes for the film, which turned out to be an impossible, frustrating task, as Dylan had his own vision of what he wanted the film to be, which mostly consisted of improvised and ad-libbed scenes about Bob Dylan played out by musicians, actors, and tour hangers-on. Shepard soon left the traveling roadshow, but capitalized on his time spent with Dylan in his tour journal, *Rolling Thunder Logbook*.

Other guests who joined the tour for one-offs or short stints included Joni Mitchell, Arlo Guthrie, Gordon Lightfoot, Ronnie Hawkins, and his (and Dylan's) former bass player, Rick Danko of the Band. Even Dylan's mother, Beatty Zimmerman, joined in the regular all-ensemble finale, "This Land Is Your Land," after being serenaded by Joan Baez and her son in a rarely heard version of "Mama, You Been on My Mind."

The tour kicked off on October 30 with a concert at the War Memorial Auditorium in Plymouth, Massachusetts. The venue was chosen for its inherent symbolism, and much was made in *Renaldo and Clara* of the "landing" of the revue at Plymouth Rock. Organized by Dylan's boyhood friend Lou Kemp, the tour proceeded throughout New England and the Northeast, playing thirty shows in theaters, college auditoriums, and small-town convention centers, with little official tour publicity but plenty of media attention, especially given the pairing of Dylan and Baez and the fact that this was the first Dylan tour in nearly two years, and the first concerts that included songs from *Blood on the Tracks* and *Desire*. This first leg of the revue culminated in the Night of the Hurricane benefit concert in New York City on December 8, and *Desire* was finally released on January 16, 1976.

The tour band featured the core group from *Desire*—Rob Stoner, Howie Wyeth, and Scarlet Rivera, augmented by guitarists T-Bone Burnett and Steve Soles and the mandolinist David Mansfield. The most surprising addition to the band was Mick Ronson, best known as David Bowie's guitarist and bandleader, and Ronson's incongruous style, from his wardrobe to the way he played guitar, lent the proceedings a unique "glam-folk" aura. It also meant that this was a guitar-heavy crew; with the addition of Dylan there were four guitarists, and they were often supplemented by Neuwirth, McGuinn, or others who all together formed a kind of guitar army. Dylan also enlisted the country singer Ronee Blakley to sing the harmony parts that Emmylou Harris laid down on *Desire*; Blakley, who had just appeared in Robert Altman's critically acclaimed film *Nashville,* about the country music business, also found her talents as an actress exploited for *Renaldo and Clara.*

Jacques Levy came along to help give the show a theatrical flair—the stage set included a Rolling Thunder backdrop and living room furniture to give it a warm, cozy feel. Levy acted as stage manager, figuring out how best to pace the show and how to deal with the many comings and goings of guests who would step up for short minisets in between the main performers, Dylan and Baez. But the theatricality was mainly to be found in Dylan's animated performance. If he was martial and stentorian two years earlier, leading his own private army called the Band, here he was alone and on fire, or breathing fire: a small, skinny projectile of naked emotion. With the aid of the thundering rhythms of Stoner, Wyeth, and the percussionist Luther Rix, Dylan spat out songs like "Isis" and "Hurricane" as if a gun were being held to his head. On the second leg of the tour, documented on the live album *Hard Rain,* he'd take this even further on numbers such as "Shelter from the Storm" and "Maggie's Farm." Songs that formerly gained their power through subtle nuance, humor, and wordplay now were fired like cruise missiles. If Dylan's electric sets of 1966 with the Hawks were the musical equivalent of heroin or acid, the Rolling Thunder aesthetic was all tense, jittery, heart-thumping cocaine.

This isn't to say that it was all thunder and no rain. Dylan turned in heartrending versions of "Simple Twist of Fate," "Oh, Sister," and "Sara," and a stunning solo rendition of "Tangled Up in Blue," included in *Renaldo and Clara* and made into a music video. But even those numbers were juiced with an additional power boost, a lethal shot of adrenaline that raised the stakes of the desperation encoded within the tunes' melodies and lyrics, so that in no small way, his performances attained the level of public catharsis, all in the service of pleading with Sara to take him back. And that dynamic would emerge as the central, unifying theme of *Renaldo and Clara,* too; after four exhilarating but exhausting hours, the film builds to a climax as the camera lingers on Sara to the sound of Dylan singing "Sad-Eyed Lady of the Lowlands."

Where the first leg of the tour through New England was marked by its informal, easygoing approach, the second leg, previewed at the Houston Astrodome on January 25—a concert billed as Night of the Hurricane II that included Stevie Wonder but not Joan Baez and that earned a measly $50,000 for the cause—had an entirely different feel. While playing the small theaters and community centers of the Northeast was a stroke of artistic genius in a region owned by Dylan, a place where one local radio station could announce the day before a concert that Dylan and friends would be playing the local auditorium and easily guarantee a sellout, that didn't pay the bills. Nor would that approach necessarily translate throughout the South, where outside of a few major cities like Atlanta and New Orleans, Dylan had never really spent much time cultivating an audience (keep in mind that, already a decade and a half into his career, Rolling Thunder was really only Dylan's third nationwide concert tour). The South hardly knew him as a live performer, and this was to present the tour with problems when, having forsaken small venues for arenas and stadiums in the hopes of upping the gross revenues and bankrolling the snowballing budget for his film, the tour's energy dissipated before less-than-sold-out crowds and the loss of camaraderie and purpose that originally drove it. The tour proper kicked off on April 18 in Lakeland, Florida, and after playing nearly two dozen dates mostly in Florida and Texas over the course of five weeks (several shows were cancelled due to poor ticket sales), the tour came to a grinding, disappointing halt the night after Dylan's thirty-fifth birthday with a concert played to a half-filled 17,000-seat arena in Salt Lake City, Utah. By that time, the musicians were exhausted, if not demoralized, by the lack of enthusiasm on the part of the audience and the stark contrast between the aesthetic of the arena and stadium shows that dispensed in large part with the theatricality and congeniality of the indoor theater shows of the previous fall's tour through New England. Heavy drug use among the musicians may have also taken its toll.

The tour did see its share of success, however. In mid-March, Rubin Carter was granted a retrial, although perhaps that took some of the wind out of the sails of subsequent concerts, since publicizing Carter's plight was no longer an immediate goal. Several concerts were filmed for an unprecedented TV network broadcast, scoring Dylan the front cover of *TV Guide* and spawning *Hard Rain.* (The album's title was a pun of sorts, referring to the song "A Hard Rain's a-Gonna Fall," but also to the torrential downpour that took place during the outdoor concert in Fort Collins, Colorado.) While the single-LP live album captured the ferocity of Rolling Thunder's glam-folk sound, it disappointed fans who were looking forward to a promised three-LP set of songs recorded during the first leg of the tour. This recording would eventually be released in 2002 as a two-CD set, *Live 1975 (Bootleg Series Vol. 5).* The TV show itself brought Dylan before an entirely new audience, no doubt many of whom were befuddled by the strange sounds, Dylan's whiteface makeup, and the Arabian-style burnooses that Dylan and the musicians now sported out west instead of the cowboy hats that were de rigueur back east. Those who looked closely at the backdrop behind the band may also have wondered why a Star of David was featured prominently among other hand-drawn illustrations.

With Rolling Thunder put to bed, Dylan took time to regroup. With reportedly hundreds of hours of raw film footage to go through, he spent the greater part of the next year and a half editing *Renaldo and Clara,* which finally saw release in January 1978. In the meantime, Dylan's only concert appearance until he ventured out again on a lengthy world tour in 1978 was at the Last Waltz, the Band's farewell concert on Thanksgiving Day, 1976, at Winterland in San Francisco—the very first theater at which the group had performed as the Band. The elegiac film of the concert made by Martin Scorsese includes guest appearances by a who's who of rock 'n' roll stars performing with the Band, including Eric Clapton, Neil Young, Muddy Waters, Joni Mitchell, Neil Diamond, and Van Morrison. But all of this is mere prologue, as the film builds to its climax featuring the reunion of Dylan with his old bandmates, reviving "Baby Let Me Follow You Down" and "I Don't Believe You

(She Acts Like We Never Have Met)" from the 1966 tour and performing "Forever Young" from *Planet Waves*. When it was released in 1978, Scorsese's film was hailed as the greatest rock concert film ever, and it remains a signpost of an era as well as a fitting tribute to the glory that was the Band.

Dylan fans had to make do with listening to their Bob Dylan records for the next year and a half, during which time he was embroiled with divorce proceedings and custody battles with Sara (she finally filed for divorce in March 1977) while working with Howard Alk to make sense of the miles of film, including concert footage and dozens of improvised scenes, they had recorded on the Rolling Thunder tour. Otherwise, 1977 was something of a lost year for Dylan as public figure; the two significant moves he made that year were to sign with Jerry Weintraub, Neil Diamond's manager, in spring 1977, and to take out a long-term lease on a converted warehouse in Santa Monica. Rundown Studios, as he called it, would provide Dylan with a kind of headquarters—part rec room, part rehearsal space, plus recording studio—from which to plan his strategy and stage his moves as a recording and touring artist for the next five years.

Renaldo and Clara opened in just a few movie theaters in New York and Los Angeles on January 25, 1978. Within a week, the movie was pulled from distribution, the casualty of scathing reviews bordering on the sadistic. New York City's leading alternative newsweekly, *The Village Voice*, considered the film important enough to send five critics to review it, each of whom came back with nothing good to say. Reviewers complained that it was an indecipherable mess, technically inept, badly filmed, a self-indulgent expression of Dylan's narcissism, and, at nearly four hours' running time, way too long.

The treatment *Renaldo and Clara* received at the hands of the press apparently stung Dylan in a way that perhaps no other bad reviews ever had before. From conception through filming and editing the finished product, he labored on the movie on and off over two years. He clearly had great hopes that the film might be the crowning achievement of his career; not for nothing did the film open with a performance of him singing "When I Paint My Masterpiece."

Faced with the commercial failure of *Renaldo and Clara,* plus the mounting legal bills incurred in negotiating the huge marital settlement that Sara eventually won, Dylan did the only thing he knew how to do: he took to the road again on a worldwide tour that some wag dubbed the "Alimony Tour." This time out, perhaps with the input of Jerry Weintraub, Dylan decided to present a slick, well-rehearsed stage show, with a large band playing renditions of his most popular songs as well as more recent tunes. After several weeks of rehearsal, the tour kicked off with a weeklong residency at Budokan, a martial arts arena–turned–concert venue in Tokyo. Dylan's band included veterans of the Rolling Thunder ensemble (Rob Stoner, Steve Soles, David Mansfield) plus the guitarist Billy Cross, the former King Crimson drummer Ian Wallace, the keyboardist Alan Pasqua, the saxophonist Steve Douglas, and, for the first time ever in concert, a trio of female backup singers.

It all added up to a new sound and aesthetic, very different from anything heard previously. And while audiences and critics throughout the Far East, the South Pacific, and Europe were thrilled to be seeing Dylan—his Japan concerts were his first ever in that nation, the European and Australian shows the first since 1966—when the tour arrived back in the United States, it was greeted with brickbats. Dylan was accused of having "gone Las Vegas" or "disco," and not entirely without merit, as he appeared for the first time in the sort of glitzy, coordinated white body suit one would expect from Neil Diamond, and the pacing, stage patter, and some of the song arrangements suggested an effort was being made (however clumsy) to court a more mainstream audience. Some of the arrangements, as heard on *Bob Dylan at Budokan,* the live album recorded at the tour's outset, *did* turn Dylan classics into bouncy, easy-listening tunes. Numbers like "All I Really Want to Do," "Blowin' in the Wind," and "I Want You" were stripped of all virtue and rendered as just so much lounge music; you could imagine hearing these songs played this way by some combo in an anonymous hotel bar. And Dylan even sang a few songs into a handheld microphone, without playing guitar, as if he were Elvis Presley or Frank Sinatra—or Neil Diamond.

(The Neil Diamond–isms, perhaps a consequence of Dylan having hired Jerry Weintraub as his manager, were also ironic, given the oft-told story of an exchange the two purportedly had at the Last Waltz concert. After his miniset, Diamond supposedly walked off-stage into the wings, where Dylan was waiting to go on, and said to him, "Try topping *that*," to which Dylan allegedly replied, "What do you want me to do? Go out there and fall asleep?")

By the time Dylan arrived at the Boston Garden in October 1978, he was facing his critics down directly from the stage. About two thirds of the way through the show, he took the opportunity to say to the crowd, "I hope you don't think this is Las Vegas music, or disco music, because you know it isn't." But there was even something in his tone, the manner in which he said "because you *know* it isn't," that suggested he was trying to put something over on everyone. Adding to the sense of ironic detachment, Dylan inscrutably followed this up immediately by saying, "And now I'd like to introduce to you the members of the band"—something he'd rarely done in the past—and took the next five minutes to go through the ensemble, giving each musician his Las Vegas–style moment in the spotlight. And on *At Budokan*, Dylan does that cheap Las Vegas thing on the final song where he says thank you and good night to the audience, leaving the stage while the band plays on.

To his credit, however, some of the new song arrangements were fascinating. Dylan recast several of his best-known tunes, including "Don't Think Twice, It's All Right" and "Knockin' on Heaven's Door," to a reggae beat. "It's Alright Ma (I'm Only Bleeding)" was recast as funk-metal—and worked in that fashion—and the gorgeous love song "Love Minus Zero/No Limit" was carried along on the winds of flute and mandolin. Dylan also teased the crowd with his introduction of the as-yet-unreleased song "Is Your Love in Vain?" by saying, "This is an unrecorded song; see if you can guess which one it is." At least he still had a sense of humor.

Dylan had begun writing a batch of new songs in late 1977 and continued coming up with the numbers that would find a home on his next studio album, *Street Legal,* released in June 1978. For the first time since working with the Hawks, Dylan went into the studio with a touring band to record an album, bringing the musicians to Rundown Studios in Santa Monica, on a break from the tour. By this time, Stoner had left the group and been replaced by Elvis Presley's former bassist Jerry Scheff (a hiring that, for all Scheff's talent, merely added fuel to those accusing Dylan of having "sold out" or "gone Elvis").

Underneath the muddy murk and unsteady rhythms of *Street Legal* were the makings of a brilliant album, with some of Dylan's best writing since the 1960s. It was certainly a more ambitious album than *Desire,* featuring several Sixties-style epics as well as some tightly written love songs—and at least one joyous hate song. Overall, *Street Legal* was a transitional album, something of a summary statement encapsulating the work he did in the 1970s from *New Morning* through *Desire.* The sound of *Street Legal* was closer to *Desire* than *At Budokan,* although it hinted at the sound of things to come, especially in its use of a female choir throughout.

The album kicked off with "Changing of the Guards," whose very title hints at transition, and whose first line, "Sixteen years," leaps out at a listener as a biographical tidbit. What year is this? 1978. What year counts as Dylan's debut? His first album was released in 1962, sixteen years earlier. So Dylan sets the scene, for the song and the album, as a kind of taking stock of what's gone down.

> *Sixteen years,*
> *Sixteen banners united over the field*
> *Where the good shepherd grieves.*
> *Desperate men, desperate women divided,*
> *Spreading their wings 'neath the falling leaves.*

Dylan sets up a dichotomy here between the sixteen united banners (presumably representing sixteen groups, or tribes of some sort, united behind a grieving leader, a shepherd of men—could be Dylan; could be one of the biblical forefathers or prophets, many of whom were shepherds) and the desperate women and men who are divided. Are they divided between each other, men against women, as entire groups? Or are they individual men and women divided against each other, politically or emotionally? Is it Bob against Sara?

The next verse takes us back sixteen years again, to when Bob Dylan first makes his presence known to the world:

> *Fortune calls*
> *I stepped forth from the shadows, to the marketplace,*
> *Merchants and thieves, hungry for power, my last deal gone down.*
> *She's smelling sweet like the meadows where she was born,*
> *On midsummer's eve, near the tower.*

Dylan is the one plucked from Greenwich Village folk music obscurity—the "shadows"—and given a worldwide platform, at a price. Others cling to him, hoping to catch a ride on his express as a way to boost themselves financially or otherwise, and he opts out in favor of a woman. Perhaps this is a poetic reckoning of his meteoric rise to fame and his sudden decision—provoked by a motorcycle accident, a nervous breakdown, or a simple choice—to go on hiatus in summer 1966, to get off the proverbial hamster wheel, and to settle into a life of domestic virtue and bliss, raising a family with Sara.

> *The cold-blooded moon.*
> *The captain waits above the celebration*
> *. . . The captain is down but still believing that his love will be repaid.*

Dylan is the reluctant captain, beset upon by merchants and thieves intent on exploitation, refusing to take part in the celebration that was Woodstock. He knew there was something bigger than all of this, symbolized by that moon, as prophesied in the book of Joel 3:3–4: "I will set portents in the heavens and on earth: blood and fire and pillars of smoke; the sun will turn into darkness and the moon into blood [red], before the great and awesome day of G-d comes." This image of the bloodred moon recurs later in the album.

Dylan portrays a traditional Jewish wedding struggling with pagan influences:

They shaved her head.
She was torn between Jupiter and Apollo.
A messenger arrived with a black nightingale.
I seen her on the stairs and I couldn't help but follow.
Follow her down past the fountain where they lifted her veil.

In traditional Orthodox Jewish weddings, a bride's hair is shorn and replaced by a wig, so that when it grows back no man other than her husband can look upon her tresses. And for thousands of years, before the husband accepted his betrothed as his wife, he lifted her veil, to make sure that she was his betrothed, so as not to be victimized in the manner of the biblical Jacob, who wound up wedded to his betrothed's sister, Leah, instead of his intended bride, Rachel, due to the deceit of their father, Lavan. Both of these rituals—the cutting of the bride's hair and the lifting of her veil—became highly stylized by the nineteenth century, and they took place hours or days before the actual wedding ceremony.

Through the next three verses, the narrator continues to struggle through challenges on and off a symbolic battlefield:

The endless road and the wailing of chimes
The empty rooms where her memory is protected
Where the angels' voices whisper to the souls of previous times

refers to the impossibility of maintaining a relationship as a touring musician, yet the lovers continue to attempt to find refuge in each other's company even while they struggle with each other:

She's begging to know what measures he now will be taking
He's pulling her down and she's clutching on to his long golden locks.

In the end, he chooses transcendence over the obligations of the "marketplace," as the day of reckoning approaches:

Gentlemen, he said,
I don't need your organization, I've shined your shoes,

I've moved your mountains and marked your cards
But Eden is burning, either brace yourself for elimination
Or else your hearts must have the courage for the changing of the guards.

It's a short leap from the warning expressed in these last two lines to "It may be the devil or it may be the Lord / But you're gonna have to serve somebody," which will be recorded just a year later. In the meantime, the song concludes on a note pitting the Jewish mystical experience against the idolatrous one, represented here by the tarot:

Peace will come
With tranquility and splendor on the wheels of fire
But will bring us no reward when her false idols fall
And cruel death surrenders with its pale ghost retreating
Between the King and the Queen of Swords.

The image of Ezekiel's chariot, first explicated by Dylan in "This Wheel's on Fire," recurs here as a harbinger of the Messianic age. But those who cling to "false idols," pagan practices such as tarot, and the voodoo Dylan sings about in the next song on *Street Legal,* will not have a share in the world to come.

That next song, "New Pony," packs a nasty attack on Sara in the garment of an earthy, sensual blues powered by a funky bass line by Jerry Scheff and understated blue notes by Billy Cross. Not only does it accuse her of practicing the black arts and warning her of payback for doing so, it actually compares her to the Devil himself. The very first line is, "I had a pony, her name was Lucifer." Dylan hardly attempts to disguise the song's reference to Sara when in the second verse he sings, "Sometimes I wonder what's going on with Miss X," as in, ex-wife. "She's got such a sweet disposition / I never know what the poor girl's gonna do to me next."

Dylan continues in this vein:

Everybody says you're using voodoo, I've seen your feet walk by themselves
Oh, baby but that God that you've been prayin' to
Gonna give ya back what you're wishin' on someone else.

This portrait of Sara stands in stark contrast to the one on *Desire*, where she was hailed as "sweet virgin angel, sweet love of my life" and "radiant jewel, mystical wife." The angel is now devilish and the mystic a practitioner of black arts.

If this sounds like a vicious or vindictive effort on Dylan's part to embarrass Sara publicly—or a misguided, self-righteous attack that says more about Dylan's state of mind than anything about Sara—he partially redeems himself in the end by implicating himself: "You're so nasty and you're so vain / But I swear I love ya, yes I do." What passes for the song's refrain is the haunting repetition by the girl singers of the phrase "How much longer," which hangs in the air, floating like an unspoken thought bubble.

"No Time to Think" is distinguished by a descending violin melody by David Mansfield that mirrors the song's lyrics, which spiral downward to a pessimistic conclusion about the individual's ability to effect change on society or himself. Through much of the song, Dylan seems to be singing to or about himself—"You fight for the throne and you travel alone"—again revisiting his career, his relationship with Sara, and his struggle for inner calm against the demands that leave him, as the refrain goes, "no time to think," and spiritually adrift: "You can't find no salvation, you have no expectations / Anytime, anyplace, anywhere." The song is peppered with images of figures of secular and spiritual authority—judges, empresses, magicians, warlords, priestesses—and of royalty, as are many of the songs on *Street Legal*, sometimes with specific reference to tarot, other times as symbols of authority. Near the end of the song, the image of the bloody moon recurs—"You turn around for one real last glimpse of Camille / 'Neath the moon shinin' bloody and pink"—again tying the song to redemption day, which, Dylan seems to say, is coming, ready or not (whereas within a year or two, he will pose that readiness for the day of the Lord as a challenge, as an opportunity that you either accept or else face the consequences).

Other songs on the album, including "Baby, Stop Crying," "True Love Tends to Forget," and "Is Your Love in Vain?" could well be exhibits in transitional relationships. They could be love songs, but they're not; they're postlove songs, or jaded love songs, or love songs from the point of view of one all too aware of the treacherous mine-field that awaits the unsuspecting lover.

Given its subtitle, "Señor (Tales of Yankee Power)" is sometimes read as a meditation on U.S. colonialism in Latin America, and the musical arrangement, with hints of mariachi-style horns and strings, supports this reading. However, there's another level to the song, in which it is a monologue delivered by the narrator to the ulti-mate Señor, a word whose linguistic roots trace back to the Latin for "lord." The second line alone suggests the narrator has the end of days on his mind:

> *Señor, Señor, can you tell me where we're headin'?*
> *Lincoln County Road or Armageddon?*

Dylan peppers the song with allusions to Sara ("Do you know where she is hidin'?"), European conquest ("There's an iron cross still hang-ing down from around her neck"), and old songs: he sings "There's a wicked wind still blowin' on that upper deck," reviving the imagery from "Blowin' in the Wind" and "Idiot Wind," tying them together and restating the importance of the wind, and wind as an evil force. But the most convincing reading of the song is as a prophet's com-plaint. He's tired of prophesying to no effect, tired of waiting for everything that G-d has said would happen and hasn't. He's ready to take the next step, which is why he asks if it's to "Lincoln County Road or Armageddon?" The prophet is exhausted, tired of waiting, wants to know what the conditions will be when they reach their ultimate destination, and what he can do to bring about change sooner rather than later. In the meantime, he feels his efforts toward admonishing the people are all for naught: "You know their hearts are as hard as leather," he complains. He can't move them, can't make them feel, can't effect any change in their behavior or understanding of how serious are the stakes.

Finally, he just requests that they bring it to an end, to its con-clusion. And he does so with language that acknowledges that the prophet is him, Dylan, and that his mode of prophecy is performance, and therefore asks to be relieved of his duties onstage—literally asks permission to unplug his guitar and microphone and walk off the stage and out of the public spotlight, where nothing makes any sense:

> *Let's overturn these tables*
> *Disconnect these cables*
> *This place don't make sense to me no more.*

Of all *Street Legal* songs, this one became the fan favorite and the one that Dylan continued to perform sporadically throughout the ensuing decades. The album was filled out with songs that included an attempt to recapture the pop charts, a "Lay Lady Lay"–type tune called "Baby, Stop Crying," and "We Better Talk This Over," another mature look at divorce that finds the narrator reconciled to the marital breakup, albeit not without some bitterness and regret: "The vows that we kept are now broken and swept / 'Neath the bed where we slept." He even acknowledges the need to enter a new phase in his life: "Oh, babe, time for a new transition," using the language of self-help psychology, before once again ruing his inability to change the situation, once again invoking pagan arts:

> *I wish I was a magician.*
> *I would wave a wand and tie back the bond*
> *That we've both gone beyond.*

The song also includes the oft-remarked-upon line "I'm exiled, you can't convert me," which many have taken as an expression of Dylan's self-identification with the Jewish people—an exilic nation—and a refusal to remake his status as something other than a Jew, making his efforts of the next few years all the more puzzling.

EIGHT

BURNT OFFERINGS

In an interview with *Rolling Stone* upon the release of the film *Renaldo and Clara*, Bob Dylan told Jonathan Cott, "Those guys are really wise. I tell you, I've heard gurus and yogis and philosophers and politicians and doctors and lawyers, teachers of all kinds . . . and these rabbis really had something going."

This made it all the more difficult to fathom when word first started leaking out in early 1979 that Bob Dylan had become a "born-again Christian" and was recording an album of songs testifying to a newfound faith in Jesus. To admirers who remained locked in their view of Dylan as an avatar of leftward opposition to the political mainstream, this seemed the worst kind of betrayal at a time when the religious right was growing increasingly powerful in American politics, culminating in the election of Ronald Reagan as president in 1980. To those who counted on Dylan to maintain his voice of independence as expressed through absurdist poetry ("Don't follow leaders / Watch the parkin' meters"), the idea that he would surrender his independence of thought and subscribe to *any* "organized religion"—much less the evangelical strain of Christianity that was often termed "fundamentalist," implying the abject surrender of one's individuality to a greater ideology (no less than to any

-ism, and something for which Dylan caught minor flak in the early 1970s when he was accused of being a right-wing follower of *Zion-ism*), and one that was associated with a litany of conservative social policies (anti-abortion, pro-guns, blind patriotism)—came as a huge letdown. And for Jewish fans, as for any Jews, for such a publicly identified and beloved Jewish figure to turn his back on the faith of his forefathers and declare his allegiance with a supersessionist Christianity was intolerable; some took it so personally they swore off Dylan for years or even decades to come, far beyond the isolated, year-and-a-half period that Dylan wrote, recorded, and performed original songs that drew their inspiration from the story of Jesus as recounted in the Gospels.

With time and hindsight, everyone's reactions and interpretations were at best misguided and at worst utterly wrongheaded—except perhaps for those who greeted the albums with mild indifference or at least with admiration that Dylan had finally made a record that *sounded* good purely from a technical point of view. With rare exception, Dylan's working process in making recordings was simply to document the playing of the songs by a group of musicians, typically pick-up musicians who ordinarily had little if any time to rehearse and often didn't even know what songs were going to be played when or in what keys. The result, in his greatest recordings like "Like a Rolling Stone," was the brilliance of spontaneous inspiration on the part of Dylan and his band.

Equally as often, however, it meant that Dylan's brilliance as a writer and vocalist begged listeners' (to say nothing of critics') indulgence: Dylan, unlike his contemporaries in the Beatles, the Rolling Stones, or even the host of so-called New Dylans that appeared on the scene in the 1970s, never opted to use the recording studio itself as part of his instrumental palette. He had little patience for multiple takes, overdubs, and painstaking efforts at mixing and remixing (although he did at times take advantage of all of these techniques, but never to the extent of his peers, and with rare exception, in efforts that too often resulted in his worrying the songs to death), preferring to let the recordings stand as documents of the spontaneous jam sessions that took place in the recording studio. (Dylan was to vary this practice somewhat in the 1980s and 1990s, turning over the raw tracks of *Empire Burlesque* to the disco engineer Arthur Baker, who put a very un-Dylanlike contemporary dance sheen on several tracks, and working with art-rock producer Daniel Lanois on 1989's *Oh Mercy* and 1997's *Time Out of Mind,* two career-defining albums that bore the unmistakable imprint of Lanois's painterly touch as a creator of soundscapes—aural landscapes that colored an album's overall sound and feel.)

All this is to say that as much as the stark religious message (which, as we shall see, wasn't quite as stark and religious—certainly not as Christian—as it's often been made out to be) of *Slow Train Coming,* the most distinctive characteristic of the album was how it was really the first Dylan album that was "professionally" produced. Dylan called on the services of the legendary R&B man Jerry Wexler (who is credited with coining the moniker "rhythm and blues" as a journalist for *Billboard,* the music-industry trade journal, to replace "race records," the despicable term used until then for records by black musicians), best known for his work with the likes of Ray Charles, Aretha Franklin, Wilson Pickett, Dr. John, and Willie Nelson, and with Dusty Springfield on her classic *Dusty in Memphis* album. Wexler was one of the founders of the Atlantic Records sound, working out of the Stax Records studio in Memphis and later out of the Muscle Shoals studio in Sheffield, Alabama. Wexler had crossed paths with Dylan in 1972, when he produced *Doug Sahm and Band,* and again the next year when the two teamed up to coproduce the debut album by "new Dylan" Barry Goldberg at Muscle Shoals. This time around, Wexler—a self-described "Jewish atheist" born in New York City in 1918 to a family of immigrants—teamed Dylan with an odd assortment of musicians including old-time soul hands such as the keyboardist Barry Beckett (who was cocredited with producing the album) of the Muscle Shoals house band; the California studio sideman Tim Drummond, who got his start playing bass with James Brown's touring band but was best known for his work with Neil Young; and the guitarist-singer Mark Knopfler of the up-and-coming English rock group Dire Straits, whose second album,

Communique, Wexler had just produced and whose vocal style was heavily indebted, to say the least, to Dylan. Dire Straits's drummer, Pick Withers, rounded out the core of the band. The album also featured the funky Muscle Shoals horn section, and three gospel-oriented backup singers—two holdovers from the *Street Legal* session plus Carolyn Dennis, who was a member of the chorus on Dylan's big-band world tour of 1978, and who was his on-and-off girlfriend for much of the next decade before becoming his second wife in June 1986, and seven months later, the mother of his child Desiree Gabrielle Dennis-Dylan. (Dylan and Dennis were divorced in 1992.) Dennis would also record and tour with Dylan throughout much of the next decade.

The role of Dylan's black female backup singers—most of with whom at one point or another Dylan had romantic relationships—in steering him toward Christianity has often been remarked upon, including by Dylan himself. A Christian revival of sorts had also been spreading through many of the musicians from the Rolling Thunder Revue, including T-Bone Burnett (who would go on to greatest renown as the producer of the hit soundtrack to the film *O Brother, Where Art Thou?*), Roger McGuinn, Steve Soles, and David Mansfield. The most significant personal relationship that may have led Dylan to studying the Christian Bible at the Vineyard Fellowship, where Burnett, Soles, and Mansfield played in the house band, was with Mary Alice Artes, a black actress and roommate of Dylan's longtime paramour Sally Kirkland. While dating Dylan, Artes herself had a born-again experience and began attending the fellowship. It was her connection to Dylan that got the leaders of the fellowship to reach out to and invite Dylan to study at the school, which he did for a three-month period in early 1979. His studies fed his muse, spurring him into a flurry of songwriting over the next year that would find him penning dozens of songs, including the seventeen originals that wound up being included on his two "Christian" albums, *Slow Train Coming* and *Saved.*

Dylan has said that the songs on *Slow Train Coming* were originally intended for a projected gospel album by Carolyn Dennis, who boasts a stellar resumé of her own as a backup singer for the likes of Stevie Wonder, Bruce Springsteen, Michael Jackson, Gladys Knight, Donna Summer, Smokey Robinson, and Tracy Chapman. What would have happened to Dennis—and Dylan—had *Slow Train Coming* been hers and not Dylan's is fodder for a great guessing game; Dylan recorded the songs himself, and the rest, as they say, is history.

The album was recorded in a week in early May, and word began leaking out soon afterward about the Christian orientation of its contents. Apparently even Wexler and Knopfler had little to no idea beforehand about the nature of Dylan's new songs. Despite his unique, signature sound, Knopfler—who would go on to produce Dylan's "postconversion" album, 1983's curiously titled *Infidels*—proved to be a sympathetic accompanist who found a way to snake through Dylan's phrasing without getting in the way or unnecessarily drawing attention to his own playing. Drummond, Withers, and Beckett formed a dynamite, funky rhythm section, and the Muscle Shoals horns as well as the female vocalists peppered the songs with colors and accents to make for what in hindsight was a more of a funk-soul-R&B effort than gospel. Or to put it another way, while the content of many of the songs hinted at gospel music (although we will see how in fact they were both more and less than gospel, especially as compared with Dylan's next album, *Saved*), the gospel was hidden in the soulful grooves of Wexler's Muscle Shoals–influenced rock, which would garner Dylan his first Top 20 hit ("Gotta Serve Somebody") in a decade and his first Grammy Award *ever* (Best Male Rock Vocal, for the same song).

While the cover imagery of a railroad worker wielding a pickaxe in the shape of a cross was immediately suggestive, as were song titles such as "When He Returns" and "I Believe in You," *Slow Train Coming* is as noteworthy for its lack of Christian material as it is for any blatant references to Jesus. The album's two key songs, the title track and the hit single, for example, contain no overtly Christian messages; in fact, "Gotta Serve Somebody" fits comfortably within a Jewish worldview in which mankind's utmost duty is seen as *serving* G-d (hence, the daily and weekly prayer *service,* which has replaced the ancient practice of burnt offerings). In his farewell speech to the Israelites, after having settled their tribal claims, Joshua offers this bit of prophecy:

> And now, revere G-d and serve Him with undivided loyalty; remove the gods that your forefathers served beyond the Euphrates and in Egypt, and serve the Lord. If it is evil in your eyes to serve the Lord, *choose today whom you will serve:* the gods your forefathers served beyond the Euphrates, or the gods of the Amorite in whose land you are settled. But as for me and my house, we serve the Lord (Joshua 24:14–15; emphasis mine).

In other words, you gotta serve somebody.

While Joshua, like Dylan, pays lip service to this being a matter of *choice,* what kind of choice can there really be between serving G-d versus serving the *other* gods, whether those of the Babylonians ("the gods your forefathers served across the Euphrates") or those of the corrupt inhabitants of the Promised Land ("the gods of the Amorite in whose land you dwell")? Joshua makes clear his choice, and Dylan certainly implies that there isn't really a choice, the only options being serving the devil or serving the Lord. Whose side are *you* on?

Given hindsight, *Slow Train Coming* was in many ways the logical outgrowth of Dylan's increasingly forthright, hardcore worldview—the logical outgrowth, really, of his prophetic inclinations. The song "Slow Train," rather than being an overtly religious one, fits comfortably within Dylan's own tradition of sociopolitical critique, albeit in this case colored in large part by the hue of apocalyptic thinking that will, depending on one's point of view, tint or cloud Dylan's work from *Slow Train Coming* henceforth into the next century. But is there as apt a modern-day paraphrase of the prophetic point of view as the opening line of the title track?

> *Sometimes I feel so low-down and disgusted*
> *Can't help but wonder what's happenin' to my companions*
> *Are they lost or are they found*

Have they counted the cost it'll take to bring down
All their earthly principles they're gonna have to abandon?

How different are the sentiments expressed here than those expressed by the likes of Jeremiah and Isaiah in form, tone, and content? Rabbi Rami Shapiro writes, "In addition to warning the kings of their political follies, Isaiah relentlessly challenges the people to live up to the moral standards set for them by God. Putting one's hope in politics is madness, Isaiah says." Dylan would more directly address this theme a decade later on the song "Political World," on the mystically infused album *Oh Mercy*.

Dylan goes on in "Slow Train" to cite a litany of things he sees wrong with the world: evidence of corruption, debasement, violence, and greed that is at once an abasement of the human spirit and of man's relationship with G-d. But more than this, as the Prophets do, he puts this in the context of man's relationship with G-d, and warns that at some point accounts will be settled, and that in this case, the day, if not nigh, is upon us: "There's a slow, slow train comin' up around the bend."

That train could be the second coming of Jesus, or at least the harbinger of the End of Days as predicted in the book of Revelation—or, more likely, as predicted in a book that apparently had as strong an influence on Dylan and on those with whom he studied in the three-month course at West Los Angeles's Vineyard Fellowship. Hal Lindsey's *The Late, Great Planet Earth*, a bestselling, populist work of pseudo-eschatology, drew upon both the Bible—particularly the books of Daniel and Ezekiel, with which Dylan was already intimately familiar—and Revelation to read signs of imminent apocalypse in recent and contemporary historical events, such as the founding of the independent state of Israel in 1948. (Lindsey's subsequent works included *Satan Is Alive and Well on Planet Earth* and *The 1980s: Countdown to Armageddon*.)

The fact that Dylan should find inspiration in the story of Jesus, with the dramatic narrative possibilities inherent in that story and its striking imagery, and in the gospel-music tradition itself shouldn't come as any surprise. Whatever his personal beliefs at the time were—how personally he identified with the story of a reluctant prophetic/messianic figure who was several times betrayed by his followers or accepted the teachings of the religion based upon that story—is really almost beside the point. Dylan's creative use of Jesus served as a culmination of where his apocalyptic and prophetic inclinations were leading, and then he set those Christian-based inclinations aside in favor of a more all-consuming, overwhelmingly biblical prophetic orientation that would fuel the best of his material for the next thirty years.

On *Slow Train Coming*, Dylan leavens the Bible-thumping message of self-righteousness with some of the funkiest music of his career, some of the most self-referential self-mockery, and, surprisingly, a lethal dose of levity on a plane not seen or heard since the mid-1960s and not equaled until *"Love and Theft."* The very format of "Gotta Serve Somebody" is almost a comic setup. "You may be an ambassador to England or France / You may like to gamble, you might like to dance." So the song begins, going on to list a dizzying array of people and types from all walks of life, all of whom must make the choice of serving either the devil or the Lord—one of the phrases most often quoted by those who were or remain infuriated by the album's whiff of self-righteousness.

But already in the second line of the song, Dylan becomes somewhat self-referential: "You may be the heavyweight champion of the world," he sings, just a few short years after opening an album with a song about a boxer who "could have been the champion of the world" (although not a heavyweight—Rubin Carter was a middleweight), one who by this time had been convicted for a second time of the crimes that Dylan proposed that he hadn't committed in an earlier attempt at a hit single, "Hurricane." The reference also could be to Muhammad Ali, who *was* the heavyweight champion of the world, a fellow defender of Carter's, and a bigger-than-life-size personality along the lines of Dylan, yet who was also a spiritual man who submitted himself to the will of a higher power (in his case, one he called Allah). It also could be an in-joke about Dylan himself—a reference to Dylan's longtime interest in boxing, which he would pursue as an earnest avocation well into his seventh decade, even to the extent of bringing a sparring partner on tour with him.

Dylan goes on to pepper the song with sly (or not so sly) references to himself: "Might be a rock 'n' roll addict prancing on the stage / Might have drugs at your command, women in a cage," shining the harshest sort of light on himself and his worst celebrity excesses, if not those of his rock 'n' roll peers. "You may be living in a mansion or you might live in a dome," he goes on to sing, the "you" here being Dylan himself, whose palace in Malibu notoriously had a living room topped by a dome.

Before he even gets to the end of the first song on the first album of his so-called born-again period, Dylan already shows evidence of his ambivalence over the whole package: "You may be a preacher preaching spiritual pride . . . ," which won't be the last time Dylan questions the role of self-proclaimed men of the cloth (again, possibly including himself). Lines like this recur in other songs on *Slow Train Coming* and on the aptly titled *Infidels* in 1983.

The song "Gotta Serve Somebody" reveals its origins in its last verse, concluding with an authentic comedy routine borrowed from Bill Saluga, whose shtick was built upon a character named Raymond J. Johnson, Jr., who after being addressed as "Mister Johnson," would reply, "You can call me Ray, or you can call me Jay," and so on, followed by other names he could be called and concluding with "but you doesn't have to call me Johnson."

Dylan models the entire last verse around Saluga's routine. The first line, "You may call me Terry, you may call me Timmy," alludes to Saluga, and presumably is a nod to Tim Drummond ("Terry" could be Terry Young, who, although he didn't play on the recording, would become Dylan's keyboardist for the ensuing tour promoting the album, as well as an instrumentalist on the next album, *Saved*). The verse's third line explicitly quotes Saluga—"You may call me RJ / You may call me Ray"—nearly undermining the seriousness of the entire song. The second line, however, implicates Dylan himself—"You may call me Bobby, you may call me Zimmy," turning Dylan into a Raymond Johnson–like character while at the same time acknowledging for the first time ever in song his original surname,

Zimmerman. The verse ends with, "You may call me anything but no matter what you say," again paraphrasing Saluga, mocking himself, and bringing the song back around to the chorus.

Sticking this verse at the end of the song raises all kinds of questions about Dylan's intentions. Is the humor of the last verse meant to offset the self-righteousness of what comes before? Is it meant to mock the song by revealing that Dylan has structured it along the lines of Saluga's comedy routine? Is Dylan winking at the listener, saying, in effect, don't take me too seriously—this is just another role, a routine, a mask, an artifice, a masquerade, that I'm assuming?

Certainly, by the evidence of what follows, Dylan doesn't seem intent on subverting the overall message of the album and the songs of this period. He echoes the central message of the first song's chorus on the song that follows, "Precious Angel," when he sings, "You either got faith or you got unbelief and there ain't no neutral ground." The song is the first to introduce Dylan's new scorching view of apocalypse, as well as the essential role that a woman played as his spiritual mentor and companion in his newfound discovery:

> *Precious angel, under the sun*
> *How was I to know you'd be the one*
> *To show me I was blinded, to show me I was gone*
> *How weak was the foundation I was standing upon?*

Dylan contrasts his newfound friend (whom we will learn later is a woman and a lover) with his "so-called friends" who seemingly are oblivious to what's really happening around them (like so many clueless Mr. Joneses), unaware of their fate as "men [who] will beg God to kill them and they won't be able to die."

Dylan addresses the fourth verse to an unspecified "sister." He tells about a vision that he had of her drawing water from a well while "suffering under the law," and how she talked about Buddha and Muhammad but not Jesus. There's no overt mention of the woman having told him about Judaism or a Jewish prophet, in the manner in which Dylan discounts Buddhism and Islam, which are by implication dismissed by the omission of any discussion about Jesus. Years later, Dylan will rewrite "Gonna Change My Way of Thinking," from the same album, and reclaim "the law" as his personal code.

The next verse turns more personal, as Dylan leaves the "sister" he's addressing and returns to the title character, the "precious angel." In this verse, Dylan reveals that he and the angel have common, but different, roots. "What God has given to us no man can take away," he sings, indicating that both he and she are part of some God-given contract or covenant (as he will sing about more prosaically on *Saved*'s "Covenant Woman"). Here Dylan hints that the "precious angel" is a black woman and that, as a Jew, they have historical and symbolic ties—both are "covered in blood," both are descendants of slaves—ties that would bind Jews and American blacks together in the 1960s civil rights movement, which drew heavily upon the symbolic imagery of the Hebrews enslaved by and then liberated from Egyptian bondage.

The chorus of "Precious Angel" harks back to the chorus of "I Shall Be Released." In the latter, the narrator clearly saw his personal destiny and the redemption of his people in a "light come shinin' from the west down to the east." Here, the narrator calls upon the woman, or perhaps Jesus, to "Shine your light, shine your light on me / Ya know I just couldn't make it by myself / I'm a little too blind to see," alluding to that most popular of spirituals, "Amazing Grace." The opening phrase of the chorus is probably derived from Isaiah 9:1, "The people that walked in darkness have seen a great light; those who dwelled in the land of the shadow of death, light has dawned."

Dylan's blindness, too, is a recurring theme throughout his work, especially in the late 1990s and 2000s. While his blindness or lack of sight is meant poetically, it has its basis in fact: Dylan is terribly nearsighted, and combined with vanity that apparently discounted the wearing of corrective lenses, he has been myopic in every sense of the word for much of his life and career. (Early photos often capture Dylan wearing glasses offstage; nearsightedness, however, can be something of a blessing for a performer, as it eliminates the possibility of clearly identifying faces and gestures of audience members, which can be extremely distracting to a performer onstage.) The blindness to which he refers here is some sort of limitation in his ability to find truth on his own: presumably meant as an expression of gratitude toward the woman (presumably his girlfriend at the time, Mary Alice Artes) who introduced him to Jesus, it is also unintentionally ironic. Bob Dylan, of all people, too blind to see? Given the certitude with which he espoused truths from day one, that's a little hard to fathom.

Dylan continues somewhat in the same vein in "I Believe in You," a more straightforward love song that could be directed variously toward Jesus, toward his girlfriend, or even toward Sara (or to all of them). The song is marked, however, by a strong sense of self-pity, portraying the narrator as a victim of his love, having paid the price of ostracism for his belief (or for his love—it's unclear if he's singing about belief or love, or a combination of the two—perhaps his friends don't like him because he's taken up with a woman who they think has polluted his mind). Given that Dylan had yet to experience the backlash that *Slow Train Coming*, his subsequent concert tour, and his reported "conversion" to Christianity would cause, it's questionable what exactly he's referring to here, unless he's already identifying himself with Jesus (with Mary Alice Artes in the Mary Magdalen role).

There's no question, however, what he's singing about on the title track. An epic sociopolitical indictment and portrayal of a bleeding, decaying America that has lost sight of its ideals, set to a bluesy, syncopated funk riff, it features some of Dylan's greatest phrasing; lines that read like clunkers on the page flow effortlessly out of his mouth and pop out at a listener as if delivered by an experienced inspirational speaker. This is not subtle or poetic prophecy; rather, this is the voice of the prophet having hit bottom. "Sometimes I feel so low-down and disgusted / Can't help but wonder what's happenin' to my companions," he starts off, taking to task peers who seem to be oblivious to the decadence surrounding them, abasement that both signals and can only be amended by an interdiction of sorts (such as a "slow train comin'" or the arrival of a messianic age). Again, Dylan echoes "Amazing Grace" when he asks about his friends, "Are they lost or are they found," once again stating in no uncertain terms the dualistic notion that many found offensive: devil or Lord, faith or unbelief. The train itself could well be the one sung of by Curtis Mayfield in his 1965 hit with the Impressions, "People Get Ready"—an inspirational gospel-soul song that Dylan included in the soundtrack of *Renaldo and Clara*. (He also recorded versions of the song with the Band during the Basement Tapes sessions and again in 1990 for the soundtrack to the film *Flashback*.)

Dylan goes on to recite a catalog of contemporary socioeconomic and spiritual ills—hunger, poverty, greed, conformity—somehow tying these all together as symptoms of a single, overarching malady, and pointing out, in several cases, the hypocrisy and stupidity lying behind social dysfunction ("People starving and thirsting, grain elevators are bursting / You know it costs more to store the food than it do to give it").

The song, however, also added fuel to the fire of those who would accuse Dylan of adopting the sociopolitical outlook of the religious right, with what some took to be a jingoistic if not downright racist analysis of America's economic situation at the time:

> *All that foreign oil controlling American soil,*
> *Look around you, it's just bound to make you embarrassed.*
> *Sheiks walkin' around like kings, wearing fancy jewels and nose rings,*
> *Deciding America's future from Amsterdam and Paris.*

While perhaps overly patriotic for the time, in the long run, Dylan's viewpoint here would prove to be right on the mark: the groundwork was laid in the 1970s for the long term destruction of America's economic engine, as the foundation of its economy became almost wholly based on foreign energy sources, Arab or otherwise, which also had incredibly destructive environmental results.

But again, Dylan finds plenty of fault on the home front, too, and here is where he falls back into the traditional prophetic mode:

> *In the home of the brave, Jefferson turnin' over in his grave,*
> *Fools glorifying themselves, trying to manipulate Satan*

And again, Dylan evidences distrust of conventional, organized religion:

> *. . . the enemy I see wears a cloak of decency*
> *All non-believers and men stealers talkin' in the name of religion*

Just exactly who are these "men stealers talkin' in the name of religion"? Presumably they are stealers of men's souls (earlier in the verse Dylan groups them with "false healers and woman haters / Masters of the bluff and masters of the proposition"). Are these the Jerry Falwells and Jimmy Swaggarts of the world? The Jimmy Carters and the Ronald Reagans?

Dylan's is an all-encompassing condemnation. He offers up little in the way of hope, little in the way of transcendence, other than the vague promise of the slow train. While the sense of the song is that the slow train is one of deliverance, as in the Curtis Mayfield song ("All you need is faith to hear the diesels comin' / Don't need no ticket, you just thank the Lord"), nowhere here does Dylan make this connection explicit; while this train, as in the Woody Guthrie song, *may* be bound for glory, a pessimistic reading of the song could have Dylan singing about a train with another destination, especially given the prominent role trains played in transporting people toward places of unspeakably horrific murder in the twentieth century.

Mixed in with the language of the prophetic tirade are a few personal verses. The song, in fact, begins in the first person, talking about the narrator's feelings of disgust and wonder about how greed and corruption have blinded his friends to the threat of the inevitable upheaval to come. The second verse then credits a "backwoods girl" in Alabama for her "realistic" take on things, and for helping the singer to see the error of his own ways. It's curious that Dylan labels the woman "realistic," as opposed to *spiritual* or some other term that might indicate her ability to see through the everyday bullshit toward the larger picture (insightful? intuitive? psychic?). He also seems to have a little bit of fun with his pronunciation of "back-woods"—in Dylan's mouth, the woman in question sounds suspiciously "backwards."

Dylan then leaves the woman for the next four verses full of prophetic condemnation, before returning to her (presumably her, although it could be a different woman) in the final verse. But unlike the woman portrayed in "Precious Angel" and "I Believe in You"—the mysterious woman who seems to have shown the narrator the path of righteousness (and who otherwise is as noticeable for her *absence* on *Slow Train Coming* as for her ubiquity on his next album, *Saved*)—the woman of "Slow Train" turns out to be "a real suicide case" who runs off to Illinois "with some bad-talkin' boy she could destroy." In the end, Dylan is left entirely alone, to bemoan her fate and the fate of all those about whom he cares: "It sure do bother me to see my loved ones turning into puppets."

Dylan uses a similar dialectical strategy in the next song, "Gonna Change My Way of Thinking," a bit of R&B-influenced rock, the fifth of nine songs on *Slow Train Coming*. Not until we get to this song, the fulcrum of the album, as it were, does Dylan explicitly mention Jesus (which is nothing new—he had mentioned Jesus plenty of times in songs dating back to the beginning of his career, including "Masters of War" and "Bob Dylan's 115th Dream"). The song begins *not* with a profession of belief in Christianity, but, in fact, an announcement of a personal change of values:

> *Gonna change my way of thinking,*
> *Make myself a different set of rules. . . .*
> *Gonna put my good foot forward*
> *And stop being influenced by fools.*

This isn't exactly the declaration of a convert to a preordained religion (at least not in this first verse); rather, the narrator of the song simply declares a reevaluation of how he thinks, and in the process, composes a new code of his own, aptly summarized in the second two lines.

In the next four verses, the narrator echoes some of the complaints from "Slow Train," describing a litany of social, political, and spiritual ills afflicting contemporary society, including oppression, perversion, violence, and greed. His complaints portray moral debasement in direct violation of biblical law and the uniquely modern ailments of celebrity culture. The latter indictment was more fodder for those who accused Dylan of becoming a sociopolitical reactionary, as he subverts the language of the Sixties counterculture ("Do your own thing," "Be cool"), holding it up as an example of the ultimate in selfishness, made explicit by the concluding couplet of the verse, "You remember only about the brass ring / You forget all about the golden rule."

The mention of the "golden rule" here, at the song's halfway mark, is the first invocation of the Bible as a guidepost to the narrator's new way of thinking. (It also telegraphs the next song on the program, "Do Right to Me Baby [Do Unto Others].") The so-called Golden Rule—popularly rendered as "Love thy neighbor as thyself" and, by logical extension, "Do unto others as you'd have them do unto you"—has its scriptural basis in Leviticus 19:18, which the sage Hillel, as quoted in the Talmud (Tractate Shabbat 31a), interpreted as "That which is hateful to you, do not do to your fellow," adding, "That is the whole [lesson of] the Torah, and all the rest is commentary." According to the Christian book of Matthew 7:12, Jesus paraphrased Hillel thus: "So in everything, do to others what you would have them do to you, for this sums up the Law and the Prophets."

Again, in the next verse, Dylan slowly works the received wisdom of religion into what began as a declaration of independent thinking. Warning of those who could "mislead a man" by taking "ahold of his heart with [their] eyes," he concludes, "There's only one authority / And that's the authority on high," poetically rendering the prohibition against idolatry as outlined in the biblical Ten Commandments in Exodus 20:3–5: "Do not have any other gods before Me. Do not represent them by any carved image or picture. . . . I am G-d your Lord, a G-d who requires exclusive worship."

Dylan continues on the path toward a new belief system, but not before a detour with a woman who vaguely resembles the backwoods girl from Alabama. This time around, the narrator has "a

God-fearing woman" who "can do the Georgia crawl" (even if she's from Alabama) and "walk in the spirit of the Lord." He can also "easily afford" the woman—presumably a dig at his ex-wife, Sara, who won a significant portion of Dylan's accumulated and future wealth in their divorce settlement. The woman portrayed here is not, as elsewhere, a lofty, religious mentor; rather, she is painted in earthy, sensual tones, her spirituality balanced by her sensuality, in a verse that's rather uncharitable—in both the Christian and non-Christian sense—to women in general, and, if it's to be read autobiographically, to the specific woman Dylan is writing about.

The penultimate verse of "Gonna Change My Way of Thinking" contains the first and one of the only direct references to Christian theology on *Slow Train Coming*:

> *Jesus said, "Be ready,*
> *For you know not the hour in which I come." . . .*
> *He said, "He who is not for Me is against Me,"*
> *Just so you know where He's coming from.*

There is a faint echo of the refrain of "Gotta Serve Somebody" here in the third line. Dylan also chooses to introduce Jesus as a harsh figure—Jesus as warrior (with the implication of a threat in the final line) rather than peacemaker, Jesus as lion rather than lamb. Dylan will cling to this portrayal of Jesus, this side of his character, throughout the time he writes songs with Christian themes; in a twist, of sorts, Dylan's view of Jesus is more "Old Testament" than "New." His is a Jesus of fire, brimstone, and wrath, not unlike the Hebrew Prophets, whose rhetoric consists largely of admonishments and warnings if not wholesale threats, without any reference to themselves as the potential objects of belief or worship, the Prophets always speaking on behalf of G-d and never equating themselves with Him.

The song's final verse refers to a "kingdom called heaven" where "there is no pain of birth" created by G-d "about the same time he made the earth." The heavenly place of Creation was the Garden of Eden, where there was no pain of birth because G-d created Adam and Eve. The pain of childbirth was an explicit punishment for Eve's transgression of the prohibition against eating fruit from the Tree of Knowledge: "In pain shall you bear children" (Genesis 3:16). Adam didn't get off scot-free, either; he, along with Eve, was banished from the Garden, condemned to a life of hard labor—the origin of "there's no free lunch," so to speak—and robbed of immortality. With no return to Eden possible, the best man could hope for was to garner a place in the world to come, ushered in by the Messiah, who would bring about the resurrection of the dead. According to the sages, it would be a world where women would conceive and give birth all in the same day (Shabbos 30B), precluding any time for birth pangs.

Dylan narrows his focus on the next song, "Do Right to Me Baby (Do Unto Others)," an easygoing bit of acoustic funk distinguished by Mark Knopfler's guitar fingerpicking and Barry Beckett's soulful organ. Dylan digs deep into the Golden Rule for all its poetic, humorous, and emotional possibilities—writing a midrash on it, really, and one that, while it coheres thematically and musically, falls apart upon close reading. In fact, the song's refrain actually *reverses* the formula suggested by Hillel and Jesus—saying, "If you do right to me, baby / I'll do right to you, too"—before restating it in the proper formulation, "Ya got to do unto others / Like you'd have them . . . do unto you." Dylan's genius is apparent throughout, however, most notably in the way he takes the lofty language of the sages and puts it into the vernacular, so that it suits his litany of things he *doesn't* want to do to others and have others do to him, including being used as a doormat, being hurt, being shot, and marrying somebody if they're already married (how gallant of him!). In content if not mood, the song most resembles "Rainy Day Women #12 & 35," with its similar litany ("They'll stone you when you're trying to go home . . . when you're playing your guitar . . . when you're at the bar") and biblical refrain ("Everybody must get stoned").

The final line of the song's final verse has the narrator putting the Golden Rule above and beyond any overarching belief system: "Don't put my faith in nobody, not even a scientist." Dylan is being somewhat ironic here, positing faith against science and then opting for neither (just minutes after he's sung, "You either got faith or you got unbelief / And there ain't no neutral ground"). Perhaps his refusal to put faith in anyone doesn't include G-d or Jesus, but Dylan makes no direct reference or appeal to Jesus in this song, either.

In fact, the most unusually resonant line in the song may well be a reference to his Jewish heritage, when he sings, "Don't wanna burn nobody, don't wanna be burned," a subtle but piercing allusion to the Holocaust (which means, literally, "completely burnt"), and not the first time Dylan has referred to Jews cast into fire ("in the ovens they fried," he sang in "With God on Our Side"). Nevertheless, the overall mood of the song is light and breezy, a whimsical meditation on the Golden Rule.

The mood darkens lyrically and musically on the next song, "When You Gonna Wake Up." A full-blown soul-funk tune, driven by the rhythm section and colored by Barry Beckett's keys and the Muscle Shoals horn section, the song is in the vein of the title track, with Dylan recounting more social and moral ills and urging listeners to "wake up" and, in this case, "strengthen the things that remain." Like a Prophet of old, Dylan opens and closes the song with invocations to G-d—"God don't make promises that he don't keep," he begins, leaving it ambiguous whether this is meant as a note of reassurance or a threat—with six verses between (plus one that also mentions G-d), depicting a world gone wrong: a world of innocents in jail, doctors who do harm, philosophies that confuse, and, as always, the strong preying upon the weak.

Among the targets of Dylan's wrath are "adulterers in churches" and "spiritual advisors and gurus" who provide "instant inner peace" but require that "every step you take has got to be approved." Dylan is presumably ranting against New Age preachers and practitioners of Eastern religions (one wonders how his good friend George Harrison, a longtime follower of guru-based Hinduism, felt about this line), but more generally, Dylan betrays his lifelong distrust of any sort of leaders; how different were the pastors of the Vineyard Fellowship from these "spiritual advisors" who monitor one's progress?

The final verse of this song, however, is Dylan's most direct statement of Christian belief on the album. The official, published lyric has him singing, "There's a Man up on a cross and He's been crucified / Do you have any idea why or for who He died?" But on the recording Dylan sings, "There's a man on the cross, and he been crucified for you / Believe in his power, that's about all you gotta do." The line seems tacked on to the end of the song; nothing that comes before prepares a listener for this statement of faith; there is no case being made that leads up to this as the logical (or illogical) conclusion; it's practically a non sequitur as it appears in the song.

The album's penultimate track, "Man Gave Names to All the Animals," is a jaunty, reggae-flavored children's song, luxuriating in its humorous rhyme scheme, elaborating on Genesis 2:19–20:

> G-d had formed every wild beast and every bird of heaven out of the earth, and brought them to the man to see what he would call each one. Whatever the man called each living thing would be its name. The man named every livestock animal and bird of the sky and all the wild beasts.

In Dylan's version, the man, who was Adam, observes each animal and comes up with a name that rhymes with a characteristic; thus,

> *an animal leavin' a muddy trail*
> *Real dirty face and a curly tail*
> *He wasn't too small and he wasn't too big*

gets called a pig. Likewise, a cow is so named because Adam "saw milk comin' out but he didn't know how," and an animal with a "great big furry back and furry hair" is named a bear.

It's a child's delight, which even Dylan recognized, consenting to the publication of the lyrics as a children's book, with illustrations by Scott Menchin, in 1999. The song was not without any other significance, however. In the final verse, man "saw an animal as smooth as glass / Slithering his way through the grass / Saw him disappear by a tree near a lake . . . ," and thus the song ends, with the music left hanging on an unresolved modulation and the snake remaining unnamed. We all know, he seemed to say, what this animal was all about.

The album closes with "When He Returns," the only real gospel tune on the album, with Dylan singing atop Barry Beckett's lush, ornate acoustic piano. Dylan's vocals are impassioned and raw, and the track sounds like a demo version that Dylan decided to keep just as is, rather than rerecord with the ensemble (although apparently the opposite is what occurred in the recording process—Dylan tossed off this version as an afterthought after having recorded a full-band version, and chose to close the album with this rendition—a good choice!). The song is Dylan's most explicit statement of messianic belief—"there'll be no peace . . . the war won't cease / Until He returns"—alluding possibly to the "second coming" of Jesus, but just as easily to the Davidic Messiah of Judaism. Dylan revisits the lines from Ezekiel, Isaiah, and Jeremiah that originally inspired "Blowin' in the Wind" when he sings, "For all those who have eyes and all those who have ears"—the song is, in some ways, an expansion of or an elaboration upon that song. The second and third verses have two lines apiece of questions beginning with "How long . . . ," echoing "How many times," and include other rhetorical devices ("Will I ever learn . . . ?") leading to the answer, which here is only slightly more specific than "blowin' in the wind." Dylan also casually bounces around the narrative voice from third to second to first person and back, tossing it like a hot potato, and by doing so implicates the listener, the narrator, G-d, and himself.

"The iron hand it ain't no match for the iron rod," sings Dylan in the song's opening line. The "iron hand" is an oft-used metaphor for the brute force of the Hebrews' taskmasters, whether they be Egyptians, Romans, or Germans; they prove no match, however, for the "iron rod"—a literal reference to Moses' miraculous staff, which parts the waters of the Red Sea, turns into a snake, and gets water out of a rock, or, metaphorically, a reference to the word of G-d, the Torah, as given to Moses and handed over to the Jewish people. We see this parallel drawn in Isaiah 11:1–4:

A staff will emerge from the stump of Jesse and a shoot will sprout from his roots [here the rod is understood as a metaphor for the Messiah stemming from the House of David]. The spirit of G-d will rest upon him. . . . He will be imbued with a spirit of reverence for G-d; and will not need to judge by what his eyes see nor decide by what his ears hear. He will judge the poor with righteousness, and decide with justice for the humble of the earth. He will strike down a land with the rod of his mouth, and with the breath of his lips he will slay the wicked.

The "rod" here is equated with the word of G-d.

Dylan also draws inspiration from the Prophets when he sings, "He sees your deeds, he knows your needs, even before you ask," echoing "G-d sees innermost thoughts and feelings . . . for I have revealed my grievance to You" (Jeremiah 20:12) and "He recounts to a person what were his deeds" (Amos 4:13).

Several songs that Dylan recorded but didn't include on this album have surfaced on subsequent collections, unofficial recordings, or in concerts that took place concurrently with the release of *Slow Train Coming* and *Saved*. Among these is "Trouble in Mind," which originally surfaced as the B side of the single version of "Gotta Serve Somebody." "Trouble in Mind" explores the inner struggle and torment of a soul being constantly tempted by sin. Dylan invokes the story of Lot's wife here, in another sly reference to his maternal family's name: "Ask Lot what he thought when his wife turned to stone." He also finds Satan struggling for the soul of the ancient Israelites: "He's gonna deaden your conscience 'til you worship the work of your own hands / You'll be serving strangers in a strange, forsaken land." The sin of idolatry, and, conversely, the prohibition against worship of material things and corporeal gods, is a running motif throughout the Bible, and the subject of one of the Ten Commandments, found in Exodus 20:3–5. The Prophets blame dispersion from the Promised Land on idolatry: "Then its land became full of false gods; each one of them bows to his own handiwork, to what his fingers have made" (Isaiah 2:8) and "G-d says to Jeremiah: 'I will argue my case against [Judah] for all their evil, for they have forsaken Me and sacrificed to the gods of others and prostrated themselves to the works of their hands'" (Jeremiah 1:16).

While certainly a watershed work, a stunning one in many ways, and one that introduced a new and heightened interest in music-as-prophecy, *Slow Train Coming* was a small step toward Dylan's temporary embrace of Christianity (and one of his best-selling albums of all time, reaching number 3 on the *Billboard* album chart on its way to being certified "platinum" for more than one million sales). The album's most powerful songs were really just newly clothed protest songs—not so different from Dylan's most pointed work of the early 1960s. They had an added veneer of apocalyptic thinking, a sterner outlook, and a suggestion that social and political ills were symptoms of spiritual crisis—a societal crisis that mirrored Dylan's own personal crisis, about which he would reveal more on *Saved*.

Where *Slow Train Coming* was mostly an impassioned album of spiritual protest in southern funk garments, *Saved*, recorded in five days in February 1980 and released in late June, was a more personal and theological exploration of Dylan's newfound fascination with the story of Jesus and its connection to his Jewish heritage. Lingering assumptions to the contrary, neither of these albums was a profession that Dylan was a "born-again Christian," a phrase bandied about at the time ("Bob Dylan has finally confirmed in an interview what he's been saying in his music for 18 months: He's a born-again Christian," wrote Robert Hilburn in the *Los Angeles Times*) and still used in otherwise respectable books about Dylan claiming to be "definitive." Very simply, as a Jew, there is no way that Dylan could be a "born-again Christian." The concept of being "born again" is a wholly Christian one that says *Christians* need to be born twice: once to their mothers, and subsequently to Jesus as part of a spiritual "rebirth." The best Dylan could do would be to convert to Christianity through baptism, but this would merely make him a convert (and, thereby, an apostate), but not "born again." Nor would it make him no longer Jewish—once a Jew, always a Jew, is the rule; even excommunication, rarely if ever practiced in the modern era, doesn't make a person not Jewish, but merely bans him from participating in Jewish communal life (which is, in a sense, the self-defined status of the vast majority of today's Jews).

Nevertheless, the term remains attached to Dylan, not helped by the fact that Dylan was often quoted using it to describe himself in interviews in 1979 and 1980. But for every time he's quoted claiming that he was or is born again, there's another quotation saying he wasn't ("I've never been a Fundamentalist. I've never been Born Again. Those are just labels that people hang on you."). Finally, the press release for 2003's *Gotta Serve Somebody: The Gospel Songs of Bob Dylan,* an officially sanctioned tribute album featuring newly recorded versions of songs from *Slow Train Coming* and *Saved* by contemporary gospel performers—plus a newly recorded version of "Gonna Change My Way of Thinking" by Dylan—never once used the term "born again" to refer to Dylan or to the period in which the songs originated.

Dylan kicks off *Saved* with a spirited, nearly a cappella, call-and-response rendition of the old country spiritual "A Satisfied Mind," which was a hit for Porter Wagoner and which Dylan had been singing since his earliest days in New York (unofficial recordings exist of him singing the tune during the *Basement Tapes* sessions, too). The album proper then kicks into gear with the title track, a full-fledged Pentecostal romp in which the singer joyfully proclaims he's been "saved by the blood of the lamb." The rollicking, driving tune, which sounds like something you'd hear emanating from any black Southern church with a large choir on a Sunday, bears the weight of Dylan's clichéd rhetoric—almost a paint-by-numbers job in composing an instant gospel classic (albeit one that unaccountably tanked when released as a single). While being saved "by the blood of the lamb," in Christian parlance, refers to the crucifixion of Jesus—rendered poetically as "the lamb"—it draws its roots in the literal salvation of the Hebrew slaves in Egypt, who were spared the ten plagues cast upon Egypt by sprinkling lamb's blood on their doorposts. The yearly Passover seder commemorates the deliverance of the Jews from Egyptian captivity, and the name of the holiday refers to the passing over of Jewish houses by the angel of death, who killed all Egyptian firstborn sons. In Hebrew, the holiday is called Pesach, which is the name of the lamb offering (hence, the *Paschal* lamb). Thus, being saved by the blood of the lamb is a cornerstone of the Passover story and the symbol of Jewish liberation.

The song also refers to two major biblical figures, Joseph and Job, in this verse:

He bought me with a price,
Freed me from the pit,
Full of emptiness and wrath
And the fire that burns in it.

The well-known story of Joseph and his brothers, recounted in Genesis 37, features his jealous brothers tossing him into a well in order to do away with him: "They took him and threw him into the well. The well was empty; there was no water in it" (Genesis 37: 24). Joseph's life was spared only by the sudden, miraculous appearance of a caravan of traveling merchants, to whom the brothers sold him. The hand of G-d is readily evident here, as it is the traders who take Joseph to Egypt, thus putting into play the series of events that will see Joseph become a prince of Egypt, in which position he is able to save his brothers and their extended clan from the famine that strikes the land, depositing them in a region where they can grow strong and prosper as shepherds, eventually giving birth to the Israelite nation, which finds its way back to its homeland under the leadership of Moses.

Similarly, in the book of Job, there is discussion of man being condemned to a grave yet being redeemed by G-d for a price. Elihu says to Job, "His flesh is consumed from sight; his bulging bones become unseen. His soul approaches the grave, and his being the killers." Through the intervention of an angel who speaks up on behalf of the man, G-d says, "Redeem him from going down to the grave." Through atonement and prayerful repentance, he is accepted anew by G-d, Who "recompenses man for his righteousness"—in other words, buys him for a price.

"Covenant Woman" is one of several songs on *Saved* addressing a woman or recounting the role of a woman as spiritual mentor, picking up from where "Precious Angel" on *Slow Train Coming* left off. A spiritual love song addressed to a woman who's "got a contract with the Lord," the song is an expression of loyalty and gratitude. Dylan hints that his newfound spirituality came at a time of desperation, even though in contemporary interviews he denied that his proclamation of faith, such as it were, was the act of a vulnerable or desperate man in need of salvation, spiritual or otherwise.

The narrator expresses his gratitude more to the woman than to G-d. He's thankful that she prayed to heaven for him and pledges his loyalty to her as a friend, but doesn't say anything about adopting her beliefs. In fact, if the song *is* talking about or to a Christian woman (for example, Mary Alice Artes, as is widely assumed), Dylan seemingly draws a distinction between her status vis-à-vis Christianity and his own:

> *You know we are strangers in a land we're passing through.*
> *I'll always be right by your side, I've got a covenant too.*

The parallels drawn between the narrator and the "covenant woman" hint at black and Jew, as they did on *Slow Train Coming*'s "Precious Angel" (echoing the line "both our forefathers were slaves" in that song). That Jews were strangers in Egypt is a motif repeated throughout the Bible, and they continued to be "strangers" throughout history—for the most part being consigned to separate territories, towns, or ghettos throughout the Diaspora, rarely granted full citizenship until recent times—segregated for the most part much like those of the African diaspora. And in the way Dylan phrases the next line, the fact that he *also* has a covenant sounds like it's a similar one but not the same one that the "covenant woman" has (his being the Jewish one, hers being the Christian).

The next song on *Saved*, "What Can I Do for You?" continues in this vein. But this time around the "you" is "You"—the narrator of the song is addressing G-d, expressing gratitude, and asking what he can do in return for being "renewed inside." Dylan employs some of the same imagery here that he used in "Covenant Woman"—freed from slavery and fed spiritually. Dylan goes back and forth between Jewish and Christian imagery here: he's been liberated from bondage (Jewish) but renewed inside (Christian), he was "chosen . . . to be among the few," presumably a reference to Jews as "the chosen people." (This is a problematic epithet. The term has often been mis-understood to carry with it a sense of self-superiority totally foreign to the phrase's origin in Deuteronomy 7:6—"G-d your Lord has chosen you to be His special people." The verse immediately fol-lows the chapter in which Moses recounts the giving of the Law at Mount Sinai, explaining that having been chosen to receive the Torah, the Jews therefore are obligated to follow the strict set of commandments contained therein. In other words, they have been "chosen" for responsibility and service, rather than for any inherent superiority. Nevertheless, the misperception of having labeled them-selves "chosen" by G-d has been used against Jews by anti-Semites to fan the flames of Jew-hatred for several millennia.)

A Christian belief called supersessionism says that with the advent of Jesus, a new covenant between G-d and man was put into place and that the previous covenant between G-d and the Jews was thus superseded. According to this equation, Christians became the new "chosen people." But in the song's phrasing, it's not clear how one would then be "among the few," Christians far outnumbering Jews. Nevertheless, Dylan draws upon Jewish imagery for some of the most striking lines in "What Can I Do for You?" He sings, "Soon as a man is born, you know the sparks begin to fly." There are numerous such references throughout the Bible to sparks and coal bearers, one of which is found in Job 5:7: "For a man is born to weariness, just as sparks fly upward." Dylan then continues, "He gets wise in his own eyes and he's made to believe a lie," a line pos-sibly inspired by no fewer than three verses from the Prophets and Writings:

The wise man has his eyes in his head, whereas a fool walks in dark-ness (Ecclesiastes 2:14)

Do not be wise in your own eyes; fear G-d and shun evil (Proverbs 3:7)

Woe to those who are wise in their own eyes, and in their own view, understanding (Isaiah 5:21)

Not for the last time, Dylan alludes to William Blake's "Auguries of Innocence," for the second half of this line: "We are led to believe a lie / When we see not thro' the eye."

"Solid Rock" is indeed just that: one of Dylan's hardest-rocking numbers of all time. While the song seemingly expresses a belief in Jesus as martyr, at the same time, it's grounded in the Jewish belief of G-d as the bedrock of existence. In the refrain, Dylan sings, "Well, I'm hangin' on to a solid rock / Made before the foundation of the world." Throughout Jewish scripture and liturgy, G-d is likened to a *tzur*, a rock. In fact, in every daily prayer service, Jews address themselves directly to G-d as Tzur Yisroel, or "Rock of Israel," a metaphor initially found in Deuteronomy 32, in which Moses chastises the gathered assembly—in song, incidentally—for their anticipated rejection of their Lord:

> The deeds of the Rock are perfect, all His ways are just. . . . Destruction is His children's fault, not His own, you crooked and perverse generation. Is this the way you repay G-d, you dull, witless nation? . . . The nation abandoned the G-d who made it, and spurned the Rock of its salvation.

Or, as Dylan sings,

> *For me He was chastised, for me He was hated,*
> *For me He was rejected by a world that He created.*
> *Nations are angry, cursed are some,*
> *People are expecting a false peace to come.*

"Solid Rock" also makes reference to the Jewish belief in the constant inner struggle between good and evil, the battle between the *yetzer tov* (the good urge) and the *yetzer hara* (the evil urge), a battle that mystics say is won through a combination of prayer, study, and the doing of good deeds, or *mitzvot*. Dylan captures the struggle thus: "It's the ways of the flesh to war against the spirit / Twenty-four hours a day you can feel it and you can hear it."

Likewise, "Pressing On" also teeters between Judaism and Christianity. It echoes the self-pity of "I Believe in You" at the same time it alludes to "Amazing Grace." Dylan juxtaposes a phrase from Isaiah 52:2 ("Shake the dust from yourself") with one of his own signature lines ("Don't look back"), the latter of which harks back to the biblical story of Lot's wife, who in defiance of an angel's warning—"Run for your life! Don't look back!" (Genesis 19:17)— gazed upon the destruction of Sodom and Gomorrah and was turned into a pillar of salt (as we've seen, Dylan also used this line for the title of D. A. Pennebaker's documentary film of his 1965 concert tour of England). The lyrics to "Pressing On" also draw upon the dark, gloomy writings (the book begins with the phrase "all is futile," and goes downhill from there to "I hated life, for I was depressed by all that goes on under the sun") of King Solomon as quoted in the book of Koheles, better known as Ecclesiastes, that veritable wellspring of lyrical inspiration for Dylan and other songwriters. In this case, Dylan's line "What's to come has already been" is a clever reversal of Ecclesiastes 1:9, "Whatever has been is what will be, and whatever has been done is what will be done." The next line is even more famous throughout literature: "There is nothing new beneath the sun." This same sentiment is repeated a few lines later: "What has been, already exists, and what is still to be, has already been" (Ecclesiastes 3:15). Or, as Abraham Joshua Heschel summarizes, "In the eyes of man, what comes about and what is still to come may be an age apart; in the eyes of God, they are one."

Surrounding these biblical verses is a wealth of material that Dylan and others drew upon. While credited to Jim McGuinn, who later changed his name to Roger, "The Ballad of Easy Rider," from the 1969 film *Easy Rider*, is widely believed to have been written by Dylan and given to McGuinn. The song's first line paraphrases Ecclesiastes 1:7 ("All the rivers flow into the sea"), which also inspired Dylan's "Watchin' the River Flow." Ernest Hemingway trod these waters for the title to his greatest book, inspired by Ecclesiastes 1:5 ("The sun rises and the sun sets"), as did the apostle Mark, who borrowed his most famous proverb, "For what is a man profited, if he shall gain the whole world, and lose his own soul?" from

Ecclesiastes 1:3, "What profit does man have for all his labor which he toils beneath the sun?" Perhaps most famously, Pete Seeger based his song, "Turn! Turn! Turn! (To Everything There Is a Season)" on a nearly verbatim use of Ecclesiastes 3 ("Everything has its season, and there is a time for everything under heaven"), to which, coincidentally, McGuinn gave full voice in his hit version with the Byrds, which went to number 1 in fall 1965. (For all its pessimism, Ecclesiastes has been very, very good to Roger McGuinn.)

Musically, "Pressing On" is one of the highlights of the album, beginning with Dylan's vocals accompanied by lush gospel piano as the song builds steam, with the help of the call-and-response gospel choir, before the full-band arrangement kicks in with a marching beat. Thus the rhythm and arrangement perfectly accentuate the song's arc and message.

Likewise, the next song, "In the Garden," is one of Dylan's finer achievements in the gospel idiom, also starting out with vocals over keyboards for several verses before the band enters and propels the story-song forward through a series of modulations (chord changes) that raise the key while the lyrics raise the stakes. In this case, the song recapitulates Jesus' story, albeit slightly out of order, from his miracles to his preaching in Jerusalem, to his arrest in Gethsemane (the garden of the song's title), through his resurrection. Once again, Dylan successfully uses the rhetorical device he first stumbled upon with "Blowin' in the Wind," writing an entire song as a series of questions—albeit here the questions are much more concrete, pointing to a clear answer (they didn't, and they were wrong), as opposed to the more open-ended inquiry of "Blowin' in the Wind."

The penultimate song on *Saved*, "Saving Grace," is another organ-drenched expression of thanks nodding to "Amazing Grace" but with both Jewish and Christian references. *Grace* itself is a Christian term referring to the forgiveness G-d grants repentant sinners; hence the song's opening lines:

> *If You find it in Your heart, can I be forgiven?*
> *Guess I owe You some kind of apology.*

The second verse drops a hint of autobiography into the otherwise gospel-by-numbers nature of the song when Dylan sings:

By this time I'd-a thought I would be sleeping
In a pine box for all eternity.

presumably referring here to the perilous rock 'n' roll lifestyle to which he succumbed at various points in his career, one that cut down many before their time, but not him (hence the suggestion that he labored under some sort of protective shield, or "saving grace"). The choice of "sleeping in a pine box" as a metaphor for death is a telling one, as Jews traditionally shun elaborate carved caskets made of expensive woods for simple boxes made of the cheapest locally available wood, such as pine. The phrase also echoes the concluding line of "Where Are You Tonight? (Journey Through Dark Heat)," the final song on *Street Legal,* in its fatalism: "I can't believe it / I can't believe I'm alive." In that case, though, the singer's amazement was tempered by the loss of his one true love—"because without you it doesn't seem right"—whereas on "Saving Grace," it's seen as evidence of a gift from G-d.

The year-and-a-half period beginning with the release of *Slow Train Coming* in late summer 1979 was also marked by a series of concert tours in which Dylan entirely or in large part played programs confined to his new, gospel-oriented songs. He also peppered many of these shows with minisermons, some of which were in response to fans heckling Dylan to play other songs or accusing him of betraying his past. The irony of such accusations was apparently lost on these hecklers, who merely became pawns in the immediate and larger drama of Dylan's career. Accusing Dylan of betrayal merely fed his growing identification with Jesus as martyr, while echoing earlier such accusations that found their most heinous realization in the infamous—now utterly ironic—cry of "Judas!"

Dylan's first public performance of his new songs took place on the late-night TV variety show *Saturday Night Live,* on October 20, 1979. Two weeks later, Dylan played the first concert of a two-week residency at the 2,000-seat Fox Warfield Theater in San Francisco.

The concerts kicked off with a six-song set of gospel performed by his trio of female singers, before Dylan took the stage and sang most of the songs from *Slow Train Coming* and several from the as-yet-unrecorded *Saved,* as well as a few others that were never committed to vinyl. Dylan continued performing in this manner in theaters in California and the Southwest into the second week of December, when the band took a break, picking up again in mid-January for a monthlong series of shows in the Pacific Northwest, the Midwest, and the South, most for multiple-day residencies. By this point, audiences knew what to expect, but they still reacted across a spectrum from outright disrespect to enthusiastic fervor.

Dylan and band returned to Muscle Shoals studio for five days in mid-February 1980 when, once again under the guidance of Jerry Wexler and Barry Beckett, they recorded the songs that would comprise *Saved*. In late February, Dylan made his first appearance at a Grammy Awards ceremony, performing "Gotta Serve Somebody," for which he wound up accepting the award for Best Male Rock Vocal, thanking "The Lord, Jerry Wexler, and Barry Beckett," in that order. In mid-April, the third leg of the gospel tour kicked off with a series of shows in Toronto and Montreal, this time with four singers, only one of whom—Regina Havis—remained from the previous legs of the tour. The band played another two dozen shows throughout upstate New York, New England, Pennsylvania, and Ohio, before bringing down the curtain on the all-gospel tour three days before Dylan's thirty-ninth birthday in Dayton, Ohio, a month before the release of *Saved*.

Dylan and band wouldn't perform again until the following November, when they returned to the Fox Warfield Theater for a dozen shows in which the gospel set was supplemented this time out by other Dylan songs, including classics such as "Like a Rolling Stone" and "Blowin' in the Wind." The San Francisco residency was marked by a series of unannounced guest appearances by the guitarist Mike Bloomfield, Jerry Garcia of the Grateful Dead, Roger McGuinn, and the folk-blues singer Maria Muldaur. The short tour wrapped up in early December with a series of shows in the Pacific Northwest, concluding with a performance at the Paramount

Theater in Portland, Oregon, chock full of early gems such as "To Ramona," "Just Like Tom Thumb's Blues," "Don't Think Twice, It's All Right," and "A Hard Rain's a-Gonna Fall," just four nights before John Lennon was murdered outside his luxury apartment building on New York's Upper West Side. News reports claimed that soon after the shooting, Dylan hired two Israeli bodyguards. When asked why Israelis, he replied, "Because they're the best."

The fall 1980 concerts premiered a few new songs Dylan had been writing, songs that suggested a shift of focus away from the direct evangelical themes of *Saved* in favor of a return to Dylan's highly stylized narrative writing. While not totally lacking in religious import, songs such as "Caribbean Wind" and "Groom's Still Waiting at the Altar" picked up where *Blood on the Tracks* and *Desire* left off in their surrealistic, time- and place-shifting imagery ("Groom" alone touches down in "the ghetto," the Mediterranean basin, Argentina, and El Salvador; "Caribbean Wind" hops from Rome to Miami, Atlantic City, and various locations throughout the Caribbean) while adopting a much more personal tone than the scripture-by-rote verses of *Saved*. While neither of these songs would be included on the initial release of *Shot of Love*—widely regarded as Dylan's first "postconversion" album—in August 1981 ("Groom," unaccountably left off initial pressings of the LP and available only as the B side to the single version of "Heart of Mine," would be added to later pressings of the album), they offered hints of the shape and sound of things to come.

Another song committed to tape as a demo during this period but never performed live nor revisited in the studio for an album version was "Yonder Comes Sin," highly revealing of Dylan's state of mind at the time. Available only on unofficially circulating recordings, "Yonder Comes Sin" is an R&B rocker with a "Jumpin' Jack Flash"–like guitar riff. This lyric stands out from the litany of complaints and admonitions that comprise most of the song:

> *Jeremiah preached repentance*
> *To those who would turn from hell*
> *But the critics all gave him such bad reviews*

> *Put him down into the bottom of a well*
> *But he kept on talking anyway.*

By no means is this the first time Dylan has hinted at self-identification with a prophet, but rarely had he been so blatant as in this direct reference to Dylan-as-prophet getting bad reviews on the basis of his "preaching repentance." He could be referring specifically to the critical barbs that greeted his early gospel concerts, but instead of fitting himself for a crown of thorns this time, he's punished by being thrown into a well like the Jewish Prophet Jeremiah. But this was only the latest incident in a career full of such; in some ways it has been the defining characteristic of Dylan's dynamic relationship to the press and select groups of listeners (folk traditionalists, political radicals, music snobs) from the outset.

Like the Prophets, Dylan's work has always been informed by a strong sense of purposefulness. He is almost always driven and present in performance, in recordings, and on stage. Those performances vary dramatically—they can easily be called erratic in the sense that there is seemingly little continuity among them (compare, for example, the easygoing country squire of *Nashville Skyline* with the manic testifier of *Live 1975*)—but Dylan is always intense, always present. This isn't always the case in popular music; in fact, it's the exception rather than the rule in a field where recordings and concerts are for the most part self-conscious performances. There is little or any self-consciousness in Dylan's work; rather, it is always in the moment, on the spot. We know that, much to the chagrin of his record producers, studio musicians, and record company executives, this is Dylan's preferred mode of recording, and we can hear the results with our own ears. And with rare exception and to degrees of success that vary with the aesthetics and arrangements of a particular tour, this is also the case on stage; Dylan has more in common with jazz musicians than pop musicians when it comes to performing his songs before a live audience (again, to the consternation of many of his listeners and musical partners, including notably Joan Baez, who could never get Dylan to commit to specific phrasing or even exact lyrics for which she could provide harmonies).

Dylan shares these performance characteristics, as it were, with the Prophets, who were addressing their people out of divine inspiration, either directly or indirectly. The Prophets were performers, too; Jeremiah was particularly theatrical as he wandered the streets of Jerusalem prophesying, engaging the use of props such as a cattle yoke to symbolize the fate that would befall backsliders who refused to give up their idolatrous practices.

Dylan could easily see himself slipping right into this tradition, starting out as a prophet to some acclaim (his early, folk-protest period); having his "tribe"—his folk-music followers—rebel against him after he "went electric" (and then, repeatedly, having his followers reject him: when he "went country" with *Nashville Skyline*, "Las Vegas" on the 1978 world tour, and when he began to "preach repentance" in 1979); and, like Moses and Jeremiah before him, finding himself "saved" by a "slave"—in his case, the descendant of slaves.

From the very beginning, Dylan shared another characteristic with the Prophets. In his lyrics, his presentation, his music (much of it blues-derived), and especially in his voice, there is a sense of futility balancing or offsetting the purposefulness of his delivery. There is a basic level of futility built into the typical blues song and vocal, but Dylan's songs aren't typical blues, and there's a different kind of world-weariness about his performance that has more in common with the Prophets than with any Mississippi Delta bluesman singing about love and betrayal. Dylan is addressing his audience on a more lofty, intellectual plane, challenging their notions and preconceptions and behaviors much like the Prophets. And while this is the task to which he was apparently born, or called, it's also one with a built-in modicum of failure (as it was, in large part, for the biblical Prophets). "Jeremiah bemoaned his own fate," writes Rabbi Nosson Scherman. "Why had he been the one chosen to not only foretell the horrors but to witness them, and even to be at the mercy of the brethren he had been trying to save?" Jeremiah's burden was not only futile, destined to fail, but it even caused him physical pain: "My word is like fire," says G-d to Jeremiah (23:29), "and like a hammer that shatters a rock."

Thus it was in large part for Dylan: a witness of his times, drawing moral lessons from the hypocrisies that surrounded him, and warning his listeners to think or to act or to bear the consequences. In response, more times than not, he was greeted with boos or, worse, indifference; got bad reviews; or found himself on the wrong end of shoddy journalism ("Someone's got it in for me / They're planting stories in the press," he sang on 1974's "Idiot Wind"). Or, as G-d said to Jeremiah, "You will tell them all these things, but they will not listen to you" (Jeremiah 7:27), which didn't stop the Prophet from continuing with his calling—through the course of being taunted, beaten, and imprisoned in a dungeon on false charges of being a deserter, only to be thrown into a deep mud pit and subjected to more indignities—until his book and his life come to an end forty-five chapters later.

Likewise, no matter the intensity of his performance, the beauty of his poetry, the conviction of his rhetoric, in songs addressing topical or political concerns, matters of the heart, or greater ethical and moral matters—into all of which Dylan pours everything he's got—there is also a sense that, like Sisyphus pushing the rock up the hill, Dylan's task is ultimately futile. His words, like those of the Prophets, are doomed to fall on deaf ears; people may hear but they don't listen; they may catch sight of him but they don't see. It's not for nothing that his first and perhaps greatest anthem, "Blowin' in the Wind," addresses this very concern. Often heard as a civil rights anthem, it is more than that: it's the cry of a forsaken Prophet: "How many ears must one man have / Before he can hear people cry / The answer, my friend, is blowin' in the wind."

Yet Dylan, like the Prophet—like the Jeremiah of "Yonder Comes Sin" (and like the Jeremiah of the Bible)—perseveres. Certainly, in the case of Bob Dylan the man, a large motivation is money: being "Bob Dylan" quickly became a profitable endeavor, due to his early success. Some artists labor in obscurity, money be damned, and have to opt for other jobs—teaching gigs, artisanship, desk work—to get by. At a very young age, Bob Dylan was freed from ever having to consider these options. And given the tremendous publishing catalog he had amassed by 1966, he could afford several periods of relative silence or commercial inactivity (or poor-selling albums and concerts) in the pursuit of his own muse, which in his case just happened to be the muse of the Prophet. This level of commercial success could have fallen upon any number of Dylan's Greenwich Village peers—Tom Paxton, Phil Ochs, Dave Van Ronk—but it didn't, and it's easy to see why: Dylan, alone among them, was speaking about transcendent concerns and to the ages. The others were all limited in their scope and vision; much to the chagrin of many fans and critics, Dylan saw no boundaries in what he could do and where he could take his art, in terms of form (electric rock; drawing and painting; films and videos) and content (traditional folk and blues; topical protest; confessional love songs; hate songs; novelty numbers, and so on). What underlined and unified almost all of it was the recurrence of the prophetic impulse in Dylan's work. And in this way, the work was both inspired and futile, and never perhaps more than during the late period of his career, which can be said to have begun with 1989's *Oh Mercy*, leading into his "Never Ending Tour" of the 1990s and 2000s and the later albums full of brooding songs about aging, illness, mortality, nostalgia, and apocalypse.

As Dylan himself remarked in a 1985 interview, "What I learned in Bible school was just . . . an extension of the same thing I believed in all along, but just couldn't verbalize or articulate. Whether you want to believe Jesus Christ is the Messiah is irrelevant, but whether you're aware of the messianic complex, that's . . . important." On some level there was little difference between Dylan's "Christian" songs and early protest anthems such as "The Times They Are a-Changin'" and "When the Ship Comes In"—they all adhere to a worldview steeped in messianism, a messianism shared by some Christians and Jews alike, and in the latter case, particularly the Lubavitcher Hasidim with whom Dylan had strongly identified in the early 1970s and again in the early 1980s and then throughout the next quarter century.

How consciously aware was Dylan of the similarity of what he was doing to the role of the biblical Prophets? As we've seen, Dylan was always an unreliable interviewee, dissembling as much as answering honestly, whether out of frustration with the stupidity of his interlocutors' questions or in a purposeful attempt to mislead in order to protect his privacy—even if it was just the privacy of his thoughts—or simply just to take the piss.

But some interviews seemed less likely to be put-ons than others. In the mid-1970s, when interviews were few and far between (until Dylan found it worth using the press to publicize pet causes such as Rubin "Hurricane" Carter and to get maximum, free public exposure for his dense, difficult film *Renaldo and Clara*), the existence of a serious running motif points to a consistent, sincere point of view about his relationship with G-d and His influence on Dylan's work. "I don't care what people expect of me," he told Jim Jerome of *People* in November 1975. "I'm doin' God's work. That's all I know." Not only is he doing G-d's work; Dylan credits G-d himself for creating "Bob Dylan": "I didn't consciously pursue the Bob Dylan myth. It was given to me—by God." Replace "Bob Dylan" with "Jeremiah" or "Isaiah"—or even "Jesus"—and one could easily imagine this sentence being spoken by one of the biblical Prophets.

A year later, Dylan sat down for an interview with Neil Hickey of *TV Guide* to promote *Hard Rain,* the network broadcast of one of the final Rolling Thunder Revue concerts. After his correspondent points out the biblical imagery that informs so much of his work, Dylan replies, "There's a mystic in all of us. . . . It's part of our nature. Some are shown more than others. Or maybe we're all shown the same things, but some make more use of it," clearly including himself in the latter category. While Dylan still has a sense of humor about his relationship with G-d—when asked how he envisions Him, he replies with a laugh, "How come nobody asks Kris Kristofferson questions like that?"—he does allow that he can "see God in a daisy." Identifying his work with prayer—specifically Jewish liturgy and the psalms, as well as anticipating the imagery that will form the 1981 song "Every Grain of Sand"—he continues, "I can see God at night in the wind and the rain. I see creation just about everywhere. The highest form of song is prayer. King David's, Solomon's, the wailing of a coyote, the rumble of the earth. It must be wonderful to be God."

In another interview a couple of years later, Dylan took umbrage at the truism "God is dead." Interviewed by Ron Rosenbaum for

Playboy in 1978, Dylan claimed that the downfall of America could be traced from the day that the phrase "Is God Dead?" appeared on the cover of *Time*. "Would you think that was a responsible thing to do?" he asked rhetorically. "What does God think of that? I mean, if you were God, how would you like to see that written about yourself?" (In 1997, *Time* plastered "Dylan Lives!" on its cover, in an article championing his comeback album, *Time Out of Mind*. Bob Dylan, 1; G-d, 0.)

Just as "Yonder Comes Sin" suggests that Dylan had found consolation in the fate of other Prophets besides the one crowned with thorns who died a criminal's death, the song itself, alongside others from the early sessions that would eventually produce *Shot of Love*, hint at Dylan's original musical goals for that album, and in greater context, for the period stretching from 1979 to 1983 and perhaps beyond. If *Slow Train Coming* and *Saved* were Dylan's forays into gospel music, musically as well as lyrically—and certainly *Saved* qualifies as such, whereas *Slow Train* was more of a grab-bag of African-American musical styles, including funk, soul, and reggae—on the basis of early sessions recorded at Rundown Studios in April 1981, he was apparently intent on making a full album's worth of R&B-influenced songs. Tapes from these sessions that circulate unofficially capture Dylan, his band, and his singers working their way through sketches of unfinished songs powered by soul and funk grooves that, when considered in context with numbers that *did* finally make it to the completed *Shot of Love*, including "Heart of Mine," "Watered-Down Love," "Dead Man, Dead Man," and the title track, suggest that Dylan's aim was to pay tribute to the black music that grew out of gospel: R&B, soul, and funk. Songs such as "Is It Worth It?" a dark, loping reggae-blues, find Dylan mining a whole new vein of personal paranoia, beyond the sort evinced by *Street Legal's* "New Pony." These tapes also offer a fascinating glimpse into Dylan's rehearsal process at the time: on a number labeled "Ah Ah Ah Ah," presumably because he had yet to come up with a chorus and just sang those words, he hums his way through verses and choruses for which he has yet to write lyrics; he sings bass lines; he teaches the complex, jazzy chord progressions to the musicians on the guitar. And at times, he also laughs (he turns his laugh into the chorus of "Ah Ah Ah Ah" at the end, singing "Hah hah hah hah").

The album that was completed at Clover Studios in May 1981 was produced by Chuck Plotkin, a Columbia Records staffer fresh off his success engineering Bruce Springsteen's album *The River* (Plotkin would go on to produce many of Springsteen's subsequent albums, including the megahit *Born in the U.S.A.*), and veered away from Dylan's total commitment to the bluesy soul and funk grooves heard on the rehearsal tapes recorded the previous month. Vestiges of Dylan's original plan can still be heard in "Watered-Down Love," a blatant attempt at a Motown-style pop tune; the gospel-laced hard funk of the title track; the infectious Southern soul of "Heart of Mine" (featuring Ringo Starr and the Rolling Stones guitarist Ron Wood); and "Dead Man, Dead Man," bringing the proceedings up to date with one of Dylan's first full-fledged reggae tracks, foreshadowing the rhythms powering much of 1983's *Infidels*.

With few exceptions, most notably "Property of Jesus," Dylan left Jesus behind him on *Shot of Love*—but even on that track, full of self-righteousness and self-pity, Dylan isn't singing about Jesus so much as complaining about the response to his supposed conversion. It's a cranky, bitter, updated version of "Positively Fourth Street," utterly lacking that song's visceral power and ingenuity. That self-pity runs through several songs on the album, including the title track, which also invokes Jesus, but again, only in the service of portraying the narrator as the victim of betrayal.

For the most part, *Shot of Love* is, as the title hints, a collection of love songs. The title track, kicking off the album, is a fiery, sensual rant by someone in need of a love fix, someone who is seemingly not satisfied nor at peace with what he currently has going on. Instead, he is paranoid, ill at ease to the point of being emotionally unbalanced, and desperate, like an addict. There's no real indication that he's talking about heavenly love, either: this guy has had it with everything and is in dire need of a physical fix.

"Heart of Mine" is lighter musically and lyrically, powered by some of Dylan's best honky-tonk piano playing ever imprinted on vinyl, and addressed entirely to the singer's heart, warning it away from the ties that bind. Dylan also uses the piano to drive "Lenny Bruce," a balladic paean to the irreverent comedian who was hounded to death by government officials for his freewheeling use of obscenities in his comic routines. "Watered-Down Love" hides another ambivalent view of love in the guise of a Motown pop tune, driven by an infectious guitar riff courtesy of James Taylor's long-time sideman Danny "Kootch" Kortchmar.

The eventual addition of "The Groom's Still Waitin' at the Altar" to the album's program opened it up somewhat, giving it more teeth and urgency. Dylan is in prophesying mode once again: "Cities on fire, phones out of order / They're killing nuns and soldiers, there's fighting on the border." The song jumps around from those kinds of sociopolitical observations to personal commentary and an obscure narrative about a woman named Claudette. To say the narrator is less than charitable about Claudette (whom he surmises "could be respectably married or running a whorehouse in Buenos Aires") and those who "persecute" him ("Try to be pure at heart, they arrest you for robbery / Mistake your shyness for aloofness, your silence for snobbery") is an understatement. But somehow all the bitterness is redeemed by the hope implied in the refrain:

> *West of the Jordan, east of the rock of Gibraltar*
> *I see the turnin' of the page, curtain risin' on a new age*
> *See the groom still waitin' at the altar.*

(These lyrics, which Dylan sings on the recorded version, differ from the officially published version of the song, which reverses the compass points.)

Besides locating the dawning of a new age in the Middle East ("West of the Jordan, east of the Rock of Gibraltar"), Dylan is playing coy here. When one pledges himself to Jesus and the Church, one enters into a relationship likened to a marriage. But this person whom Dylan is singing about hasn't gone through with his vows for some reason. He's been left at the altar—perhaps by Claudette, who doesn't appear to be the woman he thought she was at first—and still owns the status of an unwed groom. In other words, he hasn't married, nor has he entered into that sort of relationship with the church. Rather, as Dylan sang a dozen years earlier, he sees his light come shining "from the west down to the east," a reversal of the natural order, but one that is intended to bring about long-promised redemption. Dylan also injects a note of doubt or unease, which he will explore in much greater detail in the final song of the album, in the brilliant couplet

> *Got the message this morning, the one that was sent to me*
> *About the madness of becoming what one was never meant to be.*

He never says who sent the message, nor does he judge it, even though it seemingly could be one of those messages from "so-called friends" who have called him out on being a Christian. He merely follows with the refrain, locating the site of redemption in the Middle East, to where he will return in a couple of years' time.

Half the songs on the album are sung as duets with Clydie King, doubling Dylan's vocal; the rest feature King as part of a four-part choir with Carolyn Dennis, Regina McCrary, and Madelyn Quebec. If *Shot of Love* is a meandering disappointment, Dylan redeems himself in "Every Grain of Sand," a song widely considered to be one of the best of his canon. Coming at the end of the album, and given a hymnlike arrangement, with Dylan's voice mixed far out front over one keyboard drone and another keyboard riff, soft bass and drums, subdued backing vocals by the choir, and two harmonica solos, the song bears the weight of the entire album and, in form and context alone, shouts out "summary statement."

The most surprising element of "Every Grain of Sand"—inspired as much by Alexander Pope, John Keats, and William Blake as by the Bible—is the lack of certainty conveyed by the song. For the last three albums, Dylan's narrator has come across as wholly confident of his path and totally convinced of his righteousness. Suddenly,

Dylan sounds naked and unsure of himself. He has reinvested notes of ambiguity and ambivalence and doubt into his very personal narrative, and the singsongy, gospel-tinged ballad arrangement only forefronts this aspect of the work. The narration is retrospective, even nostalgic, and tinged with more than a modicum of regret. No longer is he certain of having achieved easy, guaranteed salvation through his acceptance of divine grace; he is now tormented by "this chain of events that [he] must break." He seems to have swapped theological certainty for existential despair; the bloom is off the rose, and he is "hanging in the balance."

William Blake uses the same central image of the grain of sand to open his poem "Auguries of Innocence," to which we have seen Dylan previously allude:

To see a world in a grain of sand,
And a heaven in a wild flower,
Hold infinity in the palm of your hand,
And eternity in an hour.

There is other imagery from Blake upon which Dylan builds phrases, including the "flowers of indulgence," the "sun beat down upon the steps of time," and the "broken mirror of innocence."

The song describes a moment in time of utter, total desperation, somehow connected to an accounting of oneself:

In the time of my confession, in the hour of my deepest need
When the pool of tears beneath my feet flood every newborn seed.

Anyone who has gone through the *teshuvah* process of Yom Kippur—the Jewish Day of Atonement—will recognize this imagery, both figuratively and literally. The yearly cycle of renewing one's relationship with G-d culminates on this day with the ritual and personal confession of one's sins and inadequacies—not with any intermediary, but directly between man and G-d—in order to wipe the slate clean and be written into the Book of Life for the next year. Hence, the hour of one's deepest need. The ritual process is one of intense self-examination and reflection, such that when practiced in its most intense and serious manner, including supplication through the beating of one's own breast, it is not unheard-of to shed tears as one experiences the true awe of having one's fate decided at this very moment, depending on a balance between one's piety and sincerity on the one hand versus the nature and seriousness of one's sins on the other. No priest or rabbi intercedes on one's behalf, and no sacrificial lamb—not since the biblical Azazel—in beastly or human form can assume the burden of one's guilt.

One approaches this day and this ceremony in the guise of a dead person—shrouded in white as if ready for burial (literally wearing a *kitl*, a burial caftan), neither eating nor drinking nor washing nor engaging in any other daily habits or ablutions that are the sole province of the living—existing for twenty-five hours in a state of suspended animation, somewhere between life and death. One's entire being is solely focused on the task before him: to pray for forgiveness and for another year of life:

> *There's a dyin' voice within me reaching out somewhere*
> *Toiling in the danger and in the morals of despair.*

At no other point during the year does one come so clearly face-to-face with his mortal fate, tied up in the consequence of his actions:

> *Don't have the inclination to look back on any mistake,*
> *Like Cain, I now behold this chain of events that I must break.*

And at no other time does one feel so empowered to regain control of one's life, to set oneself on a new course, to become fully aware of the contingency and the delicacy of the gift of life:

> *In the fury of the moment I can see the Master's hand*
> *In every leaf that trembles, in every grain of sand.*

The genius of the song is the manner in which Dylan skirts the particular and the universal, portraying the intense spiritual experience available to everyone (and surely the Yom Kippur ritual is not the only such framework constructed for this sort of taking stock) while revealing his own personal doubts, fears, and vulnerabilities, especially in light of what came before:

> *I gaze into the doorway of temptation's angry flame*
> *And every time I pass that way I always hear my name.*

Proclaiming one's belief in G-d, or a god—even one who allegedly died for one's sins—doesn't eradicate temptation nor does it immunize one against the *yetzer hara,* the evil inner urge, which is a wholesale part of us and which we take with us to the grave.

Dylan almost succumbs to self-pity when he sings:

> *I have gone from rags to riches in the sorrow of the night*
> *In the violence of a summer's dream, in the chill of a wintry light,*
> *In the bitter dance of loneliness fading into space,*
> *In the broken mirror of innocence on each forgotten face.*

It's another spin on, "Oh, it's lonely at the top," but it works in this case because it is utterly sincere—no one doubts the heavy toll Dylan has paid in exchange for his fame and fortune, nor the cost he's paid in terms of broken hearts and lost love, and the terrors that must accompany a life of constant movement—even in twentieth-century style in first-class seating or on a luxury tour bus, the life of a wandering minstrel is still the life of a wandering minstrel, and nighttime brings with it pain, loneliness, and sorrows.

Dylan's final confession is one of fear, paranoia, and the feeling of insignificance in the face of all that's gone on before, in the insubstantial role his existence assumes in the context of the greater narrative that unfolds from the beginning, and as just a piece of dust in G-d's Creation. In its confessionary, consolatory nature, in its implied appeal for forgiveness, in its expression of powerlessness in the face of the "Master's hand," the song functions much like one of the biblical psalms, not surprising given its origins in psalm

139:16–18, which turns on the central imagery of the grains of sand while tying it to the very Book of Life that is the centerpiece of the Yom Kippur service:

> Your eyes saw my unshaped form, and in Your book all were recorded; though they will be fashioned through many days, to Him they are one. To me—how weighty are Your thoughts, O G-d! How very great are their number! Were I to count them, they would outnumber the grains of sand, even if I were to be constantly awake and always with You.

And thus does Dylan bring to a close *Shot of Love* on a note suggesting that he has put the recent past behind him, while foreshadowing themes to come.

Dylan paid for his apparent embrace of Christianity through song in more ways than one. Besides the critical drubbing *Saved* received, his concerts during this period were hard sells. The man who attracted ten million ticket orders for his comeback tour in 1974, selling out stadium-size arenas, wound up playing to empty seats in theaters with one tenth the capacity. For the first time since 1964, a Dylan album (*Saved*) failed to crack the Top 20, and the hopes pinned on *Shot of Love,* intended in part to rectify, at least commercially, the injuries Dylan caused himself failed to materialize—the album sold even fewer copies than *Saved.* That all this happened in the wake of his expensive divorce settlement and custody battle with Sara at the same time that he was racking up huge attorneys' fees for the lawsuits and countersuits with Albert Grossman only made things more challenging for Dylan, and so once again he formed a band and took to the road, beginning a yearlong tour in Europe in June 1981. That tour, too, failed to ignite much critical or commercial excitement, even with the return of many of his classic songs from the 1960s to the program and the addition of Al Kooper to his touring band. Fans still weren't sure what to make of the gospel songs that peppered his set lists, the female backup singers whom many felt detracted from the vocal focus on Dylan, and the sprawling musical arrangements played by a large band of mostly anonymous musicians. After his longtime friend and film collaborator Howard Alk took his life over the New Year's holiday at the end of 1981, Dylan's world seemed to be crashing around him. At age forty, not even a belief in Jesus could save the man whom many once looked to as a messiah of sorts.

NINE
PSALMS

After a yearlong respite from touring and recording, reputedly study-ing Judaism with a Lubavitcher rabbi in Crown Heights, Brooklyn, Dylan returned to the recording studio in spring 1983 to record the follow-up to *Shot of Love,* with Mark Knopfler—now a huge pop star as the leader of Dire Straits—returning as guitarist and pro-ducer. While preparing for the album's release, Dylan spoke with a reporter from his home state's *Minneapolis City Pages* about his Jew-ish roots and his identification with the prophetic tradition:

> Roots, man—we're talking about Jewish roots, you want to know more? Check up on Elijah the prophet. He could make it rain. Isa-iah the prophet, even Jeremiah—see if their brethren didn't want to bust their brains for telling it right like it is, yeah—these are my roots, I suppose.

When the album was released, it turned out to be another attempt on Dylan's part, very much along the lines of *Shot of Love,* to straddle the line between overtly religious songs and nonreligious material. This time out, however, the "religious" songs were couched in lan-guage and imagery that were quintessential Dylan. Gone were the direct certitudes of *Slow Train Coming* and *Saved*. Here they were replaced by two epic poems fueled by the Jamaican rhythm section of Sly Dunbar and Robbie Shakespeare. Religious images jumped out from other songs, too, but they were all in the service of tales of woe, abstract threats, and love songs. Most suggestive was the album title itself, *Infidels*, which had no obviously direct correlative with any particular song on the album (unlike the names of his previous three recordings, which were all taken from song titles). Just who or what were the infidels in question was never made clear.

The lead track, "Jokerman," kicks off with an image drawn directly from the Jewish Days of Awe—from which Dylan would draw repeatedly over the next quarter century. Dylan opens the album with a scene from *tashlich*: "Standing on the waters casting your bread . . . ," whose source is the biblical injunction "Cast your bread upon the waters" (Ecclesiastes 11:1). This isn't the first time Dylan would refer to this ritual; as we've seen, he used the term "bread crumb sins" in his 1964 song "Gates of Eden."

Beyond that, the code of "Jokerman" is elusive, and it's difficult to give the song a unified, coherent reading. The title figure has been variously identified as Jesus, G-d, the Jewish Messiah, or Dylan himself—perhaps in reference to his earliest singing group, the Jokers—or some combination of the four (to paraphrase the old Woody Allen joke, one has to identify oneself with some sort of role model). The biblical David is also invoked on this album; Dylan seemed to identify strongly with David as a sensual loner, an outlaw king, a ruthless monarch, a musician-poet, and a great lover, but also as a figure full of inner torment, as expressed throughout the book of Psalms, which he penned—psalms that in their purest form are really songs.

Dylan overtly refers to David in the lines "Michelangelo indeed could've carved out your features," and various other phrases suit David—and Dylan—to a *t*. "Shedding off one more layer of skin / Keeping one step ahead of the persecutor within," he sings, with great insight into both his and David's ever-changing personality and evasive maneuvers in their (mostly failed) attempt to avoid temptation in the form of the *yetzer hara*, the evil urge.

"You're a man of the mountains, you can walk on the clouds / Manipulator of crowds, you're a dream twister," he sings, describing both David and himself. The image of a ruler who walks with clouds also recalls the biblical Daniel's vision of the Messiah:

> I looked on in night visions and behold! with the clouds of heaven, one like a man came. . . . He was given dominion, glory, and kingship, so that all peoples, nations and languages must serve him; his dominion would be an everlasting dominion that shall not pass, and his kingship would never be destroyed (Daniel 7:13–14).

Later, he finds Jokerman "Resting in the fields, far from the turbulent space," much like David, constantly on the run from his sworn enemy, King Saul.

"I and I" also strongly draws upon the figure of David—"some righteous king who wrote psalms beside moonlit streams." But this time it is Moses' mystical experience that serves as the central image of the song, as expressed in the refrain, "I and I / One says to the other, no man sees my face and lives."

"One" is G-d and the "other" is Moses. As it is written in Exodus 33:20, in response to Moses' plea to see G-d's face, He replies, "No man can see My face and live," although He consents to allow Moses to catch a glimpse of His back in passing (or, in some translations, to hear, know, or understand His name). The manner in which Dylan draws the parallelism of this encounter between G-d and Moses as "I and I" reflects back both on the Rastafarian belief in oneness and the "I-Thou" theology of Martin Buber.

As elsewhere on *Infidels*, Dylan seems to be drawing himself closer to the faith of his ancestors while separating himself from his dalliance with Christianity. He sings, "Took an untrodden path once, where the swift don't win the race," paraphrasing Ecclesiastes 9:11—"the race is not won by the swift"—and continues, "It goes to the worthy, who can divine the word of truth." (The published lyrics say "divide the word of truth," but to my ears it sounds distinctly like "divine," which makes a lot more sense—in the word's connotation of "to understand"—than "divide.") The "untrodden path" was Dylan's road to Damascus, but it was an empty journey. As he continues:

> *Took a stranger to teach me to look into justice's beautiful face*
> *And to see an eye for an eye and a tooth for a tooth.*

In other words, he has returned to the biblical concept of justice—the one with a "beautiful face," the one that Christianity attempted to supersede. Who the "stranger" is who taught Dylan that "justice's beautiful face" was to be found right back where he started is unknown; possibly it was one of the Brooklyn rabbis who brought Dylan back to the fold. In the next verse, two lone men are waiting for a train to arrive—an allusion to the "slow train comin'"—but this time out, there's no sign of that train. Just a few years ago, it was just "up around the bend"; now "there's nobody in sight." And finally, in an echo of the last verse of "Tangled Up in Blue," albeit darker and more desperate, the narrator is "still pushin' myself along the road, the darkest part," after having "made shoes for everyone, even you, while I still go barefoot." That "even you" in the middle of the line is classic Dylan, punctuating the phrase, making it leap out at the listener, who is now directly implicated, Dylan seeing himself as the tireless servant of his devoted followers, the reluctant prophet who serves up testimony in the form of songs, or here, "shoes," that clothe the soul, while he remains, like Moses to the ungrateful, stiff-necked Israelites, a figure repaid with scorn.

Anyone looking for clarity on *Infidels* could find it most blatantly on "Neighborhood Bully," a Rolling Stones–style rocker (featuring the playing of the former Rolling Stones guitarist Mick Taylor) that was a thinly veiled paean to Israel and Jewish peoplehood. Never had Dylan so clearly identified in song or in any other statement where his political and personal sympathies lie on one of the most important issues of the twentieth century (and this without ever using the words "Israel" or "Jew"). And never did anyone so perfectly encapsulate three thousand years of history as Dylan achieved in this full-tilt rock song, portraying both Israel and the Jewish people as the perennial underdog, doomed to be opposed but scrappy as all get out.

The song has a point of view, too, making the case that Zionism is inextricably linked with Judaism. The two are practically equated here, as Dylan jumps back and forth with verses about modern-day Israel's struggles against its enemies and ancient Jewish history, drawing parallels between the two and suggesting that the contemporary nation-state is vital to the continued survival and prosperity of the contemporary people of the Bible.

Dylan opens the song describing the status of Israel today vis-à-vis its Arab neighbors. He also introduces the sarcasm behind the term "neighborhood bully" by positing the preposterousness of viewing Israel as an aggressor in the face of an enemy a millionfold its size. Dylan continues in this vein, describing a neighborhood bully that is "not supposed to fight back" but "to have thick skin," to "lay down and die when his door is kicked in."

In verse three, using the same format of the first two verses, Dylan shifts the connotation of "neighborhood bully" from Israel to the Jewish people:

> *The neighborhood bully been driven out of every land*
> *He's wandered the earth an exiled man.*
> *Seen his family scattered, his people hounded and torn,*
> *He's always on trial for just being born*

—recounting the history of violence, expulsion, and oppression that has been the case more often than not since the Jews were driven out of ancient Israel, first by the Babylonians in 607 B.C.E. and then by the Romans in the year 70 C.E. Later in the song (which jumps around in time), he names "every empire that's enslaved him . . . Egypt and Rome, even the great Babylon," pointing out that they're all gone while Jews still live. Dylan pulls some of his language from scripture—"He's wandered the earth an exiled man" echoes Isaiah 49:21: "I have been bereaved and alone, an exile and a wanderer." Dylan boasts of Jewish accomplishments in the face of adversity and, taking the long view of history, emphasizes that these accomplishmcnts have been for the most part those of a people without friends. Dylan even digs deep into modern politics in lines referring to the expulsion of the PLO from Lebanon, the condemnation of Israel by a United Nations–sponsored women's conference on human rights, and the bombing of the Iraqi nuclear reactor

> *Well, he knocked out a lynch mob, he was criticized,*
> *Old women condemned him, said he should apologize*
> *Then he destroyed a bomb factory, nobody was glad.*
> *The bombs were meant for him. He was supposed to feel bad.*

There was prescience in this final couplet: Israel's pinpoint air strike on the French-built Iraqi nuclear reactor, which was engineered to produce weapons-grade plutonium, postponed by several decades Saddam Hussein's campaign to amass the "weapons of mass destruction" that President George W. Bush used as justification for the U.S. invasion of Iraq. Israel's clean, efficient removal of the threat versus Bush's clumsy and ill-advised land invasion that led to a nearly decade-long quagmire—including the deaths of thousands of Iraqi civilians and U.S. military personnel—could not have been more different.

Dylan directly ties himself to the image of Israel or the Jews forever standing on the hill—presumably a reference to Jerusalem—waiting for the end of time ("Running out the clock") by including a photograph of himself on thc LP's inner sleeve kneeling on a hill overlooking the Old City of Jerusalem. Dylan's strong identification with Israel, however, didn't endear him to the American left—including the left-leaning music critics of *The Village Voice,* who took the sentiments expressed in this song, and added to them a willful misreading of "Union Sundown" and who knows what else, to call Dylan the "William F. Buckley of rock and roll" in the alternative newsweekly's review of *Infidels.*

The refrain of "Man of Peace" goes: "You know that sometimes Satan comes as a man of peace," but it's not clear if the narrator is referring to false messiahs or the original man of peace. Dylan paints a series of portraits of hypocrites, thieves, and tricksters passing themselves off as do-gooders, but who are in fact the Devil incarnate, or at least his henchmen. For example, in the first verse—with another of Dylan's great opening lines that vie with the one in "Like a Rolling Stone"—he sings:

> *Look out your window, baby, there's a scene you'd like to catch,*
> *The band is playing "Dixie," a man got his hand outstretched*
> *Could be the Führer*
> *Could be the local priest.*
> *You know sometimes Satan comes as a man of peace.*

So here we have a gentleman taking part in what presumably is a second line—a New Orleans postfuneral procession—trying to raise money for the bereaved. But for some reason, the man is not to be trusted. Even though on the surface he is a "man of peace"—in this case, a man of the cloth, the local priest—he could in fact be Adolf Hitler in priest's clothing, since sometimes Satan is known to disguise himself as a priest.

This sets up the basic strategy of the song, in which the "good intentions" of men who sing love songs or whose tongues easily flatter "can be evil." The man of peace preys upon all kinds; he's a beast whose eyes "are looking like they're on a rabbit hunt." Especially vulnerable to his deceitful ministrations are those whose "troubles feel like they weigh a ton," for these people are easily manipulated or taken advantage of—a reference, perhaps, to Dylan himself, who at one of the most vulnerable times in his life succumbed to those who came to succor him in the guise of men of peace.

This raises the question as to whether Dylan is suggesting here that his "conversion" was encouraged by those whose "good intentions" were "evil," causing "trees that've stood for a thousand years suddenly [to] fall," meaning the ancient lineage of his Judaism giving way to a foreign faith in one fell swoop. Dylan personalizes the song, as he often does, in the final verse, which in tone bears a resemblance to the final verse of "Neighborhood Bully"—and it's in context with the latter song especially, as well as with "Jokerman" and "I and I," that this speculative reading gains conviction:

Somewhere Mama's weeping for her blue-eyed boy,
She's holding them little white shoes and that little broken toy
And he's following a star,
The same one them three men followed from the East.
I hear that sometimes Satan comes as a man of peace.

Dylan hasn't often evoked his mother in song, but when he has, it's been as "Mama." While at the time she didn't acknowledge it publicly, insisting to interviewers that her son was still Jewish, Beatty Zimmerman supposedly intervened and took him to visit his boyhood friend Howard Rutman, under the guise of his needing to get his teeth cleaned (Rutman was a dentist). As an old friend from Herzl Camp days—and by this time, Beatty having married Rutman's uncle, a cousin of sorts—Rutman was one of the few people in the world able to confront Dylan directly, without pretense or having to beat around the bush; when Rutman spoke to Bob Dylan, he was one of the few people in the world really speaking to Bobby Zimmerman. While examining Dylan's mouth, he supposedly pointed to a cross Dylan was wearing around his neck, and asked him, "Bob, what's up with this? . . . Bob, you're Jewish." Rutman, who had remained religiously observant or grown even more so over the years, invited Dylan to his house for dinner. Dylan brought his girlfriend at the time and wound up incredibly embarrassed by the manner in which she carried on about Jesus to Rutman and his wife, who were having no truck with such talk. Dylan realized it was a huge mistake having brought her with him in the first place, but more than that, one gets the sense that his convictions lay more with the woman than with the ideology she was spouting.

So Dylan paints a picture of his mother forlorn about the fact that her boy has converted to Christianity, but then twists the understanding of the refrain 180 degrees, because in this verse, the man of peace that he's singing about is none other than Jesus. So when he sings the refrain, with a slight twist in the first two words, from "You know" to "I hear," so that now he sings "I hear that sometimes Satan comes as a man of peace," the meaning is now that Jesus himself is Satan.

For the first time since *Desire,* Dylan recorded an album without the use of a female backing choir. The only woman's voice heard on the entire album is Clydie King's, harmonizing on the chorus of "Union Sundown." Otherwise, the album was a relatively stripped-down affair compared to the five albums preceding it and several that would follow, all of which made extensive use of female choruses and an instrumental palette larger than the typical rock lineup of guitars, bass, drums, and keyboards employed on *Infidels.*

Along with the picture of Dylan overlooking the Old City of Jerusalem, with a perfect view of the Temple Mount, this only added to suspicions that he had returned to the faith of his forefathers. The photo, shot by his former wife, Sara, was apparently taken on a recent trip to Israel, where their son Jesse celebrated his bar mitzvah on the plaza in front of the Wailing Wall.

Released in the MTV era, the album produced Dylan's first official music video to go along with the ill-chosen single, "Sweetheart Like You," which consisted in its entirety of an older waitress sweeping up a restaurant after closing time while Dylan and band performed the song from a small stage in the same room. *Infidels* was given a mixed reception in the press. While some reviewers hailed it as a return to form, Dylan still seemed to be suffering a backlash that wouldn't quit. If *Infidels* was a failure, it was at least a noble one. Knopfler was reportedly unhappy with the way the album was finally mixed, and, as was typical for Dylan, probably the best song he recorded for the album, "Blind Willie McTell," was left off.

As it turned out, *Infidels* marked a high point in Dylan's recording that wouldn't be surpassed until the end of the decade, with his masterful work *Oh Mercy.* In the interim, with only rare exceptions, Dylan churned out second-rate material that found him seemingly growing more indifferent by the year, from *Empire Burlesque* in 1985 until the point in 1988 when he released *Down in the Groove,* which wasn't even a coherent album in the sense of one planned and executed, but rather one consisting of leftovers from various other albums and projects, aborted or otherwise, from the last few years (although it wasn't presented as such a compilation, but rather as a regular album).

This period of time was also marked by some of the most disappointing concerts of Dylan's career. His tours, for the most part, paired him with other superstar acts, no doubt in order to boost attendance for his shows at a time when he probably couldn't sell out theaters, much less arenas. In several cases, Dylan used these other acts, including Tom Petty and the Heartbreakers and the Grateful Dead, as his backing bands. It's easy to see why Tom Petty and the Dead's Jerry Garcia would have agreed to these arrangements. While on their own they could easily fill stadiums, they still were in awe of Dylan: Petty was probably the single most successful artist to build a career in large part on Dylan's sound (albeit interpreted secondhand by the Byrds), and while Garcia and the Dead had their own thing going on musically, they always borrowed liberally from Dylan's songbook and felt a kinship—musical, spiritual, chemical, and otherwise—with him.

While Dylan's pairing with Petty was probably the most successful of the decade, it wasn't enough to save him from embarrassments, including the 1986 album *Knocked Out Loaded,* which featured the Heartbreakers' accompaniment on several tracks. Columbia Records failed to release a live album of the Dylan/Petty concerts, instead opting to document his 1984 European tour backed by a band composed of washed-up English rockers (Mick Taylor again, Ian McLagan, formerly of the Faces) and the guitarist Carlos Santana on the wholly forgettable *Real Live,* as undistinguished as its title, and *Dylan and the Dead,* which featured meandering performances, including the spectacle of Dylan forgetting the words to several of his own songs.

The title of *Empire Burlesque,* an album full of filmic references and dialogue, refers to movie theaters of that name back in the mid-century—the era when Dylan's extended family's business interests included a privately owned chain of such cinema palaces (none of which was called Empire or Empire Burlesque). Over the years, scribes have parsed every line of this album to find a remarkable number of phrases lifted right out of the movies. "Seeing the Real You at Last" is made up almost in its entirety of dialogue from films, especially Humphrey Bogart movies and Westerns.

The title also was a nod to the cinematic quality of at least one song, "When the Night Comes Falling from the Sky," a kind of extended elaboration on "All Along the Watchtower," pieced together with film dialogue and perfect Dylanisms, such as "It was on the northern border of Texas where I crossed the line." The refrain, which consists of the song's title, hints at a kind of apocalypse, and the song is phrased in a prophetic stance:

> *Look out across the fields, see me returning,*
> *Smoke is in your eye, you draw a smile.*
> *From the fireplace where my letters to you are burning,*
> *You've had time to think about it for a while.*

It's an opening gambit that pays off, both in narrative form—it quickly sets a scene between a couple or between someone trying to get a message across and someone else unwilling to heed it—and in its self-reflective aspect, as Dylan saying (as Dylan and/or as prophet), "Here I am again, are you going to listen to me now?"

He continues in that vein, having "walked two hundred miles" like a Prophet of old, testifying on the eve of destruction, "It's the end of the chase and the moon is high." He preaches more doom and gloom about a time when earthly pursuits, even romantic ones, will prove meaningless, superfluous, given the nature of what's to come. Again, he styles himself as a reluctant prophet—"I can't provide for you no easy answers"—while at the same time reminding his interlocutor of the price others have paid for not heeding his words:

> *I saw thousands who could have overcome the darkness,*
> *For the love of a lousy buck, I've watched them die.*

He then offers an admission of having himself been duped that harks back to the album's opening track, "Tight Connection to My Heart (Has Anybody Seen My Love)," in which he sings, "Never could learn to drink that blood / And to call it wine," disavowing the Christian belief in transubstantiation. He repeats the same sentiment here, attaching it to his obsessive need for the approval of a loved one:

> *I don't want to be a fool starving for affection,*
> *I don't want to drown in someone else's wine*

—suggesting that his temporary acceptance of wine as Jesus' blood had more to do with a love relationship than it did with any conviction on his part, and terming himself a "fool" for having done so.

Dylan originally recorded this song with members of Bruce Springsteen's E Street Band, perhaps as a test to see if they could make a whole album together (much as he would in years to come with Tom Petty's Heartbreakers, sort of stealing back the thunder from two "New Dylans"). The version used on *Empire Burlesque* was recorded with other musicians and was the grossest example of the dance-floor hitmaker Arthur Baker's crass attempt at remixing Dylan's sound into something "contemporary" with the addition of canned percussion and synthesized loops. The rest of the album is filled with mostly forgettable songs, perhaps of interest only to those who find it a worthwhile diversion to play "name that film quote." But one song does stand out among all the rest. "Trust Yourself" could well be the answer song to Dylan's own "Gotta Serve Somebody." (It's certainly more imaginative and convincing than John Lennon's unreleased, seemingly drunken, bitter, unfunny parody, "Serve Yourself.") While the song doesn't rule out a belief in G-d or a faith tradition, it does return the responsibility for belief back to the individual, under no guise of threat of unintended consequences or punishment. But it also represents an explicit rejection of the harsh, judgmental prophesying of *Slow Train Coming* and *Saved*.

Empire Burlesque was released in June 1985. That year also marked Dylan's most active in terms of publicly lending his fame, influence, and performances for good works. He took part in the superstar benefit recording "We Are the World"—organized by Quincy Jones, Michael Jackson, and Lionel Richie—the previous January. As seen in a "making of" documentary for the charity single,

Stevie Wonder had to coach him with a spot-on Dylan imitation. Later that summer, Dylan, joined by the Rolling Stones' guitarists Keith Richards and Ronnie Wood, headlined the Live Aid benefit concert at JFK Stadium in Philadelphia, where a bad sound system and noise behind the stage curtain rendered the trio's performance nearly unintelligible to the musicians themselves along with the billion people watching the show on a worldwide satellite feed. Dylan's off-the-cuff comments about donating some of the event's proceeds—intended to help feed millions of starving people in Africa—to America's family farmers inspired Willie Nelson, John Mellencamp, and Neil Young to found Farm Aid, an organization that staged benefit concerts annually well into the twenty-first century. Dylan performed at the first Farm Aid benefit show, which took place the following September. Later in the year, he would also lend his imprimatur to Bruce Springsteen's guitarist "Little" Steven Van Zandt's anti-apartheid song and video, "Sun City," as one of many superstar artists contributing vocals to the effort and appearing in the video. A cynic would say Dylan's willingness to lend his name, voice, and hand to these charity efforts—something he only rarely did in the past (most notably for George Harrison's relief efforts for Bangladesh)—was motivated at least as much by the free publicity such goodwill could garner him at a time he needed all the goodwill and publicity he could get.

The 1980s—the era of MTV, bad haircuts, and dubious one-hit wonders—weren't kind to popular music or to Bob Dylan. Even with his considerable cinematic experience—including the promotional short for "Subterranean Homesick Blues" that played at the beginning of *Dont Look Back,* in hindsight, the proto–music video—he seemed as confounded by the form and aesthetics of MTV-style videos as he was by the gaudy fashions of the yuppie years. His lone attempt at playing a leading role in someone else's scripted film led to the debacle of 1987's *Hearts of Fire,* an English effort in which he played a washed-up rock star (please don't say "typecasting"), which was so bad it never received a stateside theatrical release, going straight to video in 1988, and to oblivion shortly thereafter.

Dylan returned to Israel in early 1985 to initiate planning for his first concert there, which finally took place in September 1987, when he played concerts in Tel Aviv and Jerusalem as part of a European tour with Tom Petty and the Heartbreakers. He marked the occasion of his first concert in the Promised Land by concluding the show with the traditional spiritual "Go Down Moses."

Dylan salvaged what looked to have been mostly an erratic, if not entirely lost, decade beginning in 1988, when he hit the road once again, this time with a stripped-down backing trio led by the *Saturday Night Live* bandleader-guitarist G. E. Smith. In retrospect, what was eventually dubbed the Never Ending Tour, which continued in some form or fashion throughout the next two decades, kicked off with a four-month U.S. tour launched in Concord, California, on June 7, 1988. Forever gone were the female backup choirs that had become standard features of his ensembles for the previous decade. Forever gone were the big-name backup bands such as the Heartbreakers and the Grateful Dead, having been replaced by mostly anonymous journeymen musicians chosen for their ability to think quickly and improvise and for their familiarity with American roots music. The personnel would change over the years, and the sound would evolve over time, but the bands would never be called anything other than "His Band," as in "Bob Dylan and His Band," and outside of the devoted legion of Dylan followers, the musicians would remain unheralded, like complete unknowns. And the overall aesthetic would remain the same, as Dylan refined a classic American roots style, where rockabilly, swing, folk, country, blues, and bluegrass were all merely accents for a timeless brand of postrock that Dylan patented uniquely as his own.

Early in 1988, one of the greatest accidents in rock 'n' roll history grew out of George Harrison's urgent need to record a B side for a European single. Harrison was enjoying the fruits of a commercial comeback spurred by the success of his album *Cloud Nine,* released in late 1987. As the story goes, Harrison called Dylan to see if the latter's home studio in Malibu was available. Jeff Lynne, best known as the leader of the pop group ELO, had produced *Cloud Nine,* and came along to work with Harrison on the single, bringing with him Roy Orbison, with whom he was working at the time, in hopes of garnering for the long-forgotten rockabilly legend a late-career comeback. On his way to Dylan's, Harrison had to stop by Tom Petty's place to pick up a guitar he'd left there, and Petty joined Harrison and the rest at Dylan's place. And thus were the Traveling Wilburys born.

No one had intended to create a rock 'n' roll supergroup, nor was there ever a serious effort to combine forces creatively in the way that David Crosby, Stephen Stills, Graham Nash, and Neil Young had done nearly two decades earlier. And even if there had been such a plan, it would have been preempted by the untimely death of Orbison that December, less than two months after *Traveling Wilburys: Volume I* (with its cheekily implied promise of more to come) was released. In any case, the combined talents of the quintet proved magical if evanescent, especially on numbers such as the hit single, "Handle with Care," which featured vocal turns and harmonies by four of rock's most distinctive singers. Among Dylan's more memorable contributions to the first Traveling Wilburys album were "Dirty World," a catalog of automotive-based sexual double-entendres that began where Prince's "Little Red Corvette" left off, and "Tweeter and the Monkey Man," a gentle parody of Bruce Springsteen chock full of song titles borrowed from the Boss's repertoire.

Before heading back out on the road for a half-year tour that would take him to Europe and across the States from May through November, Dylan settled in New Orleans in late winter and early spring to work with the Canadian producer Daniel Lanois on his next album. Best known at the time as a protégé of Brian Eno, with whom he worked fashioning U2's breakthrough album, *The Joshua Tree*, Lanois had previously produced Peter Gabriel's hit album *So*, and Robbie Robertson's eponymous debut album. The result of his collaboration, *Oh Mercy*, marked a full-fledged comeback for Dylan, certainly his best album since *Infidels* and perhaps even since 1975's *Blood on the Tracks*. While the album was heavily flavored by Lanois's swampy, ambient soundscapes, they suited the haunted, mystical nature of the songs, which, given the benefit of hindsight, marked a new progression in Dylan's songwriting that he would pick up once again when he'd reunite with Lanois for his next "comeback" album, 1997's *Time Out of Mind*.

With *Oh Mercy*, Dylan returned full throttle to latter-day prophecy. The album opens with "Political World," the suggestive title of which only hints at the stinging indictment of a corrupt society that Dylan portrays in the song. The word *political* in the song is an epithet, used in its purest meaning as "the exercise of power," in the sense that "power corrupts."

Over a hard-driving funk riff, Dylan sings,

> *We live in a political world,*
> *Love don't have any place.*
> *We're living in times where men commit crimes*
> *And crime don't have a face*

sounding as cranky as ever over what he sees of a world gone wrong.

> *We live in a political world*
> *Where peace is not welcome at all,*
> *It's turned away from the door to wander some more*
> *Or put up against the wall,*

presumably to be shot. Dylan concludes the song that introduces the album's theme with a reference to Jewish martyrdom. Whereas Judaism frowns upon martyrdom by intent, in the case where one's life is threatened—especially in the course of what we now call a hate crime—or when one refuses to dishonor G-d by renouncing one's Judaism, praying to an idol, or committing murder or a sexual crime, even upon pain of death, one thereby dedicates one's life to G-d in the act of *Kiddush HaShem*, literally "sanctification of the name of G-d," by dying with the name of G-d on one's lips, either literally or figuratively.

The only problem is, no one knows G-d's name; it remains a mystery and one of the eternal pursuits of mystics. The closest we can come is by uttering probably the best-known Jewish prayer, the Sh'ma—*Sh'ma Yisroel, Adonay Eloheynu, Adonay Echad* (Hear Israel, the Lord our G-d, the Lord is One)—at the moment of death. This is the *Kiddush HaShem* with which the victims of the Crusades, the Inquisition, and the Holocaust ended their lives.

Thus Dylan sings,

> *We live in a political world*
> *Everything's hers or his,*
> *Climb into the flame and shout God's name*
> *But you're not even sure what it is.*

Dylan would allude to the same Sh'ma blessing on another *Oh Mercy* song, "Ring Them Bells," when he sings, "Ring them bells so the world will know that God is one." He follows this line with one derived from Ezekiel, presumably describing those in need of awakening to the resonant truth implied by the bells:

> *Oh the shepherd is asleep*
> *Where the willows weep*
> *And the mountains are filled*
> *With lost sheep.*

Speaking for G-d, Ezekiel says:

> Woe to the shepherds of Israel who have tended themselves! Is it not the flock that the shepherds should tend? . . . My sheep wander on all the mountains and upon every lofty hill; My flock is scattered upon the whole face of the earth, but no one seeks and no one searches (Ezekiel 34:2, 6).

G-d goes on to say that He Himself will gather in His sheep, and see that they are tended to through the agency of His servant, David.

David also plays a role in "Where Teardrops Fall," a love song to someone "far away and over the wall," apparently someone who has died, in this verse:

> *I've torn my clothes and I've drained the cup*
> *Strippin' away at it all,*

Thinking of you when the sun comes up
Where teardrops fall.

When a parent, sibling, or child dies, it is customary for a Jew to rend his garment, in a ritual act called *k'riah*. The ritual has a biblical basis going back at least as far as the patriarch Jacob, who when he heard the false report of his son Joseph's death, "tore his robes in grief" (Genesis 37:34). King David builds upon Jacob's spontaneous act of mourning, ordering all who are in attendance upon receiving the news of Abner's death to tear their clothes (II Samuel 3:31). Regarding the drained cup, David prays to G-d for the day of redemption, when evil will be destroyed, in psalm 75, saying:

> For neither from sunrise nor from sunset, nor from the wilderness comes greatness. For G-d is the Judge—He lowers this one and raises that one. For there is a cup in G-d's hand, with strong wine . . . all the wicked of the earth drink, draining it to the very dregs.

Dylan continues in the prophetic vein of *Oh Mercy* on "Everything Is Broken," one of the funkiest blues-rock efforts of his career. While the song is presented simply as a litany of things that are broken—springs and strings, heads and beds, plates and gates—Dylan's phrasing, wordplay, and humor laced with disgust make this more than just a mere list of things gone wrong. Throughout the song, Dylan mixes up abstractions and objects ("rules" and "tools"), lending power and import to both, and tying them together so that each is symptomatic of the other. In other words, he seems to be saying, it's no wonder that nothing works right in a world where nothing *is* right. Yet somehow, even through the desperation, he has the wit to have people exhibit such corruption that they will *bend* rules that are *already broken*! And not only that, they will do so with a voice—like Dylan's on this song—that combines the howling of a dog with the croaking of a bullfrog.

The concept that we live in a world where everything is broken—and that it is mankind's task to repair the brokenness of the world—

is central to Jewish mysticism. The Jewish mystics of the sixteenth century taught that before G-d created the world, His presence was infinite, filling all time and space. In order for Him to make room for the universe, therefore, He had to contract voluntarily. In doing so, He filled vessels with his "light" or "energy," some of which shattered, thereby bringing about an imperfect Creation comprised of a broken world. Hence, it is through the carrying out of *mitzvot,* or religious obligations, such as prayer and the giving of *tzedakah,* or charity, that man can help repair the broken vessels, toward the eventual restoration of a unified, spiritual existence, as represented by the Messianic era.

This process of repairing the world is called *tikkun olam,* literally "fixing the universe," a term often erroneously used as a synonym for social justice devoid of any spiritual or mystical implications. While these so-called acts of *tikkun olam* are certainly worthy in and of themselves, and while many of them, intentionally or not, may fulfill obligations of religious merit, it is only through their relationship to the spiritual world that they are worthy of the term *tikkun olam.* To think otherwise would be an act of hubris. As Heschel wrote, "messianism implies that any course of living, even the supreme efforts of man by himself, must fail in redeeming the world. In other words, human history is not sufficient unto itself." Dylan understood this intuitively when he resisted the partisan demands placed on him by the protest movement of the early 1960s, and thus it's no surprise that when he came around to understanding the religious basis of this tension after studying Kabbalah with Hasidic rabbis that he would choose to sing about it—to turn it into musical prophecy.

In the context of Dylan's publicly professed identification with Lubavitcher Hasidism—one of the most popular mystical sects of Orthodox Judaism—it wasn't surprising that Dylan would produce an album infused with Jewish mystical themes. As far back as 1983, he was rumored to have recorded an album of Hasidic tunes (since such recordings have never surfaced, it's not even clear if the rumor refers to a recording of Dylan singing actual *nigunim,* the wordless vocal melodies used by Hasidim to invoke heightened levels of spirituality, or original songs inspired by Hasidic teachings). Dylan first publicly acknowledged his support of Chabad, the organizational arm of the Lubavitchers, when he made the first of three appearances on a Los Angeles–based "To Life" fundraising telethon for the group in 1986, prerecording a performance of Hank Williams's "Thank God," backed by Tom Petty and the Heartbreakers. He also spoke directly to the camera about Chabad in a message taped while filming *Hearts of Fire* in Great Britain, paying tribute to the organization's work with drug addicts, "helping to set them free from the misconceptions and devastation which is destroying their lives from within."

Along with his longtime actor friend Harry Dean Stanton and his Orthodox Jewish son-in-law, Peter Himmelman, Dylan made his second appearance on a Chabad telethon on September 24, 1989, at which the trio performed three songs—none in English. Himmelman introduced the Yiddish lullaby "Shlis tsu, mayn kind, dayne eygelekh (Close your eyes, my child)," crediting his grandmother with having taught it to him. Dylan accompanied Himmelman on flute on this number. Dylan moved to recorder on "La Adelita," a famous Mexican Revolution folk song about a courageous woman warrior, on which he traded Spanish-language vocals with Stanton, perhaps a nod to their having met in Mexico on the set of *Pat Garrett and Billy the Kid*. For the finale, the Hebrew-language "Hava Nagila," Dylan pulled out his harmonica.

Dylan appeared live on the telethon a third time, on September 15, 1991, when he joined the show's host in urging Mikhail Gorbachev to release a collection of books in the Lenin Library that once belonged to the Lubavitcher Rebbe. "Tell them to give back the books," says the rabbi to Dylan, who replies, "Oh, yeah. Give back the books. And give plenty of money to Chabad. It's my favorite organization in the whole world, really. They do nothing but good things with all the money, and the more you can give, the more it's going to help everybody." Later on in the show, Dylan backs his musician friend Kinky Friedman on guitar as the latter performs his song "Sold American." Both Friedman and Stanton had accompanied Dylan on the Rolling Thunder Revue in 1975–76, the tour that first put Dylan directly in touch with evangelical Christians.

Oh Mercy contains other hints of Dylan's connection to mysticism via Hasidism. One of the distinguishing features of contemporary Hasidim is their dress; even in the heat of a Brooklyn summer, the sidewalks in Crown Heights, where Chabad's worldwide headquarters is located, teem with men in long black coats. And in Dylan's song "Man in the Long Black Coat," the title figure is known to quote the Bible. He also greets a woman's invitation to dance with "a face like a mask"—a Hasidic man would never dance with a woman other than his wife. Once again, Dylan toys here with the aspect of identity as seen through a mask. The lyrics also portray men as unable to rely on their conscience alone for moral guidance; a code of ethics needs to come from without. And finally, this is one of very few songs in which Dylan rhymes "June" and "moon."

In "What Good Am I?" Dylan returns to the rhetoric of "Blowin' in the Wind," this time personalizing the questions that powered that early anthem, while constructing the lyrics around the same imagery the latter tune borrowed from Ezekiel and Isaiah:

> *What good am I if I know and don't do,*
> *If I see and don't say, if I look right through you,*
> *If I turn a deaf ear to the thunderin' sky,*
> *What good am I?*

While bogged down by its awkward, central conceit, "Disease of Conceit" is another song in which Dylan addresses the spiritual ills of mankind blinded by material concerns instead of acting as the holy beings, created in G-d's image, that we are intended to be. Dylan draws on boxing imagery to describe symptoms of the affliction—it "comes right out of nowhere / And you're down for the count"—and warns against its power to confuse an individual's sense of his place in the greater scheme of things:

> *Give ya delusions of grandeur*
> *And an evil eye*
> *Give you the idea that*
> *You're too good to die*

"What Was It You Wanted" is one of the album's most perfect songs, evoking the dusky mood with tremolo-laden electric guitar like the setting sun shimmering over a lake and harmonica slicing through the mist like birds settling in for the night. There's a slight sense of danger or even paranoia, as Dylan seems to address an obsessed fan or a stalker, or merely those who still project their own needs or desires onto him as a would-be savior ("What was it you wanted / When you were kissing my cheek?"). He uses the language of the music industry to interrogate his nemesis, asking, "Has the record been breaking / Did the needle just skip?"—sort of a polite way of saying something like, "Do you not speak English?" He acknowledges that time, as marked by fashion, may have passed him by:

> *Is the scenery changing,*
> *Am I getting it wrong,*
> *Is the whole thing going backwards,*
> *Are they playing our song?*

But he's not about to let that stop him at this point:

> *What was it you wanted*
> *You can tell me, I'm back,*
> *We can start it all over*
> *Get it back on the track.*

And indeed, with *Oh Mercy*, he did.

Although not included on *Oh Mercy*, several songs recorded for that album would see later release, including "Dignity" and "Series of Dreams." The latter song, which was included in the original *Bootleg Series Vol. 1–3*, is a vivid description of the sensation of waking from a layer of dreams inside dreams. The musical arrangement features a throbbing pulse, like "in a dream where someone wakes up and screams," and his heart is racing. The tension builds over the length of two verses and a bridge, before the crescendo bursts in the third verse and the dreams themselves are finally described:

> *In one, numbers were burning*
> *In another, I witnessed a crime*
> *In one, I was running, and in another*
> *All I seemed to be doing was climb*
> *Wasn't looking for any special assistance*
> *Not going to any great extremes*
> *I'd already gone the distance*
> *Just thinking of a series of dreams*

It's hard to hear the phrase "numbers were burning" in a song ostensibly about nightmares and not think about Jews in death camps—their arms tattooed with numbers—being burned alive, especially when the image echoes the one about *Kiddush HaShem* in "Political World." In "Dignity" (which would first surface on *Greatest Hits Volume 3* and in a live version on *MTV Unplugged*), Dylan refers to "Steps goin' down into tattoo land," where he "met the sons of darkness and the sons of light / In the bordertowns of despair." The song is another litany—in this case a lament for the disappearance of dignity—and portrays an assortment of characters looking all over for it, including one right out of the Zohar. Dylan sings, "Wise man lookin' in a blade of grass," alluding to a midrashic dictum favored by Jewish mystics, "Every blade of grass has its angel that bends over it and whispers, grow, grow." (The pop singer Madonna, a self-professed follower of Kabbalah, quoted this saying in her acceptance speech upon being inducted into the Rock and Roll Hall of Fame.)

The singer searches for dignity everywhere—to "where the vultures feed," in a "crowded room full of covered up mirrors" (that is, a Jewish house of mourning, where tradition has it to cover the mirrors), "on a rollin' river in a jerkin' boat," and "into every masterpiece of literature." Finally, he goes "into the valley of dry bone dreams," like Ezekiel before him, where in chapter 37 G-d commanded the latter to prophesy over dry bones in order to provide hope to Israel in exile and to symbolize the resurrection of the dead in the Messianic age.

Unfortunately, Dylan did not take this sort of care with his next album, *Under the Red Sky*. The songwriting, the performance, and the production do not live up to the new standard he had set for himself with *Oh Mercy*. Instead of a small core band like the one that Daniel Lanois put together for *Oh Mercy*, lending that album its distinctive sound, *Under the Red Sky*, coproduced by Don Was and David Was of the funk-rock group Was Not Was along with "Jack Frost"—making his first credited appearance on a Dylan album, and better known to you and me as Bob Dylan—featured a revolving all-star cast of backup musicians including George Harrison, Slash of Guns N' Roses, Stevie Ray Vaughan, Jimmie Vaughan, David Lindley, Robben Ford, and Waddy Wachtel on guitar; Bruce Hornsby, Elton John, and Al Kooper on piano; and David Crosby and members of Was Not Was on background vocals. Dylan himself played piano on nearly half the songs, and contributed accordion to an album for the first time.

The recording blends a few angry social critiques ("Unbelievable," "T.V. Talkin' Song") with a few more reflective, prophetic tunes originally written and recorded for *Oh Mercy* but heard here in rerecorded versions ("Born in Time," "God Knows"). The bulk of the album, however, consists of catchy, nursery-rhyme-like tunes ("Wiggle Wiggle," "Handy Dandy," "Cat's in the Well")—although even this last group of songs embed an undertone of dread inside their otherwise frivolous nature. It wasn't lost on savvy followers at the time that Dylan had become a father once again in 1986 (with Carolyn Dennis) as well as a grandparent for the first time, when his daughter Maria gave birth to a son, Isaac, in November 1989, and the liner notes include a dedication to "Gabby Goo Goo," presumably a reference to his daughter Desiree.

Under the Red Sky, recorded in early 1990 and released in September, still has some things going for it. "T.V. Talkin' Song," powered by a funky, Talking Heads–like groove, displays some wit underneath its grouchy but wholly deserved attack on the idiocy of television ("Sometimes you gotta do like Elvis did and shoot the damn thing out"), and uses the same device of a surprise ending Dylan first employed on *Desire*'s "Black Diamond Bay." "Handy Dandy," built on the riff from "Like a Rolling Stone," with Warren Zevon's guitarist Waddy Wachtel doing his best Mike Bloomfield imitation and Al Kooper reviving his signature organ fills, puts Dylan himself in the hot seat that Miss Lonely used to occupy. "Controversy surrounds him," he sings about a man named Handy Dandy, who shares some essential biographical highlights with Bob Dylan, such as a mystery surrounding an injury (think motorcycle accident), a much-criticized female backup group, and a mansion on a hill, all of which are made out to be signs of some sort of evil import, in the vein of "Idiot Wind" and "Gotta Serve Somebody" among other portraits of paranoia.

Several of the album's counting songs are inspired by scripture. "10,000 Men" alludes to King David, about whom it is repeatedly said in the Bible, "Saul has slain his thousands and David his ten thousands." Ten thousand men is also the number of troops Barak mustered to wage war against Sisera, on his way toward defeating the Canaanites (Judges 4:10–14). The song "2 x 2" refers to the story of Noah's ark ("Two by two, they step into the ark"). "God Knows," to which Dylan would frequently return in concert throughout the next two decades, is built on the figure of speech "God knows . . . ," but Dylan employs it as a pun in both its figurative and literal meaning in his description of a coming apocalypse:

> *God knows it's a struggle*
> *God knows it's a crime*
> *God knows there's gonna be no more water*
> *But fire next time.*

The reference to there being "no more water" is from the original covenant between G-d and man, contracted through Noah after the Great Flood. "I will make My covenant with you, and all life will never be cut short by the waters of a flood. There will never again be a flood to destroy the earth," the Lord says to Noah (Genesis 9:11).

After recording *Under the Red Sky*, Dylan regrouped with the remaining members of the Traveling Wilburys and recorded the undistinguished follow-up album, *Volume III,* sans the late Roy Orbison, in April, before heading back out on tour crisscrossing North America and Europe for well over a year, with hardly a break.

One of those breaks did come on February 20, 1991, when, at one of the low points of his career as a recording artist, Dylan was honored with a Lifetime Achievement Award by the National Academy of Recording Arts and Sciences at the thirty-third Grammy Awards ceremony, held at Radio City Music Hall in New York. After an introductory tribute by his self-professed number-one fan, the actor Jack Nicholson, Dylan and band performed a nearly unrecognizable, unintelligible version of "Masters of War"—presumably a reference to the U.S. attack on Iraqi forces, "Operation Desert Storm," which began just a few weeks earlier, in response to the Iraqi army's occupation of Kuwait the previous fall.

After the song, Nicholson gave a visibly awkward Dylan his Grammy plaque, and left Dylan at the microphone to say a few words. After stumbling a bit, Dylan launched into a speech that, although nearly as unintelligible and mystifying as was his delivery on "Masters of War," he seemed to have prepared and even memorized beforehand. He confused a worldwide TV audience of many millions by saying:

> Well, my daddy, he didn't leave me much—you know he was a very simple man, and he didn't leave me a lot—but what he did tell me was this. He did say, son, he said . . . he said so many things, you know. . . . He say, you know it's possible to become so defiled in this world that your own mother and father will abandon you, and if that happens, G-d will always believe in your own ability to mend your own ways.

While this undoubtedly left most people scratching their heads, a few watching that night, however, recognized these words as a paraphrase of a key verse in psalm 27—a psalm recited every day for the month leading up to and the weeks following the High Holidays of Rosh Hashanah and Yom Kippur. The psalm, according to the

Metsudah Siddur, "voices our prayer that God will be our light on Rosh Hashanah, enabling us to repel the darkness of sin through true repentance, and that He will be our salvation on Yom Kippur, through His compassionate atonement of our sins."

Dylan apparently was familiar with the translation of psalm 27 contained in the Metsudah Siddur—a modern prayerbook with English translation favored by *baalei teshuvot,* or returnees to Judaism, for its clarity of arrangement, its explanations of the prayers, and its linear, Hebrew–English translation. The passage to which Dylan referred in his speech—"When my father and mother abandon me, G-d will gather me up" (Psalms 27:10)—is appended in the Metsudah Siddur by an elaboration of Rabbi Shimshon Rafael Hirsch, the spiritual leader of traditional German Jewry in the mid-nineteenth century, rendered here as:

> Even if I were so depraved that my own mother and father would abandon me to my own devices, God would still gather me up and believe in my ability to mend my ways.

Dylan clearly based his words on Hirsch's elaboration of the verse in question, strongly suggesting that he was familiar with and in possession of this Orthodox Jewish prayerbook, perhaps recommended to him by a Chabad rabbi or by his Orthodox Jewish son-in-law, Peter Himmelman.

Dylan continued his seemingly never-ending tour the rest of the year, performing throughout the United States, in South America, and in Italy, Yugoslavia, Germany, and Scandinavia. In spring 1992 he returned to Australia and New Zealand, and throughout the rest of the year he continued to crisscross the States, Canada, and Europe, with only a short break at the end of the year before heading back out on the road for a swing through Britain and Western Europe in early 1993, before *another* U.S. tour in the spring and a summer tour through southern Europe and the Mediterranean, including three concerts in Israel in June, for which he added the old Carter Family tune "Little Moses," to his set list. In late summer and into the fall Dylan teamed up once again with Santana for a double bill, playing sheds and outdoor amphitheaters. In early 1994, Dylan toured Japan and other Far East destinations, including Malaysia, Singapore, and Hong Kong, before a springtime swing through the Midwest, a July tour of Europe—with stops in Poland, Austria, Germany, and the Czech Republic—and a late summer and fall return to the United States, including an appearance at Woodstock '94, marking the twenty-fifth anniversary of the original Woodstock concert at which Dylan refused to appear.

Throughout this period, Dylan peppered his live shows with a host of traditional folk, blues, bluegrass, and country songs. Emboldened by his renewed interest in American roots music—and possibly suffering from a lack of writerly inspiration for new songs—he recorded two solo acoustic albums, *Good as I Been to You,* released in November 1992, and *World Gone Wrong,* which came out a year later. Although few of the songs on the albums made their way into his live sets, they fed into an overall aesthetic rejuvenation in Dylan's live performances, and would strongly influence the sound and feel of his career-reviving albums of new songs in the late 1990s and in the first decade of the twenty-first century.

Dylan continued to slog through his Never Ending Tour year after year in the 1990s. On any given night he could seem wholly inspired or utterly indifferent. But he never just phoned in his performances, which is what kept fans coming, in the hopes of catching him on one of his better nights, perhaps a night in which he threw in a rarely played number such as "I Threw It All Away" or "Visions of Johanna." Although his set lists did not change as much as legend has it—an informed concertgoer generally knew what to expect, and in what order, although a certain slot may have been a revolving one, so that every night's show was different from the previous one—his concerts were always spontaneous affairs, driven by a certain amount of improvisation, including Dylan's own meandering electric guitar solos and his quirky, unpredictable phrasing and arrangements of old and new songs alike.

In addition to pleasing old fans, Dylan was also intent on reaching new, younger ones. Through his association with the Grateful Dead, he was able to achieve this to some extent. For a year or so after Jerry Garcia died in August 1995, Dylan made it a regular practice to play two or three Dead songs, including the popular "Friend of the Devil" and "Alabama Getaway," nearly every night, as well as "Silvio," which he had cowritten with the Grateful Dead's lyricist Robert Hunter (with whom he would reteam for lyrical assistance on his 2009 album, *Together Through Life*). Left without their favorite band to follow, Grateful Dead fans—with their signature tie-dyed dress and trademark behavior including pot-smoking and noodle-dancing—began flocking to Dylan shows, exerting their strong presence, not always welcomed by longtime Dylan fans, who found the concert decorum of Deadheads to be out of sync with what was happening on stage (although Dylan himself didn't seem to mind their youthful enthusiasm at all—his own security force welcomed and even seemed to encourage a nightly, mass stage rush at the end of his mid-concert acoustic sets).

In late May 1997, just a few days after Dylan turned fifty-six, fans around the world were panicked by reports that he had been hospitalized with a potentially fatal heart infection. He had apparently contracted the fungus-based infection histoplasmosis while riding his motorcycle through a windstorm near the Mississippi River, and the spores he inhaled caused pericarditis, an inflammation of the sac surrounding the heart. Down for the count and in severe pain for several weeks, Dylan fought off the infection, and while it was touch and go for a while—upon leaving the hospital, Dylan famously told reporters, "I thought I was going to meet Elvis"—Dylan eventually regained his health and went back on the road, where, much to the chagrin of some of his more devoted followers, he continued to ride that motorcycle that seemingly wanted him dead.

When a few months later he finally released his first album of original songs since 1990's *Under the Red Sky*, listeners were stunned by the brooding sense of mortality that hung over the proceedings. That the songs were all written and recorded before Dylan's brush with death was beside the point—*Time Out of Mind*, at least initially, seemed like Dylan's response in song to having almost met his maker. "Now I feel like I'm coming to the end of my way," he sang in "'Til I Fell in Love with You." "It's not dark yet, but it's getting there," he sang in "Not Dark Yet." And as the title indicates, in "Tryin' to Get to Heaven," he's trying to get there "before they close the door."

While Dylan may have tried to reassure listeners in 1988 when he sang "Death Is Not the End" on *Down in the Groove,* the fact is it nearly *was* the end for Dylan's fans, if not for the soul inhabiting Dylan's mortal frame, in 1997. And if it was merely a bizarre coincidence that so many of the songs he had recorded before his brush with death were about reconciling oneself with one's life before handing one's ultimate destiny over to G-d to be judged, that only added to their import and their mystical significance.

From the earliest days of his career, Dylan never shied away from invoking G-d in song. But he may never have so directly portrayed himself in an I-Thou relationship than in the songs on *Time Out of Mind,* songs that border on the obsessive in the manner in which they address the *cheshbon,* the ultimate accounting, that takes place at the end of one's life, between man and G-d. In Judaism as before the Internal Revenue Service, this accounting is updated on a yearly basis, in the case of the former in the period culminating with Yom Kippur, the Day of Atonement, in which a truly repentant person hopes to have his slate wiped clean in order to be inscribed in the Book of Life for another year. The entire Yom Kippur liturgy is one of fear and confession and pleading for mercy; the ritual, in a sense, is structured so that one is like the walking dead. When carried out to its fullest extent, the Yom Kippur ritual of fasting and praying and personal anguish induces a trance of awe and resignation, often accompanied by tears, as the evening approaches and the skies grow dark and one begs for forgiveness as the doors of redemption are quietly closed.

The title, *Time Out of Mind,* is a poetic description of this state of consciousness. (The term itself literally means "time immemorial," and has many literary antecedents, including Shakespeare and Charles Dickens, but Dylan likely knew it from his friend Warren

Zevon's song "Accidentally Like a Martyr," which Dylan sang in concert several times in tribute to Zevon after the latter publicly announced he was dying of cancer in fall 2002.) And the songs, including "Standing in the Doorway," "Tryin' to Get to Heaven," and "Not Dark Yet," in large part explore the mystical experience that is induced on this day. At least as far back as 1981's "Every Grain of Sand," Dylan has been drawn to this ritual—since the 1980s, Dylan-spotting on Yom Kippur has been something of a sport, and reports consistently place him in synagogue services in whatever city or town he finds himself, typically at the nearest Chabad House.

G-d is everywhere, they say, and he certainly is all over *Time Out of Mind,* as is the Bible. The album leads off with the dark, dismal anti–love song, "Love Sick," which sets the tone for the album with the immortal opening line, "I'm walking through streets that are dead." On Dylan's midnight walk, where his mind is racing with thoughts of a former lover, he is haunted by images of "lovers in the meadow" and "silhouettes in the window." The narrator is torn by inner conflict: the desire he still has for his lover versus his need to erase the memory of her. All this adds up to the refrain:

> *I'm sick of love; I hear the clock tick*
> *This kind of love; I'm love sick*

It gives new meaning to the term "lovesick," which typically is, if not entirely a desirable feeling, also not one generally equated with physical illness, but rather, with intense emotion. Here, however, the feeling has the narrator utterly and totally out of sorts.

It also puts one in mind of the Song of Songs—one of the shortest books of the Tanakh—a love poem written by King Solomon, commonly understood to be an allegory for the love that exists between G-d and the exiled people of Israel. Early in the poem, Israel speaks to G-d, seeking His comfort from afar, from exile, explaining, "for bereft of Your Presence, I am sick with love" (Song of Songs 2:5). Or, in other words, Israel is "lovesick" for G-d.

The next song, "Dirt Road Blues," has its most obvious roots in traditional American blues songs, and the first verse is typical, finding the narrator searching for his "baby." But in the second verse, as he's "pacing 'round the room, hoping maybe she'd come back," he resorts to "praying for salvation." Soon, the narrator's walk down the dirt road (as in "Love Sick," the narrator is walking, as do many of the narrators of songs on *Time Out of Mind*) in search of his lost baby transforms into a different kind of walk on a different kind of road. He is going to keep walking, he says, until his "eyes begin to bleed," until "there's nothing left to see, 'til the chains have been shattered and I've been freed." He could be referring to the shattering of the chains of love, or shattering the chains of slavery, or, perhaps, the freedom is one of a spiritual, transcendent sort—shattering the chains of material existence.

Most directly, this verse from "Dirt Road Blues" refers to the biblical tale of Samson—whose story Dylan previously made use of in 1965's "Tombstone Blues." Samson was blinded when his eyes were put out with hot pokers, and after praying to G-d to restore the strength that was taken away from him after Delilah cut his locks, he repaid his tormentors by shattering his chains and bringing the temple of the idol worshippers crashing down upon them, killing more of his enemies than he had in an entire lifetime of battling the Philistines.

Samson's freedom from imprisonment came at the cost of his own life. So, too, does the narrator of "Dirt Road Blues" seemingly find his own freedom in earthly transcendence. This interpretation gains credence over the next few verses, which find the singer looking at his "shadow" and "watching the colors up above." In the published lyrics, which differ from the words Dylan sings on the album version of the song, the narrator is going to keep on walking, he says, until he is "right beside the sun," where, in a Dylanesque twist, he says, "I'm gonna have to put up a barrier to keep myself away from everyone." Oh, to hear Dylan sing that line!

"Standing in the Doorway" finds the narrator walking once again, this time "through the summer nights," pondering another old flame and unable to shake her memory. Again, he's conflicted and not entirely sure how he feels about her: "Don't know if I saw you, if I would kiss you or kill you." The specter of some sort of capital crime haunts the singer and is hinted at throughout the song, such that ultimately he is resigned to his fate being in the hands of the Lord:

Maybe they'll get me and maybe they won't
But not tonight and it won't be here
There are things I could say but I don't
I know the mercy of God must be near.

Lines like this last one lend the album its overall feel of a man facing death. And lines like "my heart just won't give in" add to the feeling of prescient doom that haunts many of the songs on *Time Out of Mind*.

In "Tryin' to Get to Heaven," the singer is again desolate over a long-lost love and a broken heart (no pun intended) that's never healed. But as bad as he feels about his broken heart, it's his spiritual longing that the song rides on:

Now you can seal up the book and not write anymore
I've been walking that lonesome valley
Tryin' to get to heaven before they close the door

As we have previously noted, these lines portray the culmination of the Yom Kippur ritual, which climaxes at sundown with a penitent's final plea to be inscribed in the book of life for the coming year, and not to be left to wander in "that lonesome valley"—presumably the valley of the shadow of death enumerated in that most famous and comforting of psalms, psalm 23, which begins, "The Lord is my shepherd, I shall not want," and continues a few verses later, "Though I walk in the valley of the shadow of death, I will fear no evil, for You are with me." The psalm ends with a plea for a good life, culminating in admission to the house of the Lord: "May only goodness and kindness pursue me all the days of my life, and I shall dwell in the House of the Lord for long days." Or, as Little Richard, Dylan's teenage idol, sang forty years earlier, "You keep a-knockin' but you can't come in / Come back tomorrow night and try it again."

"'Til I Fell in Love with You" is another song that finds the narrator knockin' on heaven's door. Again distraught over the loss of a woman's love, the only comfort he finds is in the knowledge that G-d is on his side: "I know God is my shield and he won't lead me astray," a paraphrase of David's song of gratitude in II Samuel 31–33: "He is a shield for all who take refuge in Him. . . . He cleared my way with perfection."

These songs of pain and desperation culminate in "Not Dark Yet," Dylan's fullest description of the two, as he stands before the Lord, beseeching his forgiveness one last time before the sun goes down. He sets the scene of the Yom Kippur prayer service in the song's first line, "Shadows are falling and I've been here all day"—since everything is basically forbidden (eating, study, idle chatter), all that's really left to do on Yom Kippur is to pray, to achieve that state of mystical union with G-d by putting oneself through the spiritual ringer. Or as Dylan has it:

> It's too hot to sleep time is running away
> Feel like my soul has turned into steel . . .
> It's not dark yet, but it's getting there.

After describing a life that has led to his "sense of humanity . . . gone down the drain," where "behind every beautiful thing there's been some kind of pain," in the first line of the final verse, the narrator reconciles himself to a life that is, after all, fundamentally not one of our own choosing: "I was born here and I'll die here against my will," he sings. The phrase recalls Judah HaNasi's redaction of biblical wisdom gathered in the Mishnah around the year 200 c.e., where it is written, "Against your will you were born, against your will you die" (Mishnah 4:29). The connection to the Yom Kippur liturgy is in the line that follows, "And the living are destined to be judged." The adage has come down to us as part of the Pirkei Avot, the "Sayings [or Ethics] of the Fathers," which are contained in every traditional prayerbook as part of the Sabbath ritual, to be studied on Saturday afternoons for the period between Passover and Rosh Hashanah.

The singer concludes with a vivid description of the final moments of the Neilah service:

> *I know it looks like I'm moving, but I'm standing still*
> *Every nerve in my body is so vacant and numb*
> *I can't even remember what it was I came here to get away from*
> *Don't even hear a murmur of a prayer*
> *It's not dark yet, but it's getting there.*

The album's penultimate song, "Can't Wait," finds the narrator at a precipice, fully connecting the few dots remaining between lost love and heavenly judgment. He's standing at a gate—the gate to heaven? The gate to hell?—waiting for her to arrive, watching people, "some on their way up, some on their way down." Amid a flurry of lyrics drawn from friends' song titles—Johnny Cash's "I Walk the Line," Leonard Cohen's "I'm Your Man"—once again the singer is trying to recover love, and it's giving him heart trouble.

The final verse begins with one of the most unlikely lines ever put to song or poem: "It's mighty funny; the end of time has just begun." Given the desperation that follows—

> *I'm strolling through the lonely graveyard of my mind . . .*
> *I thought somehow that I would be spared this fate*
> *But I don't know how much longer I can wait*

—this seems anything but funny.

Remarkably, this dark, grimmest of Dylan albums was hailed as a full-fledged artistic comeback, topping many of the major critics' polls as album of the year. More remarkably, it was a huge commercial success, his best-selling album since the 1970s. Dylan was back on the covers of major magazines—not only music magazines but also newsweeklies hailing his return as a creative force. The near-unanimous chorus of hosannas hailing his return culminated at the Grammy Awards ceremony that took place in February 1998, when Dylan and band performed "Love Sick" and when, by the end of the night, he'd accepted three trophies, including his first ever Best

Album Grammy. It took the academy only thirty-five years, during the course of which he recorded thirty studio albums, to recognize Dylan in this fashion—none of his recordings, not *The Freewheelin' Bob Dylan*, *Highway 61 Revisited*, *Blonde on Blonde*, *Blood on the Tracks*, nor *Oh Mercy*, were previously even so much as nominated for the best album award.

With *Time Out of Mind*, interest in the Never Ending Tour kicked up several notches, as fans old and new came out to hear Dylan play his strong new material. And he didn't disappoint, with songs such as "Love Sick" and "Cold Irons Bound" finding regular slots on his set lists. The commercial and critical success of *Time Out of Mind* invigorated Dylan, and over the course of the next decade, well into his sixties, he seamlessly transitioned into the role of elder rock 'n' roll statesman as he gained more gravitas, befitting a rock 'n' roll prophet.

In the wake of Dylan's critical and commercially successful comeback, no effort was spared by Bob Dylan Inc.—by that I simply mean those folks in charge of marketing, licensing, publishing, and merchandising his work—to cash in on the "Bob Dylan brand." In addition to being the most heralded artist of his generation, Dylan was a cultural icon. That status brought countless commercial opportunities and ways to exploit Dylan's past and current work. By the late 1990s, Dylan had many people directly or indirectly in his employ, as well as a growing extended family. No one could begrudge him the chance to use his fame and his legend to insure a comfortable future for himself, his family, and his close friends, as well as all those who worked for him or relied upon him in other ways.

Thus, the machinery surrounding Dylan spun into overdrive. Dylan songs, old and new, showed up more often on film and TV soundtracks. The 1998 soundtrack album for the TV show *Touched by an Angel* included a version of "Dignity." In 2002, the soundtrack album for the Callie Khouri film *Divine Secrets of the Ya-Ya Sister-*

hood—which was produced by the Rolling Thunder Revue guitarist T-Bone Burnett—included the previously unreleased song "Waitin' for You." And the next year, the soundtrack album for the Steven Spielberg TV special *Token* revisited Dylan's "Man of Constant Sorrow" from his very first album.

In 2000, Dylan wrote and recorded a new song, "Things Have Changed," especially for the Curtis Hanson film *Wonder Boys*, and was rewarded with his first Academy Award, for Best Original Song, in 2001. (It was likewise honored by the Golden Globe Awards.) Dylan and his band performed the song live via satellite from Australia for the Oscar ceremony, and he gave a sharp acceptance speech, referring to the song as one "that doesn't pussyfoot around nor turn a blind eye to human nature." Apparently tickled by the honor, Dylan perched his Oscar trophy on his guitar amplifier at every show for several years.

Once again, Dylan received kudos for a song that was a bitter lament full of weariness and disgust—anything but feel-good pop fodder. The refrain throughout is:

> *People are crazy and times are strange*
> *I'm locked in tight, I'm out of range*
> *I used to care, but things have changed.*

Pundits had a field day with the surface meaning of these lines, that seemed to renounce any commitment to social or political progress as expressed in early songs such as "The Times They Are a-Changin'." Only those who hadn't listened closely to Dylan since 1964 could really come to such a conclusion. More telling, perhaps, are these lines, portraying a prophet at the end of his rope:

> *I've been walking forty miles of bad road*
> *If the bible is right, the world will explode . . .*

Curtis Hanson would later include two Dylan numbers, "Huck's Tune" and "Like a Rolling Stone," on the soundtrack of his 2007 movie, *Lucky You*.

In 2002, Dylan returned to the Newport Folk Festival for the first time since the infamous 1965 "going electric" concert. Somewhat perversely, Dylan and band were fully outfitted in Civil War regalia—including wigs and false facial hair that made Dylan look like a Hasidic Jew. It turned out that the band had just completed filming of a full-costume music video for "'Cross the Green Mountain," a new song Dylan wrote for the soundtrack of the Civil War epic *Gods and Generals,* released the next year.

Dylan songs also showed up with increasing frequency on other people's albums—sometimes even before they showed up on his own. Billy Joel's version of "Make You Feel My Love" appeared on his *Greatest Hits Vol. III* a month before the release of *Time Out of Mind,* cracking the Top 10 Hot Adult Contemporary Tracks chart. A few months later, the country singer Garth Brooks took the song to the top of the country charts. Other artists who covered the ballad include Neil Diamond, Trisha Yearwood, Joan Osborne, Kelly Clarkson, Bryan Ferry, the Irish vocalist Mary Black, and the English pop-soul singer Adele. Likewise, a song left off *Time Out of Mind,* "Mississippi," was first heard in a version by Sheryl Crow, when she included a rendition of the tune—which would eventually surface in several different versions on subsequent Dylan albums—on her 1998 album, *The Globe Sessions.*

Back in 1965, a reporter asked Dylan for what, if anything, he would "sell out." His witty riposte was, "Ladies' undergarments." Dylan had the last laugh in 2004, when he lent his persona and his song "Love Sick" to a truly bizarre TV ad for the Victoria's Secret line of lingerie, in which a scantily clad, busty model writhed around while a leering Dylan looked on. In 2006, Dylan lent his silhouetted image to a TV ad for Apple's iPod and iTunes digital music service. It should be noted that by this time, given the struggle all but a few hot young pop artists endured to get radio airplay, many performers sought alternative means to reach the public with new songs, including video adverts, such as the one Dylan did in 2008, in which he drove a Cadillac Escalade SUV, and asked, "What's life without the occasional detour?" That ad was a cross-promotion for Cadillac and

XM satellite radio, which broadcast Dylan's radio program, *Theme Time Radio Hour.*

Begun in May 2006, the weekly show presented fans and listeners with an entirely new side of Dylan. Totally reticent onstage for nearly a quarter century—and even a bit of a gnomic presence in his films—here Dylan was garrulous, witty, and enthusiastic, telling jokes, spinning yarns, and sharing his musical enthusiasms. He even occasionally broke into song, and offered recipes and tributes to his fellow artists. The program spanned all music genres, including classic pop, jazz, and novelty tunes, offering an entirely new, unique, and at times offbeat window into Dylan's musical influences, which ranged from Charles Mingus's "Eat That Chicken" to Slim Gaillard's novelty western-swing number "Matzoh Balls." To Dylan's credit, it was one of the only such free-form radio shows where a listener could hear the likes of Nat King Cole, Graham Parker, James Brown, and Les Paul and Mary Ford played back-to-back. In 2008, Ace Records released a two-CD compilation of music played on the program.

While September 11, 2001, has been forever marked in history as the day America was attacked by Islamic terrorists, in the coordinated suicide-airplane attacks on the Twin Towers in New York and the Pentagon in Washington, D.C., it was also the date marking the release of the first Dylan studio album since *Time Out of Mind.* While attention was on Al Qaeda and the subsequent anthrax-by-mail poisonings that followed in the wake of the 9/11 attacks, eventually people got around to realizing that Bob Dylan had a new album, *"Love and Theft,"* which had been, coincidentally, released on 9/11.

A rootsy album recorded with his touring band at the time and produced by "Jack Frost," meaning Dylan himself, the aptly titled *"Love and Theft"* is a freewheeling display of allusions, paraphrases, and quotations cut up, pieced back together, and turned into a dozen gems of Americana music. The album borrows its title (hence the quotemarks) from a university-press book called *Love and Theft: Blackface Minstrelsy and the American Working Class*. The lyrics draw from literature (Lewis Carroll's *Through the Looking-Glass*, Ernest Hemingway's *For Whom the Bell Tolls*), drama (Shakespeare's *Romeo and Juliet* and *Othello*; Tennessee Williams's *Streetcar Named Desire*), movies (Alfred Hitchock's *To Catch a Thief*), blues songs (Big Joe Turner, Charley Patton, and Robert Johnson are among those invoked by name or quotation), and, as one particularly earnest literary archaeologist discovered through a comparative search on the Internet, a Japanese crime novel, *Confessions of a Yakuza*.

The album kicks off with "Tweedle Dee & Tweedle Dum," a rollicking rockabilly number (used in the 2001 film *Bandits,* starring Bruce Willis and Billy Bob Thornton) that updates the Lewis Carroll characters, placing them in a typically Dylanesque apocalyptic landscape, where they are likened to "Two big bags of dead man's bones" who are "Trustin' their fate to the Hands of God." As in the original nursery rhyme upon which Carroll based his characters, the two are fated to live their lives side by side, mirror images of each other. In Dylan's version, the two are symbols of beings that are perpetually doomed to cooperate while growing increasingly resentful of the other's proximity. After three days, fish and company begin to stink.

"Mississippi" is another in a series of late-career narratives sung from the point of view of a prophet scorned. Dylan juxtaposes biographical details ("I was raised in the country, I been workin' in the town") with expressions of futility: "All my powers of expression and thoughts so sublime / Could never do you justice in reason or rhyme." He combines the two in the song's central verse, signifying the prophet's disappointment at his inability to effect change but also compassion for those who have followed him on his journey.

"Lonesome Day Blues" is a scorching blues-rocker that, as the title indicates, finds the narrator mulling over his fate all by himself. Violence and death have wracked his world—his parents dead, his brother killed in a war, his "captain" forlorn over the death of many of his "pals," even nature offering no solace but merely trouble. Nevertheless, he hasn't given up on his duty to prophesy:

> *I'm gonna spare the defeated, boys, I'm going to speak to the crowd*
> *I am goin' to teach peace to the conquered*
> *I'm gonna tame the proud.*

Biblical motifs run throughout *"Love and Theft,"* from the floodwaters of "High Water" to the "crimson clouds" and "the earth and sky that melts with flesh and bone" of "Moonlight," in which the narrator is "preachin' peace and harmony / The blessings of tranquility."

The album closes on a mournful note in "Sugar Baby," an accordion-flecked ballad that would have fit comfortably on *Time Out of Mind.* Whereas earlier in the album he mocks the idea that he's a washed-up star who can't repeat past successes, here he is more resigned: "You can't turn back—you can't come back, sometimes we push too far." The narrator addresses his comments to a woman from whom he's been separated for a long time; one can imagine Dylan reaching out once again to Sara, his "sugar baby" in the sense that he is her "sugar daddy," having signed over millions of his earnings to her over the years. She veritably tortures him with her absence, and in the end, his final appeal to her is the ultimate tragedy of mortality, as foreshadowed by the appearance of the angel Gabriel:

> *Just as sure as we're living, just as sure as you're born*
> *Look up, look up—seek your Maker—'fore Gabriel blows his horn.*

Once again, Dylan digs into the book of Daniel, where Gabriel interprets the latter's vision of a horn:

"Understand, Son of Man, that the vision refers to the time of the End. . . . I am ready to inform you what will be after the fury, for at the appointed time will be the End" (Daniel 8:17–19).

Even through the darkness, however, Dylan finds himself able to lighten the mood. Many interpret the line "Some of these bootleggers, they make pretty good stuff" to refer not to old-time whis-key bootleggers—which the old-time sound of the music might imply—but to those ardent Bob Dylan fans and collectors who trade or peddle unofficial Dylan recordings of increasingly high quality (presumably inspiring the official *Bootleg Series* of recordings, to take some of the wind—and dollars—out of their sails/sales).

In 2003, Dylan once again appeared in a feature film in a lead role, as in *Renaldo and Clara* and even *Hearts of Fire,* playing a character that in many ways resembled Bob Dylan. Dylan shared screenwriting credits for *Masked and Anonymous* with the director Larry Charles, an award-winning TV writer who worked with the comedian Larry David on comedy series including *Seinfeld* and *Curb Your Enthusiasm.* (As screenwriters, Dylan and Charles were credited with the pseudonyms Sergei Petrov and René Fontaine, a whimsical attempt at keeping themselves masked and anonymous.) Dylan played Jack Fate (not to be confused with Dylan's record-producer alter ego, "Jack Frost"), a musician sprung from prison by a crackpot dictator, who may or may not be his father, to play a benefit concert. When it comes time to rehearse for the show, Fate employs a Jack Fate tribute band with the name Simple Twist of Fate—which just happens to be the name of a Bob Dylan song (as well as a pretty clever name for a Jack Fate tribute band). The musicians constituting Jack Fate's backup band in the film are played by the musicians who were in Bob Dylan's touring band at the time—probably the strongest lineup the Never Ending Tour ever boasted, featuring the guitarists Larry Campbell and Charlie Sexton—and the group's repertoire is composed of songs we know as Bob Dylan songs, including "Down in the Flood," "Drifter's Escape," "Dirt Road Blues," and "Cold Irons Bound," along with old folk songs such as "Diamond Joe" and a stirring rendition of "Dixie." The other songs heard throughout the film are Bob Dylan songs in versions by the likes of Shirley Caesar, the Grateful Dead, and Sophie Zelmani, as well as several Dylan numbers performed in other languages, such as a Japanese version of "My Back Pages" by the Magokoro Brothers, an Italian version of "If You See Her, Say Hello" by Francesco de Gregori, and an English-Spanish version of "On a Night Like This" by Los Lobos.

Given the fact that so much of the music in the film is Bob Dylan music, including that played and sung by Jack Fate, it's not too much of a leap to conclude that the filmmakers intended to draw some kind of connection between the fictional character Jack Fate and the real life Bob Dylan. We've seen this sort of thing before—the first words we hear in *Eat the Document* are Bob Dylan asking no one in particular, "Have you ever heard of me?" Even more so, the layering of Bob Dylan upon a fictional character was a primary theme throughout *Renaldo and Clara,* in which Bob Dylan played Renaldo, who was often seen on stage singing Bob Dylan songs (in scenes that were filmed at actual Bob Dylan concerts), and the rockabilly legend Ronnie Hawkins played a character named Bob Dylan.

Masked and Anonymous also featured performances by well-known actors, including Jeff Bridges, Penelope Cruz, Jessica Lange, Luke Wilson, Angela Bassett, Ed Harris, Mickey Rourke, and Bruce Dern. A dystopian portrayal of an America beset by a Third World–style insurrection, the film has its share of in-jokes—Jack Fate's services are called upon to headline the benefit concert only because Bruce Springsteen, Paul McCartney, Sting, and Billy Joel have declined, and Fate is apparently the best the promoter, Uncle Sweetheart (played by John Goodman, doing his best Albert Grossman impersonation), can come up with in their absence. It remains a question throughout the film whether or not Fate will actually show up for the concert, and who will pay with their lives if he doesn't. Dylan is a gnomic presence throughout, saying little, but everything he says resonates like a proverb from on high—for example, "Sometimes it's not enough to know the meaning of things: sometimes we have to know what things don't mean as well." Put *that* in your pipe and smoke it!

What differentiated *Masked and Anonymous* from *Eat the Document* and, to some extent, *Renaldo and Clara,* was an attempt, however thinly veiled, at constructing the film around a sequential narrative. With its apocalyptic setting, its absurdist scenario, and its surrealistic cast of characters, *Masked and Anonymous* was the splendid cinematic equivalent of one of Dylan's sprawling, hallucinatory mid-1960s epics like "Desolation Row" or "Just Like Tom Thumb's Blues." As is perhaps to be expected, the film garnered little acclaim and plenty of brickbats, but it was great fun for Dylan fans and a fitting culmination of Dylan's cinematic efforts begun with *Dont Look Back* and running through *Renaldo and Clara* and *Hearts of Fire*.

In 2004, Dylan published a book called *Chronicles*, with the suggestive subtitle, "Volume One." I call it a "book," because as with everything Dylan has created, there is some question as to how literally to take its contents, which, at least on the surface, resemble a memoir. The book consists of five chapters, each one dealing with a specific period of Dylan's life and career, including three chapters on his early days in Greenwich Village, one on his Woodstock days around the time of the *New Morning* album, and one about the making of *Oh Mercy* in New Orleans with Daniel Lanois. Dylan goes on tangents, however, so we hear about his childhood in Minnesota— "Mostly what I did growing up was bide my time"—his folk apprenticeship in Dinkytown, his work with Tom Petty and the Grateful Dead, and his guitar style, which he claims to have learned firsthand from Lonnie Johnson.

"Lonnie took me aside one night and showed me a style of playing based on an odd- instead of even-number system," he writes. "The system works in a cyclical way. Because you're thinking in odd numbers instead of even numbers, you're playing with a different value system." Dylan goes on at length, offering a veritable lesson in music theory, one that eventually detours into numerology and mysticism: "I don't know why the number 3 is more metaphysically powerful than the number 2, but it is. . . . You can manufacture faith out of nothing and there are an infinite number of patterns and lines that connect from key to key—all deceptively simple." Who needs Theodor Adorno when we have Bob Dylan?

The most striking thing about *Chronicles* is how it introduces an entirely new voice—that of Bob Dylan, the colorful, garrulous story-teller. Less important than how closely he adheres to the facts is the language that he uses to recount his life and times, and the detours and byways down which he leads the reader, through literature, music, philosophy, and life's learned lessons. As in his songs, Dylan exhibits a natural gift for the rhythms of the written word, which in itself provides its own visceral pleasures. Take this passage in which he talks about a script he was sent by Archibald MacLeish, who had wanted Dylan to write songs to accompany his play:

> MacLeish's play was delivering something beyond an apocalyp-tic message. Something like, man's mission is to destroy the earth. MacLeish was signaling something through the flames. The play was up to something and I didn't think I wanted to know. That being said, I told MacLeish I would think about it.

There is an inner, consistent rhythm running through the second, third, and fourth sentences of this six-sentence paragraph, a meter that is almost like poetry—or song lyrics. And there is a freedom in Dylan's use of language, especially in the sentence "MacLeish was signaling something through the flames," that characterizes the book as a whole and makes it such a delight to read.

Dylan's tangents sometimes take the reader down surprising back roads. In talking about the song "Disease of Conceit" from *Oh Mercy,* he recounts the story of the shamed Baptist preacher Jimmy Swaggart, caught in a sex scandal, and surmises that he might have been inspired by Swaggart's downfall to write the song. But he also compares Swaggart's actions to the ancients:

> The Bible is full of these things. A lot of those old kings and leaders had many wives and concubines and Hosea the Prophet was even married to a prostitute, and it didn't stop him from being a holy man.

Dylan, apparently familiar with the smallest details of the Prophets' lives, goes on to explain the concept of "conceit"—it's "not necessarily a disease," he writes. "It's more of a weakness." But more inspiring is his description of his creative process: "The song rose up until I could read the look in its eyes. In the quiet of the evening I didn't have to hunt far for it."

Another such tangent led Dylan to express his strong feelings about Zionism. Dylan introduces the reader to Ray Gooch, a denizen of the Village with whom Dylan says he bunked a lot in the early days. (The characters of Gooch and his partner, Chloe Kiel—"They lived as husband and wife, or brother and sister, or cousins, it was hard to tell, they just lived here, that's all"—had never been heard of before the publication of *Chronicles*, and are presumably composites, or masked and anonymous.) Gooch's colorful backstory includes having attended military academy and divinity school, and working on an assembly line. Gooch also once labored in an abbatoir. Dylan says he asked him what that was like, and Gooch replied, "You ever heard of Auschwitz?" From there, Dylan recounts the story of the kidnapping and trial of the Nazi death camp mastermind Adolf Eichmann, concluding, "The trial reminds the whole world of what led to the formation of the Israeli state."

In addition to being the title of Bob Dylan's memoir, *Chronicles* is the title of the final book of the Tanakh. The original Chronicles comes in two parts, volume one and volume two. As of this writing, Dylan fans eagerly awaited the second installment of Dylan's own *Chronicles*.

In 2005, Dylan joined a growing lineup of artists who came to public attention in the 1960s and 1970s—folks including James Taylor, Ray Charles, Joni Mitchell, and John Fogerty—by striking a deal with Starbucks for the exclusive release of *Bob Dylan: Live at the Gaslight 1962* on the coffeehouse chain's in-house record label, Hear Music. Dylan also participated in Hear's Artist Choice series, in which music legends such as Tony Bennett, Johnny Cash, and Sheryl Crow selected tunes that were particularly influential or beloved. The disk Dylan programmed included songs by the likes of the bluesman Junior Wells, the Tex-Mex accordionist Flaco Jimenez, the country legends the Stanley Brothers, and the jazz great Billie Holiday.

Abraham Joshua Heschel wrote, "It is an act of evil to accept the state of evil as either inevitable or final. Others may be satisfied with improvement, the prophets insist upon redemption." On his 2006 album, *Modern Times,* Dylan showed no sign of letting up on his prophetic inclinations or his insistence upon redemption. From the opening lines of "Thunder on the Mountain," which leads off the sequence, Dylan is in his apocalyptic, preacherly mode:

> *Thunder on the mountain, fires on the moon*
> *There's a ruckus in the alley and the sun will be here soon*
> *Today's the day, gonna grab my trombone and blow*
> *Well, there's hot stuff here and it's everywhere I go*

The scene he portrays recalls the one that faced the ancient Israelites on the day of the Revelation at Sinai, when G-d presented Himself for the first and only time to the assembled masses:

> On the third day when it was morning, there was thunder and light-ning and a dense cloud on the mountain, and the sound of the shofar was very powerful, and all the people in the camp trembled. . . . All of Mount Sinai was smoking because G-d had descended upon it in fire. . . . The sound of the shofar grew louder and louder; Moses would speak and G-d would respond to him in thunder (Exodus 19:16–19).

In the Bible, what follows is the presentation of the Ten Command-ments.

In the otherwise wistful, sensual "Spirit on the Water," a jazzy dance tune, one verse stands out from the rest with its allusion to the biblical story of Cain, who committed the first murder in history and was thus condemned to be "a vagrant and a wanderer on earth" (Genesis 4:12):

I wanna be with you in paradise
And it seems so unfair
I can't go back to paradise no more
I killed a man back there.

There is, however, a midrashic basis for connecting the story of Cain and Abel to love for a woman, and, as in "Spirit on the Water," for the resultant lifetime spent longing for a woman one cannot have. While the literal text in the Bible suggests that Cain rose to slay his brother over jealously regarding offerings to G-d, rabbinical legend has it that Cain's crime was motivated by sexual jealousy. Many have wondered over the years how the human race was propagated if Adam and Eve only had sons (Cain, Abel, and later on, Seth). The midrash says that a girl, destined to be his wife, was born with each of the sons. As it turned out, Abel's "twin sister" was a hottie, and Cain wanted her for his own, which makes a lot more sense than Cain killing his brother over some vague sense that G-d favored Abel over Cain because of an over-cooked lamb chop. With this reading, and with the verse that seemingly refers to Cain, "Spirit on the Water" gains narrative coherence as a song sung by Cain as a forlorn love song to Abel's intended.

Modern Times reveals its main concerns to be theological. "When the Deal Goes Down" is Dylan's version of an invocation or a prayer, an acknowledgment of the need to settle one's accounts before one is judged on the day of redemption. "Someday Baby" wears its sense of frontier (or biblical?) justice on its sleeve—"I try to be friendly, I try to be kind / Now I'm gonna drive you from your home, just like I was driven from mine"—while "Workingman's Blues #2" pleads the case for a warrior who has beaten his swords into plowshares. In "Nettie Moore," Dylan sings, "I'm beginning to believe what the scriptures tell," and in "Beyond the Horizon," the narrator once again emphasizes his penitence: "My repentance is plain."

Dylan closes *Modern Times* with "Ain't Talkin'," another walk-ing song, along the lines of those on *Time Out of Mind,* in which the narrator surveys the landscape and finds nothing but cause for despair. Even the Garden of Eden, it turns out, isn't immune from the violence and decay that the lone figure sees everywhere:

As I walked out tonight in the mystic garden
The wounded flowers were dangling from the vines
I was passing by yon cool and crystal fountain
Someone hit me from behind.

In spite of this pessimistic outlook, the narrator still clings to the Golden Rule and a belief that prayer can heal:

They say prayer has the power to help
So pray from the mother . . .
I'm trying to love my neighbor and do good unto others
But oh, mother, things ain't going well.

The walker still sees—or believes in—signs of hope, in the promise of the Messianic age, when G-d will reveal Himself to mankind, riding in on that chariot with wheels on fire:

It's bright in the heavens and the wheels are flying
Fame and honor never seem to fade
The fire's gone out but the light is never dying
Who says I can't get heavenly aid?

When all hope seems lost, in the face of millennia of wandering in exile, where "The suffering is unending . . . In the last outback, at the world's end," the narrator still clings to an ancient faith, one that long ago ceased to center itself around the sacrificial altar, having replaced it with a program of highly codified rituals, laws, and deeds, a *path,* a way of life, called *halakha*—the system of belief called rabbinic Judaism:

All my loyal and much loved companions
They approve of me and share my code

I practice a faith that's been long abandoned
Ain't no altars on this long and lonesome road.

Modern Times, once again recorded with Dylan's touring band of the moment, went to number 1 on *Billboard*'s album chart within two weeks of its release, in September 2006. It was the first Dylan album to occupy the top spot since 1976's *Desire.* By the end of the year it had sold well over ten million copies worldwide.

AFTERWORD
SONG OF SONGS

In late April 2009, just a month or so shy of his sixty-eighth birthday, Bob Dylan released his thirty-third studio album, *Together Through Life*. Dylan continued on his Never Ending Tour that spring through cities across Europe before returning home to the United States for a nationwide summer tour of minor-league ballparks, headlining a triple bill featuring the country singer Willie Nelson and the Midwestern rocker John Mellencamp. There truly seemed no end in sight for Dylan as a performing and recording artist; his new album garnered widespread attention throughout the media; and once again his blue-eyed grin—at this point surrounded by graying curls and more than a few wrinkles—graced the cover of *Rolling Stone* magazine.

Together Through Life found Dylan digging deep into American roots music, down to the Texas-Mexico border. Recorded with members of his road band and a few guest musicians, the album was given an authentic Tex-Mex touch courtesy of the accordion playing of David Hidalgo, of the Mexican-American rock band Los Lobos. Dylan also drafted Mike Campbell, of the Heartbreakers, for added heft on blues-rock numbers that acknowledged the spirit and influence of Dylan's old friend and musical collaborator Doug Sahm.

Campbell's mandolin, as well as the multi-instrumentalist Donny Herron's steel guitar, banjo, mandolin, trumpet, and violin, also lent some numbers a mariachi-band feeling; not since "Romance in Durango," from 1976's *Desire,* had Dylan so fully engaged his love of musical sounds from south of the border.

While Dylan has occasionally collaborated with other writers on individual songs—Sam Shepard on "Brownsville Girl," Carole Bayer Sager on "Under Your Spell," Tom Petty on "Got My Mind Made Up"—not since *Desire* was a cowriter granted the sort of credit that accrued to Robert Hunter on *Together Through Life;* the lyrics of nine of the album's ten numbers are "by Bob Dylan with Robert Hunter." (There is a subtle but significant distinction between the "with" in that formation and the full "and" cocredit granted to Dylan's other songwriting collaborators, including *Desire's* Jacques Levy.) Dylan had previously worked with Hunter on "Silvio" and "Ugliest Girl in the World" from *Down in the Groove.* The nature of Hunter's contributions to *Together Through Life* is difficult to ascertain: Was he just a partner sitting around kicking ideas back and forth and helping Dylan come up with an occasional rhyme? Or was he a full-fledged creative collaborator, contributing song ideas, lyrical themes and stratagems, and coinages such that any speculation about Dylan's intentions on the album are suspect until we know more about the precise extent of Hunter's work on the songs?

While the album is more of a travelogue than his previous efforts, befitting its origins in a request by the French filmmaker Olivier Dahan that Dylan contribute a handful of songs to his road film, *My Own Love Song* (in the end, only "Life Is Hard," featuring Dylan in his best cabaret-crooner persona, was written for the film), it stands beside Dylan's late-1990s, early-2000s albums in its hardbitten vision of a world gone wrong. Singing deep from within a bluesman's groove—on "My Wife's Home Town" he seems to be channeling Muddy Waters's elastic glue in his vocals—Dylan has lost none of his irascibility even as he seems to be having more fun with the music. On "Forgetful Heart," he once again conflates lost love—Sara, again?—with a lost chance at salvation, returning to the image of the door that played such a prominent role in "Tryin' to Get to Heaven" from *Time Out of Mind.*

By the time the album gets around to the penultimate number, "I Feel a Change Comin' On"—an easygoing R&B tune whose title alludes to Sam Cooke's "A Change Is Gonna Come," which in turn was inspired by "Blowin' in the Wind"—Dylan has returned to his prophetic mode. He sees change coming in the form of a woman he finds far off in the eastern part of the world; she's described as a "whore" at one point, perhaps an allusion to the whore of Babylon. The singer has "the blood of the land" in his voice and rails about materialism run amok. Nevertheless, he senses change, as the title of the song indicates, and he ends each refrain noting that "the fourth part of the day's already gone," a reference to the mass demonstration of repentance by the Israelites—denoted in the first few verses of the book of Nehemiah, chapter 9—who confessed their sins for a quarter of the day. (Incidentally, this exhibition of public penance occurred on the twenty-fourth day of the month; Robert Zimmerman was born on the twenty-fourth day of May.)

The album ends with a vision of the end of days cloaked inside an upbeat, Tex-Mex modal blues built upon the most wretchedly annoying catchphrase of the year, "It's all good." The singer portrays civilization crumbling as evidenced through an epidemic of physical and moral decline—a veritable litany of gossip, lies, sickness, destruction, infidelity, poverty, and violence—only to turn around at the end of each verse and reassure listeners with the self-satisfied phrase, "It's all good." In the year 2009, no prophet could offer more cutting damnation than that sort of world-weary sociocultural mockery. If these were to be the final words Dylan ever offered on recording, one couldn't ask for a more suitable conclusion to the book of Bob Dylan.

NOTES

Page

vii   "Those guys are really wise. . . ." As quoted by Jonathan Cott in *Rolling Stone*, January 26, 1978, from *Bob Dylan: The Essential Interviews*.

vii   "Listen, I don't know how Jewish I am . . ." ibid.

1   "He decided to raise the level . . ." Rubin, *Voices of a People*, pp. 262, 107.

1   "was a pious merrymaker . . ." Liptzin, *Eliakum Zunser*, p. 87.

2   "was becoming more and more . . ." Liptzin, ibid., p. 31.

3   "Undoubtedly, his ability to transmute . . ." Liptzin, ibid., pp. 122–23.

4   "To do justice to his . . ." Zunser, *Selected Songs of Eliakum Zunser*, p. 7.

4   "He pleads with his people . . ." Idelsohn, *Jewish Music*, p. 446.

9   Heschel, *The Prophets*, p. 185.

10   Bono in Blake, *Dylan: Visions, Portraits, and Back Pages*, p. 8.

16   Scaduto, *Dylan*, p. 27.

21   Dylan in Blake, *Dylan*, p. 18.

61   Heschel, *The Prophets*, p. 185.

117   "first biblical rock album." As quoted by Neil Hickey, "The TV Guide Interview," in Ellison, *Younger Than That Now*, p. 104.

134   Williams, *Dylan: A Man Called Alias*, p. 119.

136   Shelton, *Bob Dylan*, p. 413.

189   "Those guys are really wise. . . ." As quoted by Jonathan Cott in *Bob Dylan: The Essential Interviews*.

195   Shapiro, *The Hebrew Prophets*, p. xxxix.

211   "Bob Dylan has finally confirmed . . ." As quoted by Robert Hilburn in the *Los Angeles Times*, in Cott, *Bob Dylan: The Essential Interviews*, p. 279.

212   "I've never been a Fundamentalist. I've never been Born Again. . . ." As quoted in Trager, *Keys to the Rain*, p. 540.

217   Heschel, *The Prophets*, p. 179.

223   "Jeremiah bemoaned his own fate. . . ." Scherman, *Tanach*, p. 1071.

226   "I don't care what people expect of me. . . ." As quoted by Jim Jerome in *People*, in Ellison, *Younger Than That Now*, pp. 96–97.

226   "There's a mystic in all of us. . . ." As quoted by Neil Hickey, "The TV Guide Interview," in Ellison, *Younger Than That Now*, pp. 104–105.

243   Dylan's mother takes him to see Howard Rutman, as per Sounes, *Down the Highway: The Life of Bob Dylan*, pp. 334–35.

254   Heschel, *The Prophets*, p. 186.

261   The connections tying together Dylan's Lifetime Grammy Award acceptance speech, psalm 27, and the Metsudah prayer book were first publicized by Ronnie Schreiber on the website *Tangled Up in Jews* at www.radiohazak.com/Dylgramm.html.

BIBLIOGRAPHY

Barker, Derek, ed. *Isis: A Bob Dylan Anthology*. London: Helter Skelter Publishing, 2004.

———. *20 Years of Isis: Anthology Volume 2*. Surrey, U.K.: Chrome Dreams, 2005.

Bauldie, John, ed. *Wanted Man: In Search of Bob Dylan*. New York: Citadel Underground, 1991.

Benson, Carl, ed. *The Bob Dylan Companion: Four Decades of Commentary*. New York: Schirmer Books, 1998.

Birnbaum, Philip. *Daily Prayer Book*. New York: Hebrew Publishing Company, 1949.

Blake, Mark, ed. *Dylan: Visions, Portraits, and Back Pages*. New York: DK, 2005.

Cott, Jonathan, ed. *Bob Dylan: The Essential Interviews*. New York: Wenner Books, 2006.

Davis, Rabbi Avrohom. *The Metsudah Siddur*. New York: Metsudah, 1983.

Day, Aidan. *Jokerman: Reading the Lyrics of Bob Dylan*. Oxford, U.K.: Basil Blackwell, 1988.

Dowley, Tim, and Barry Dunnage. *Bob Dylan: From a Hard Rain to a Slow Train*. New York: Hippocrene Books, 1982.

Dylan, Bob. *Tarantula: Poems*. New York: MacMillan, 1971.

———. *Writings and Drawings*. New York: Alfred A. Knopf, 1973.

———. *Drawn Blank*. New York: Random House, 1994.

———. *Lyrics: 1962–1985*. New York: Alfred A. Knopf, 1998.

———. *The Definitive Dylan Songbook*. New York: Amsco Publications, 2001.

———. *Chronicles: Volume One*. New York: Simon & Schuster, 2004.

———. *Lyrics: 1962–2001*. New York: Simon & Schuster, 2004.

Dylan, Bob, and Barry Feinstein. *Hollywood Foto-Rhetoric: The Lost Manuscript*. New York: Simon & Schuster, 2008.

Ellison, James, ed. *Younger Than That Now: Collected Interviews*. New York: Thunder's Mouth Press, 2004.

Engel, Dave. *Just Like Bob Zimmerman's Blues: Dylan in Minnesota*. Rudolph, Wis.: River City Memoirs, 1997.

Gill, Andy. *Don't Think Twice, It's All Right: Bob Dylan, the Early Years*. New York: Thunder's Mouth Press, 1998.

Gill, Andy, and Kevin Odegard. *A Simple Twist of Fate*. Cambridge, Mass.: Da Capo Press, 2004.

Gilmour, Michael J. *Tangled Up in the Bible: Bob Dylan and Scripture*. New York: Continuum, 2004.

Gray, Michael. *Song and Dance Man III: The Art of Bob Dylan*. New York: Continuum, 2000.

———. *The Bob Dylan Encyclopedia*. New York: Continuum, 2006.

Griffin, Sid. *Million Dollar Bash: Bob Dylan, the Band, and the Basement Tapes*. London: Jawbone Press, 2007.

Hajdu, David. *Positively 4th Street*. New York: Farrar, Straus and Giroux, 2001.

Hedin, Benjamin, ed. *Studio A: The Bob Dylan Reader*. New York: Norton, 2004.

Helm, Levon, with Stephen Davis. *This Wheel's on Fire: Levon Helm and the Story of the Band*. New York: William Morrow, 1993.

Heschel, Abraham Joshua. *God in Search of Man: A Philosophy of Judaism*. New York: Farrar, Straus and Giroux, 1955.

———. *Moral Grandeur and Spiritual Audacity*. New York: Noonday Press, 1996.

———. *The Prophets*. Peabody, Mass.: Hendrickson Publishers, 2007.

Heylin, Clinton. *Bob Dylan: The Recording Sessions (1960–1994)*. New York: St. Martin's Griffin, 1995.

———. *A Life in Stolen Moments: Day By Day, 1941–1995*. New York: Schirmer Books, 1996.

———. *Bob Dylan: Behind the Shades Revisited*. New York: William Morrow, 2001.

Hinchey, John. *Like a Complete Unknown: The Poetry of Bob Dylan's Songs, 1961–1969*. Ann Arbor, Mich.: Stealing Home Press, 2002.

Hinton, Brian. *Bob Dylan Complete Discography*. New York: Universe, 2006.

Hoskyns, Barney. *Across the Great Divide: The Band and America*. New York: Hyperion, 1993.

Humphries, Patrick, and John Bauldie. *Absolutely Dylan: An Illustrated Biography*. New York: Viking Studio Books, 1991.

Idelsohn, Abraham Z. *Jewish Music: Its Historical Development*. New York: Dover Publications, 1992.

Johnson, Tracy. *Encounters with Bob Dylan: If You See Him, Say Hello*. San Francisco: Humble Press, 2000.

Kaplan, Rabbi Aryeh. *The Living Torah*. Brooklyn, N.Y.: Maznaim, 1981.

———. *Sefer Yetzirah: The Book of Creation*. York Beach, Me.: Samuel Weiser, 1993.

Ledeen, Jenny. *Prophecy in the Christian Era*. St. Louis: Peaceberry Press, 1995.

Lee, C. P. *Like the Night: Bob Dylan and the Road to the Manchester Free Trade Hall*. London: Helter Skelter, 1998.

———. *Like a Bullet of Light: The Films of Bob Dylan*. London: Helter Skelter, 2000.

Liptzin, Sol. *Eliakum Zunser: Poet of His People*. Springfield, N.J.: Behrman House, 1950.

Mackay, Kathleen. *Bob Dylan: Intimate Insights from Friends and Fellow Musicians*. New York: Omnibus Press, 2007.

Marcus, Greil. *Invisible Republic: Bob Dylan's Basement Tapes*. New York: Henry Holt, 1997.

———. *Like a Rolling Stone: Bob Dylan at the Crossroads*. New York: Public Affairs, 2006.

Marqusee, Mike. *Wicked Messenger: Bob Dylan and the 1960s*. New York: Seven Stories Press, 2003.

Marshall, Scott M., and Marcia Ford. *Restless Pilgrim: The Spiritual Journey of Bob Dylan*. Lake Mary, Fla.: Relevant Books, 2002.

Matt, Daniel C. *Zohar: The Book of Enlightenment*. Ramsey, N.J.: Paulist Press, 1983.

———. *The Essential Kabbalah*. New York: HarperSanFrancisco, 1995.

———. *The Zohar: Volume I and II*. Stanford, Calif.: Stanford University Press, 2004.

———. *The Zohar: Volume III*. Stanford, Calif.: Stanford University Press, 2006.

Mellers, Wilfrid. *A Darker Shade of Pale: A Backdrop to Bob Dylan*. London: Faber and Faber, 1984.

Nogowski, John. *Bob Dylan: A Descriptive, Critical Discography and Filmography, 1961–1993*. Jefferson, N.C.: McFarland & Company, 2008.

Pickering, Stephen. *Bob Dylan Approximately: A Portrait of the Jewish Poet in Search of God*. New York: David McKay Co., 1975.

Pinsky, Robert. *The Life of David*. New York: Schocken Books, 2005.

Polizzotti, Mark. *Highway 61 Revisited*. New York: Continuum, 2006.

Ricks, Christopher. *Dylan's Visions of Sin*. New York: HarperCollins, 2004.

Riley, Tim. *Hard Rain: A Dylan Commentary*. New York: Vintage Books, 1992.

Rinzler, Alan. *Bob Dylan: The Illustrated Record*. New York: Harmony Books, 1978.

Rotolo, Suze. *A Freewheelin' Time*. New York: Broadway Books, 2008.

Rubin, Ruth. *Voices of a People: The Story of Yiddish Folk Song*. New York: Thomas Yoseloff, 1963.

Santelli, Robert. *The Bob Dylan Scrapbook 1956–1966*. New York: Simon & Schuster, 2005.

Scaduto, Anthony. *Dylan: An Intimate Biography*. New York: Grosset & Dunlap, 1971.

Scherman, Rabbi Nosson, ed. and trans. *Tanach*. Brooklyn, N.Y.: Mesorah, 1996.

———. *The Chumash*. Brooklyn, N.Y.: Mesorah, 2000.

———. *The Complete Artscroll Siddur*. Brooklyn, N.Y.: Mesorah, 2001.

Scobie, Stephen. *And Forget My Name: A Speculative Biography of Bob Dylan*. Victoria, B.C.: Ekstasis, 1999.

———. *Alias Bob Dylan Revisited*. Calgary: Red Deer Press, 2004.

Shapiro, Rabbi Rami. *The Hebrew Prophets*. Woodstock, Vt.: Skylights Paths, 2004.

Shelton, Robert. *No Direction Home: The Life and Music of Bob Dylan*. New York: William Morrow, 1986.

Shepard, Sam. *Rolling Thunder Logbook*. New York: Penguin Books, 1978.

Sloman, Larry. *On the Road with Bob Dylan: Rolling with the Thunder*. New York: Bantam, 1978.

Smith, Larry David. *Writing Dylan: The Songs of a Lonesome Traveler*. Westport, Conn.: Praeger, 2005.

Sounes, Howard. *Down the Highway: The Life of Bob Dylan*. New York: Grove Press, 2001.

Spitz, Bob. *Dylan: A Biography*. New York: Norton, 1989.

Steinsaltz, Adin. *The Essential Talmud*. New York: Basic Books, 1976.

Tanakh. Philadelphia: Jewish Publication Society, 1985.

Thompson, Toby. *Positively Main Street: An Unorthodox View of Bob Dylan*. New York: Paperback Library, 1972.

Thomson, Elizabeth, and David Gutman. *The Dylan Companion: A Collection of Essential Writing about Bob Dylan*. New York: Delta, 1990.

Trager, Oliver. *Keys to the Rain: The Definitive Bob Dylan Encyclopedia*. New York: Billboard Books, 2004.

Varesi, Anthony. *The Bob Dylan Albums*. Tonawanda, N.Y.: Guernica, 2002.

Vernezze, Peter, and Carl J. Porter, eds. *Bob Dylan and Philosophy*. Chicago: Open Court, 2006.

Webb, Stephen W. *Dylan Redeemed: From* Highway 61 *to* Saved. New York: Continuum, 2006.

Wex, Michael. *Born to Kvetch*. New York: St. Martin's Press, 2005.

———. *Just Say Nu*. New York: St. Martin's Press, 2007.

Williams, Christian, ed. *Bob Dylan: In His Own Words*. New York: Omnibus Press, 1993.

Williams, Paul. *Bob Dylan: Performing Artist, the Early Years 1960–1973*. Novato, Calif.: Underwood-Miller, 1991.

———. *Bob Dylan: Performing Artist, the Middle Years 1974–1986*. Novato, Calif.: Underwood-Miller, 1992.

———. *Bob Dylan: Performing Artist 1986–1990 and Beyond, Mind out of Time*. New York: Omnibus, 2004.

Williams, Richard. *Dylan: A Man Called Alias*. New York: Henry Holt, 1992.

Williamson, Nigel. *The Rough Guide to Bob Dylan*. New York: Rough Guides, 2006.

Zunser, Eliakum. *Selected Songs of Eliakum Zunser*. New York: Arno Press, 1975.

ACKNOWLEDGMENTS

Thanks for years of support and encouragement to my agents Gareth Esersky and Carol Mann. Thanks to my editor, Brant Rumble, at Scribner, for his unstinting encouragement and for patience bordering on the heroic. Thanks also to the publisher Susan Moldow, and to the staff at Scribner, including Anna deVries, Rex Bonomelli, Dan Cuddy, Carla Jayne Jones, Elisa Rivlin, Jonathan Sainsbury, Meredith Wahl, and Brian Belfiglio, and to copyeditor John McGhee.

Special thanks to Harold Lepidus, my high school friend, who encouraged my efforts on this project as early as 1978, got me tickets to my first Dylan concert that same year, and worked tirelessly with me on the manuscript to insure its accuracy as well as to challenge the integrity of my judgments where necessary.

Thanks to friends who helped out along the way, including Peter Stone Brown, Jeffrey Gaskill, Amanda Gordon, Jeff Klepper, Deborah McDowell, Chris Newbound, Michael Paul, Leonardo Quiles, Ira Transport, and Michael Wex.

Thanks to those who've passed through the ranks of the Roaring Thundering Revue, my Dylan tribute band, including Dave Barrett, Lucas Harrigan, "Dangerous" Bill Meier, Lizzie Meier, Matt Meier, Paul Rapp, Rob Sanzone, Tom Werman, and my beautiful friends Annette Ezekiel and Alicia Jo Rabins, a.k.a. the Golem Girls.

Thanks to my colleagues at *Berkshire Living*: Lesley Ann Beck, Amanda Rae Busch, Church Davis, Mary Garnish, Josh Getman, Jen Hines, Jen Kain, Alison McGee, Laura Morris, Adam Michael Rothberg, Stephanie Skinner, Cara Vermeulen, and Michael Zivyak.

Thanks also to friends, colleagues, and associates, including Karl Erik Andersen, Susan Barnett, Anne Braithwaite, Scott Barrow, Alan Berg, Barbara Lepidus Carlson, Tom Cording, Dan Friedman, Aleba Gartner, Libby Goldberg, Randy Haecker, David Holzel, Wolf Krakowski, Phoebe Legere, Dan Levy, Frank London, Claire Mercuri, David Minton, Sheryl Meyer, Alana Newhouse, Renee Pfefer, Charlie Rothschild, Marc Schafler, Zelda Shluker, Matthew Tannenbaum, Sheila Weller, Larry Yudelson, and Linda Ziskind.

Thanks to my family: my father, Larry Rogovoy; my sister, Ruth Rogovoy Berkman; Greg Berkman (he is the brother I never had); my ninety-seven-year-old grandmother, Rose Peretz (*ad me'ah v'esrim*); the *mekhutonim* in Boston; and my cousin Paul Hershl Glasser, who doubles as my in-house Yiddish expert.

I can never repay the unceasing love and support given me over the years by Karin Watkins. To say that this book could not have happened without her is a woeful understatement.

And to Anna Rogovoy and Willie Watkins (who doubles as my drummer), for once again sharing their father with an obsession and the need to work it out through the writing of a book. May you go from strength to strength, and may you stay forever young.

PERMISSIONS ACKNOWLEDGMENTS

INDEX

Printed in the United States
By Bookmasters